MICROSOFT WORD 365 FOR BEGINNERS

COMPLETE BEGINNER TO PROFESSIONAL PRACTICAL
GUIDE FOR MASTERING MICROSOFT WORD 365
2022 EDITION

JOE WEBINAR

Copyright © 2022 JOE WEBINAR

All Rights Reserved

This book or parts thereof may not be reproduced in any form, stored in any retrieval system, or transmitted in any form by any means—electronic, mechanical, photocopy, recording, or otherwise—without prior written permission of the publisher, except as provided by United States of America copyright law and fair use.

Disclaimer and Terms of Use

The author and publisher of this book and the accompanying materials have used their best efforts in preparing this book. The author and publisher make no representation or warranties with respect to the accuracy, applicability, fitness, or completeness of the contents of this book. The information contained in this book is strictly for informational purposes. Therefore, if you wish to apply the ideas contained in this book, you are taking full responsibility for your actions.

Printed in the United States of America

CONTENTS

CONTENTS III

CHAPTER 1 1

INTRODUCTION TO MICROSOFT WORD 1

   THE CONCEPT OF MICROSOFT WORD 365 1
   FEATURES OF MICROSOFT WORD 365 2
   GETTING MICROSOFT WORD 365 3
   COMPONENTS OF MICROSOFT WORD 365 3
   GETTING INTO MICROSOFT WORD 5
   THE WORD ENVIRONMENT 5
   STARTING THE WORD PROGRAM 7
   WORKING ON THE WORD START SCREEN 8
   OPENING A NEW DOCUMENT 8
   CHANGING THE SIZE OF TEXT 9
   QUITTING WORD 10
   SETTING THE WORD ASIDE 10

CHAPTER 2 11

THE TYPING CHAPTER 11

   INPUT DEVICES SET UP 12
   PUTTING WORDS ON A DOCUMENT 14
   USING THE ONSCREEN KEYBOARD 14
   UNDERSTANDING HOW THE MOUSE POINTER WORKS 18
   KEYBOARD "DO'S AND DON'TS." 20
   INSERTING PAGE BREAKS MANUALLY 25
   REMOVE THE PAGE BREAK 25

CHAPTER 3 27

BASIC THINGS ABOUT WORD 365 THAT YOU SHOULD KNOW 27

   MOVING TO AND FRO IN A DOCUMENT 27
   DOCUMENT SCROLLING AND SCANNING THROUGH A FILE 27
   MOVING THE INSERTION POINTER 32

Taking Control of the Insertion Pointer 33
Return to The Last Edit 35
Auto-Scrolling in Microsoft Word: How to Make It Happen 35
The Go-To Command 36

CHAPTER 4 37

EDITING OF TEXT ON MICROSOFT WORD 365 37

Deleting a Single Character 37
Deleting a Word 38
Deleting More Than a Word 38
Remove a Line of Text 38
Delete a Sentence 39
Deleting a Paragraph 39
Deleting a Page 40
Split and Join Paragraphs 40
Making a single paragraph out of two separate ones 41
Soft and Hard Return 41
The Undo Command 42
The Redo Command 42
The Repeat Command 43

CHAPTER 5 45

SEARCH FOR WORDS ON MICROSOFT 365 45

Introduction 45
How to Search for Word on Microsoft Word 365 45
How to Find and Replace Text in Microsoft Word 365 46
Advanced Find and Replace Features 47

CHAPTER 6 50

BLOCK OF TEXT 50

What Does Block Mean in Microsoft Word 365? 50
How To Mark a Block of Text 51
Blocking a Whole Document 53
How to Deselect A block 53

    Manipulating a Block of Text 54

CHAPTER 7 61
CHECK YOUR SPELLING ON MICROSOFT WORD 365 61

    Introduction 61
    Checking Your Spelling 61
    Turning On or Off Spell Check on Microsoft Word 63
    Fixing Words That Aren't Spelled Right 63
    Words That Have Been Mistakenly Flagged. 63
    AutoCorrect in Microsoft Word 365 64
    How To Turn On and Off AutoCorrect on Microsoft Word 64
    Undoing a Correction Made by AutoCorrect 65
    Adding a New AutoCorrect Entry 65
    Adjusting AutoCorrect Settings 66
    Grammar Check 66
    Turning on Grammar Check 67
    An All-in-One Document Proofing 67
    Checking a Document Again 68
    Settings for Document Proofing 69
    How to Hide a Word Document That Has No Spelling or Grammar Errors. 72

CHAPTER 8 74
NEW, SAVED, AND OPENED DOCUMENT 74

    What a Document is All About 74
    A New Document 76
    Setting up a New Blank Document 76
    Save Your Document 77
    Saving a File for the First Time 78
    Changing Where The Saved Document Are Kept 80
    Document-save errors: How to fix them 81
    Making a mistake and not saving your work before you quit 82
    Open a Document 83
    How to Insert a Document into another Document 84

v

To Get Back a Draft 85
To find a document that has been lost 86

CHAPTER 9 88

PUBLISH YOUR DOCUMENT ON MICROSOFT WORD 365 88

Introduction 88
Document On Paper 88
Previewing Before You Print 88
Printing The Whole Document on Microsoft Word 365 90
Printing a Certain Page 90
Printing a Range of Pages 91
Odd and Even Pages are Printed on Both Sides of the Paper 93
Printing a Block on Microsoft Word 365 93
Mark the text you want to print 93
Printing More Than One copy 94
Choosing a Different Printer 95
Cancelling a Print Job 96
Publishing Your Document Electronically on Microsoft Word 365 97
Convert a Document to PDF Using Microsoft Word 97
Other Ways to Make a PDF from a DOCX File 98
Close Your Document 98

CHAPTER 10 99

HOW TO FORMAT CHARACTERS ON MICROSOFT WORD 365 99

Introduction 99
The Basic Text Formats 99
The Basic Formatting Tools 100
Paragraph Formatting 104
How to Format Paragraphs 105
Alignment of paragraphs 105
Spacing in Paragraph 107
Paragraph indentation 108
Indent the First Line of a Paragraph 108

vi

How to Indent a Whole Paragraph	108
Tab Formatting	109
Seeing Tab Characters	109
Tab Stop	110
Setting Tab Stops	111
The Standard Left Tab Stop	113
Creating a simple Two Column List	113
The Centre Tab Stop	114
Making a Right-to-Left List	115
The Decimal Tab	116
To use the decimal tab	116
The Fearless Leader Tab	118

CHAPTER 11 120

HOW TO FORMAT A PAGE ON MICROSOFT WORD 365 120

Page Setup	120
Page Numbering	126
How to Add Page Numbers in Microsoft Word	126
How to Format Page Numbers	127
How to Remove a Page Number from the First Page	128
How to Start Numbering From Second Page	128
Page Background	129

CHAPTER 12 134

SECTION FORMATTING 134

Sections Breaks	134
Uses of Section Breaks	134
How to create A Section Breaks	135
How to Remove Section Break	136
Headers and Footers	136
How to Add Headers to Word Document 365	136
How To Add Footer to Word Document 365	137
How To Delete Headers and Footers	138
To Insert Any Word on the Header and Footer	139

vii

How to Add Border to Headers or Footers in Word 141
How To Create Cover Page in Microsoft Word................................ 141
To Create Custom Cover Page.. 142
To Delete a Custom Cover Page 144

CHAPTER 13 145

STYLE FORMATTING ON MICROSOFT WORD 365 145

Uses of Styles.. 145
Creating a Customized Table of Content 147
How to See All Styles In Microsoft Word.. 149
Why Uses Styles in Words 150
Types of Styles in Microsoft Word 365... 150
How to Apply Styles on Microsoft Word 365................................. 151
Modifying a Style... 152
Creating a New Style 153
How to Delete Styles 154
Restricting Styles Changes on Microsoft Word 365 155
Turning Off These Style Restrictions 158
Template Formatting 158
Creating a Template 159
Making a New Template from Scratch 160
Theme Formatting 160
To Apply a Theme in Word 160
How To Remove an Applied Theme From Your Document 161

CHAPTER 14 166

BORDERS, TABLES, ROWS, AND COLUMN ON MICROSOFT WORD 365 166

Borders 166
How to Add a Page Border in Microsoft Word 365 166
How to Add Border to a Part of Text... 167
How to Add Border to a Paragraph 167
To Remove a Border... 168
The table on Microsoft Word 365.. 168

viii

How to Insert a Table 168
Quick Table 169
How Do I Enter Text into a Table 169
Table Styles 170
To create your table styles 171
Insert Rows and Column 171
Cut, Copy, Paste, and Delete Rows and columns 171
Resize Rows, Column, and Tables 172
Split and Merge Cells 172
How to Convert Text to Table 173
Placing a Column Break 173
How to Create Bulleted List in Microsoft Word 174
How to Create a List from an Existing Text 175
To Remove the Bullet and Numbering 175
How to create an index in Word 175
How to Insert Endnote and Footnote on Microsoft 365 176
Graphical Works in Microsoft Word 365 178
How to Insert Shape into Your Document 179
How to Create Picture Layout on Microsoft Word 365 180
How to Wrap Text Around an Image 181
How to Resize an Image 182
How to Crop an Image 183

CHAPTER 15 184

MAIL MERGE 184

Working with Labels And Envelopes in Microsoft Word 365 187
Multiple Document 190
How to Customize Your Ribbon on Microsoft Word 365 191
How to Add Commands to Quick Access Toolbar on Microsoft Word 365 192

CHAPTER 16 194

TOP TIPS AND TRICKS IN MICROSOFT WORD 365 194

Dark Mode 194

TURN YOUR WORD DOCUMENT INTO AN INTERACTIVE WEB PAGE 195
CONVERT PHOTO OR DOCUMENT PDF TO AN EDITABLE WORD DOCUMENT . 196
USING EQUATION/FORMULAS IN MICROSOFT WORD 197
SORT LIST IN WORD 197
COLLABORATE WITH OTHERS 198
PIN DOCUMENT 199
HOW TO REWRITE A TEXT 200
RESUME ASSISTANT POWERED BY LINKEDIN 201
TRANSLATOR 201
CITATION 202
FORMAT PAINTER 203
READ ALOUD VOICE 204
DICTATION 204
CONVERT WORD TO POWERPOINT 205
AUTOSAVE OPTION 206
DROP CAP 206
LOCK YOUR DOCUMENT ON MICROSOFT WORD 207
BOOKMARK IN WORDS 208
SIDE-TO-SIDE PAGE MOVEMENT 209
ACCELERATE THE RIBBON 209
CLICK-AND-TYPE 209
INSERT VIDEO ON YOUR DOCUMENT 210
HIDDEN TEXT 210
DOCUMENT PROPERTIES 211
DOCUMENT VERSION HISTORY 211
THE COMMON KEYBOARD SHORTCUT FOR SHIFT KEY 211
COMMON KEYBOARD SHORTCUTS OF THE CONTROL KEY ....

x

CHAPTER 1

INTRODUCTION TO MICROSOFT WORD

It can be presumed that almost everyone uses Microsoft Word. This is because word processing tasks are so common in our lives today. A word processor can help you write letters, memos, reports, and even emails which are part of our daily lives. Word processors can go as far as editing, correcting, and rearranging text easily and quickly.

Therefore, in the chapter of this book, you'll learn the basics of Microsoft word 365 and how to use the most important features as well as features that will help you write documents easily

Note: Microsoft Word can be found in the Microsoft Office Suite and there are other applications in the Microsoft Suite Office, such as Microsoft Excel, Microsoft PowerPoint, Microsoft OneNote, Microsoft Outlook, Microsoft Access, and Microsoft Publisher. However, we're only going to focus on just Microsoft Word.

The Concept of Microsoft Word 365

Microsoft Word is simply a word Processing Software created by Microsoft in 1983 made to help people write. It can be used on your pc, desktop, laptop, or mobile device. It is part of the Microsoft Office suite used by different groups, teachers, students, professionals, business owners, and people of all ages and backgrounds. It is used to make professional-looking documents, letters, reports, resumes, and so on. Another benefit of a word processor is that it makes it easy to make changes, like correcting spelling, adding, deleting, formatting, and moving text. Once the document is done, it can be printed quickly and accurately and further be saved for later changes.

Features of Microsoft Word 365

Microsoft Word has different versions from its inception. But what makes the Microsoft word 365 version unique include;

- **Simplified Word Processing** - Make, manage, and even edit documents without ever having to work hard. Users from all over the world use Microsoft Word to make and share all of their documents and this current version makes it easier to achieve this.
- **Rapid Document Editing** – Make changes to documents with unmatched ease and speed. Correct a document's spelling, test its readability, and change its grammar with tools that are meant to make the document better.
- It lets you save any original file in a lot of different formats. .doc,.pdf,.txt,.rts,.dot,.wps, and many more formats which can be used to make documents.
- You can make beautiful and well-designed documents with no problems at all. Thanks to this great user interface! Microsoft Word has a simple interface that even the most novice computer users can use to make great documents.

Getting Microsoft Word 365

It is possible to get Microsoft Word 365 applications in various ways:

- The first option, which is popular with students, is to buy a license and then download and install Word on your computer. This option is often chosen by students because Microsoft gives a big discount to students.
- The second option is to pay for a year's worth of service (Office 365).
- Another option is to use Word on the Internet. You can use the online version of Word for free, but you have to go to your browser to get to it. However, you will need a Microsoft word 365 account and the online version will grant you access to documents saved on your one drive.

Components of Microsoft Word 365

Now, let's talk about the components or parts of MS Word. These features let you do a lot of different things with your documents, like save, delete, style, modify, or look at the content of your documents.

1. **The File**: It has options like New, which is used to make a new document; Open (which is used to open an existing document); Save, which is used to save documents; Save As (which is used to rename a document and save it, info, options etc.

2. **The Home Tab**: In MS Word, the "Home" tab is the one that comes up when you open the program. It's usually broken down into groups: the Clipboard, Font, Style, and Editing. It lets you

choose the color, font, emphasis, bullets, and where your text is. Besides that, there are also options to cut, copy, and paste in it. After selecting the home tab, you will get more options to work with.

i. **Insert:** This part can be used to input anything into your document. Examples of things you can insert are tables, words, shapes, hyperlinks, charts, signature lines, time, shapes, headers, footers, text boxes, links, boxes, equations, and so on.

ii. **Draw:** Freehand drawing can be done with this tool in Ms. Word. Different types of pens for drawing are shown on this tab

iii. **Design**: Here, you can choose from documents with centred titles, off-centered headings, left-justified text and more. You can also choose from a variety of page borders, watermarks, and colors in the design tab.

iv. **Layout**: You can use it to make your Microsoft Word documents look the way you want them to look. It has options to set margins, show line numbers, set paragraph indentation, apply themes, control page orientation and size, line breaks, and more.

v. **The References Tab:** This tab allows you to add references to a document and then make a bibliography at the end of the text so you can look back at it. It's common for the references to be stored in a master list, which is used to add references to other documents. It has options like a table of contents, footnotes, citations and bibliography, captions, index, table of authorities, smart look etc.

vi. **Review:** The Review Tab has commenting, language, translation, spell check, word count, and other tools for you to use.

A good thing about it is that you can find and change comments very quickly. These options will display when you click on the review tab.

vii. **Mailing:** One of the best things about Microsoft Word is that you can write a letter, report, etc and send it to a lot of people at the same time, with each person's name and address in the letter.

viii. **View**: In the View tab, you can switch between a single page and a double page. You can also change how the layout tools work. You can use it to make a print layout, outline, website, task pane, toolbar, and rulers, as well as to make a full-screen view, zoom in and out, and so on.

Figure 1 below shows the Home tab features

Getting into Microsoft Word

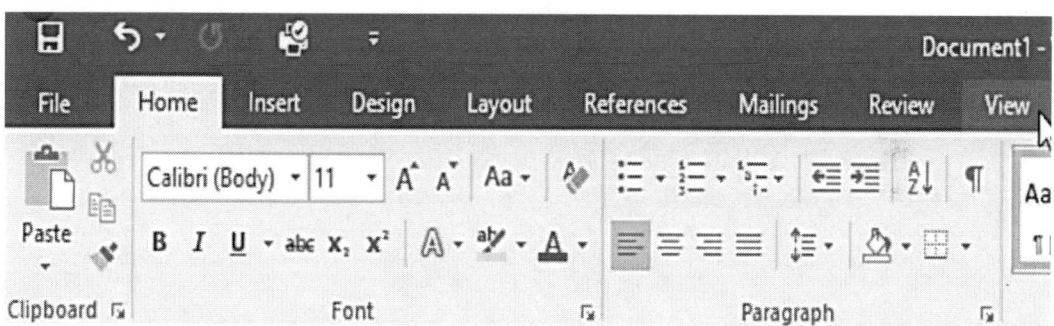

The Word Environment

The Quick Access Toolbar

The Quick Access Toolbar has icons for the tools you use the most. You can add buttons to this bar that you use a lot, and you can make them bigger. An image of the quick access toolbar is illustrated in figure 2

The Ribbon

Word Ribbon is a very important part of the word interface. It can be an inappropriate form of a button, an input box, and a menu.

The Ribbon is divided into tabs, and each has a different group which each has a commanding button. There are many different ways you can use the ribbon. You can click on a tab, then look through the group names to find what you need. Finally, click the button to make the command work. This is illustrated in figure 3.

The Status Bar

This is a bar that shows up at the bottom of Word's window. It has information and icons on the left and right sides. The information on the left shows how many pages and how many words are in the text. You can work with grammar and spelling tools by clicking the grammar icon. We'll talk about them later.

Across the right side of the status bar, some icons can be used to change how the document is shown to you. Most of the time, there are three views: Print view, which is used for editing and seeing how the pages would look if they were printed; read mode, which is like a magazine layout; and HTML view, which is how the text looks when it is viewed with a browser. Another tool that you can use while viewing a document on the right side is a zoom slider. This lets you change the size of the document as you look at it.

Figure 2: An image of the Quick Access Toolbar and its features

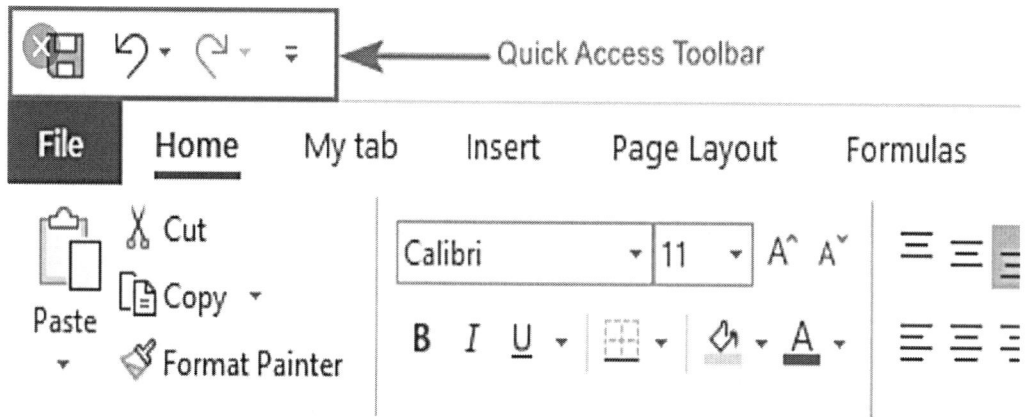

Figure 3: Different tabs and groups of the Ribbon

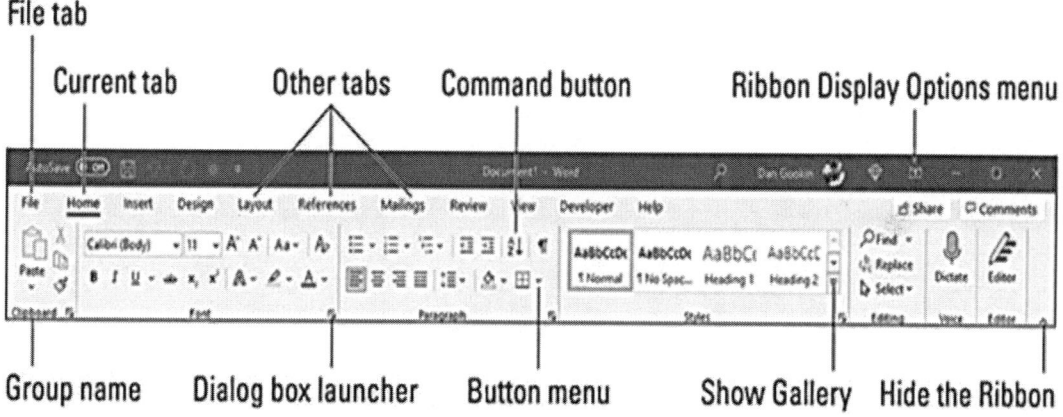

Starting The Word Program

First, you will need to find and open Microsoft Word (MS) on your computer.

From the computer's home screen:

- Double-click on the MS Word icon if it's on your computer's home screen.

But if it's not on your home screen, then do the following:

- Find the Start menu.
- Then click on Programs.
- Then click on Word, 365.

Note: Keep in mind that sometimes Microsoft Word will be in a folder called Microsoft Office. If this is the case, Microsoft Office is the first thing you click on before you click on the "Word." Then a blank document pops up where you can write your content and do different things with that content.

Working on The Word Start Screen

Start screen: You can use it to open an already-opened document, start a new document from a template, or start from scratch with a blank document. Choose to start a new document once and open it. Then, start writing.

Opening a New Document

- To open a document:
- Click on the **File tab** on the ribbon and click on the **Open option**.
- Then the screen opens where you can click the blank document to start a new document
- The document is opened and shown on the screen. It's ready for anything.

Note: You can save the document and when you save a document for the first time, you give it a name.

An example of a blank document is shown in figure 4 below

Figure 4: A View of a Document on Ms word

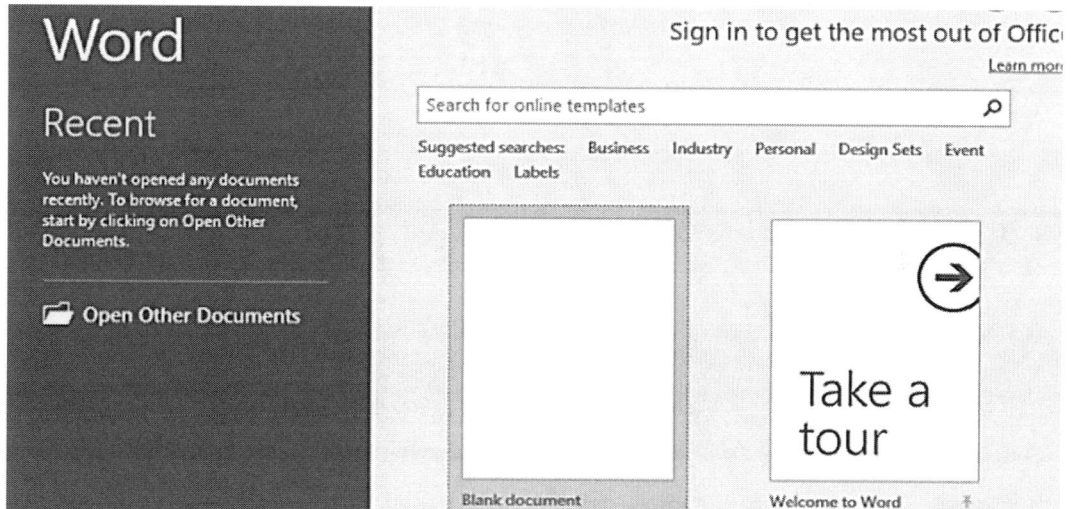

Changing the Size of Text

A zoom command can help you enlarge or shrink a presentation, making it easier to see what you're looking at. You don't have to change the font size to make the information in Word bigger. To zoom in or out, go to the Zoom command as shown in figure 5.

Figure 5: Image of a zoom slider on Word 365

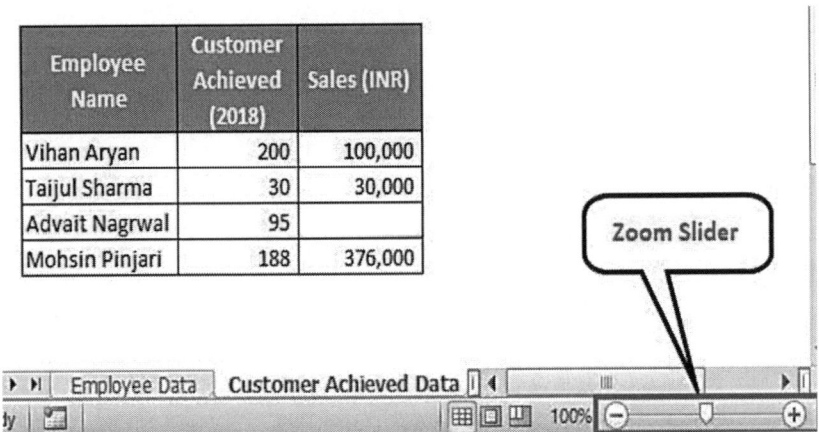

Quitting Word

It's best to close the word processor when you are done with it and don't plan to use it again soon. You can do this by clicking on the "**X**" icon in the upper right corner of the screen.

The first thing to remember is that you have to close all the word document windows that are open before you can say that you're done with the word document. It's also a good idea to save your document before you shut down the word processor.

Setting The Word Aside

You can minimize your word document to work on other things on your computer The minimize button is on the upper right corner of the screen.

To shrink the word window to a button on the taskbar, click the **Minimize** button and it will be possible for you to do other things with your computer. To bring the word document back to the screen fully, then you can click on the maximize button. How the Minimize and maximize icon looks is shown in figure 6. The first is the minimize icon and the second is the maximize icon.

Figure 6: The Minimize and Maximize Icon on Word 365

CHAPTER 2

THE TYPING CHAPTER

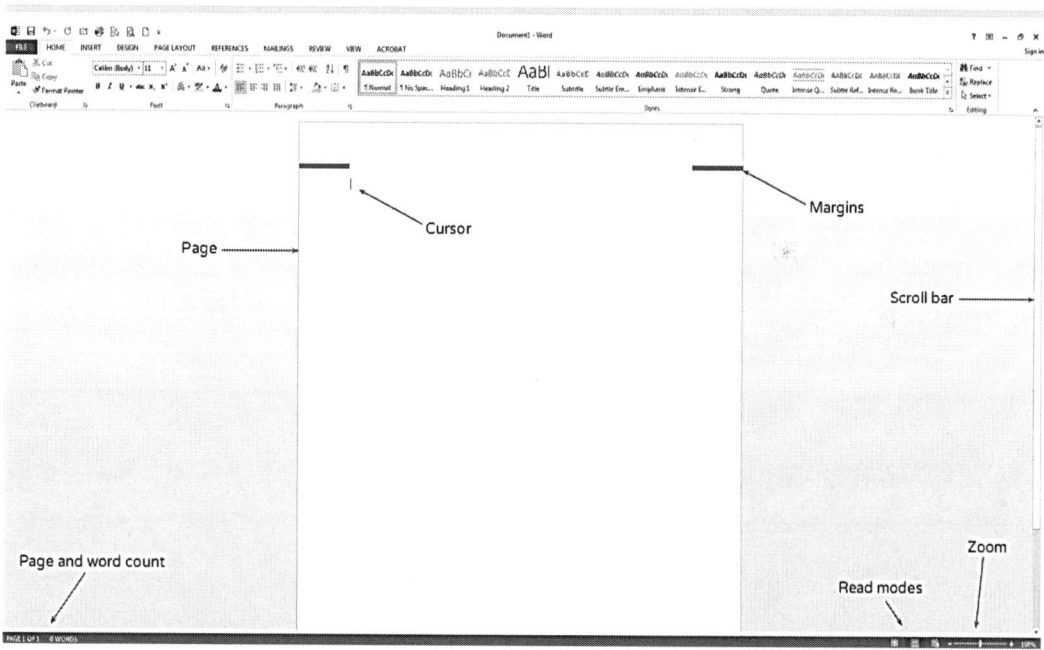

The computer will make no sense if there are no other devices that function with it. These different devices can be used to interact with the computer and perform various important tasks. This chapter will cover the two major input devices that can be used for typing and everything that covers typing in Microsoft word. How the typing screen looks is shown in the image above.

Input Devices Set Up

You can enter information into a computer with a device called an input device. The two most important input device is the Keyboard and the Mouse. These two input devices are very important for you to be able to communicate with your computer.

1. The PC Keyboard

A computer keyboard is a piece of hardware that lets you type in data (text, number, punctuations, etc) and commands to a computer. In most cases, your keyboard is the best way to get information into your computer. You can type a letter, number, symbols, punctuation Mark's, etc and you do this by pressing the keys on your keyboard.

How the keys are put together

The keys on your keyboard can be broken down into different groups based on how they work:

- **Using (alphanumeric) keys to type.** These keys have the same letter, number, punctuation, and symbol keys that you would find on a typewriter.
- **The function keys.** The function keys are used to do certain things. They're called F1, F2, F3, and so on, until F12. These keys can do different things in different programs.
- **The navigation keys**. These keys are used to move around in documents or web pages and to change the text. Each of

these buttons has an arrow next to it. They also have the Home and End keys.
- **The numeric keypad**. It makes it easy and fast to enter numbers. All the keys are in a block like on an old calculator or adding machine.

A picture of a keyboard with different types of keys is shown in figure 1

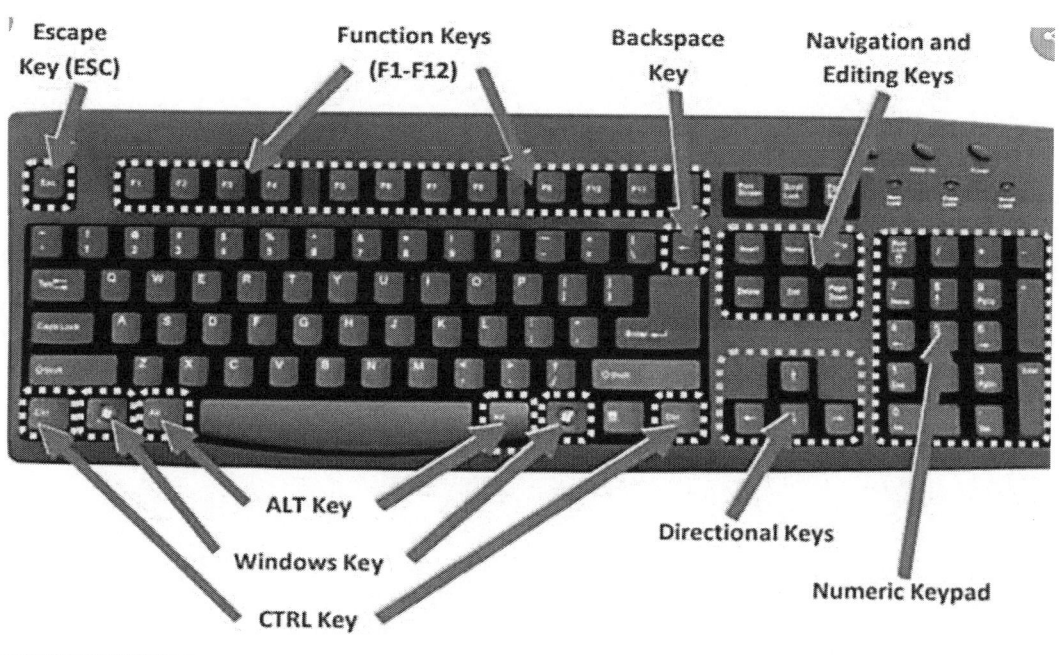

Figure 1: *A keyboard showing different important keys*

Some major keys in the keyboard are the Shift key, Caps lock, Tab, Enter key, Spacebar, Backspace, Alt key, Arrow Keys.

Note:

- There is a Desktop Keyboard and the Laptop Keyboard.
- Most laptop keyboards don't have a numeric keypad.
- The cursor keys are close together around the typewriter keys in weird and creative ways.
- The function keys may be accessed by pressing certain keys together.
- Each key has two symbols on it, which show that the person has two different personalities.

Putting Words on a Document

There is a vertical line that blinks when you need to type something in a program, email, or text box. This line is called the cursor or insertion point. It shows where the text you write will start. You can move the cursor by clicking where you want it to go with the mouse, or by using the keys to move it. In Microsoft Word, you can move your cursor with the four arrow keys that move up, down, and to the left and right.

Using the Onscreen Keyboard

When you want to use the On-Screen Keyboard;

- Go to **Start** on your computer
- Then select **Settings**
- Click on **Ease of Access**
- And then click on the Keyboard and turn on the toggle next to Use the On-Screen Keyboard to use the keyboard on the screen

- Immediately, you will see a keyboard that you can use to move around the screen and type text. The keyboard will stay on the screen as shown in figure 2 until you shut it down.
- Open a document in any program where you can write text. Then, with your mouse, click the keys on the onscreen keyboard to type in the text you want.
- To close it, Choose "Close" and then click "OK" on the screen keyboard to get rid of it from your screen.

Note: Here are some things to note about using an on-screen keyboard:

- The onscreen keyboard works almost the same as a real keyboard. You type text with your fingers, but you probably won't be able to do it as quickly as on a real keyboard.
- Some of the special keys (function keys, cursor keys, and so on) are hard to get to. Some of the time, you can get them by switching to a different touchscreen keyboard layout, but most of the time, they're not there at all.
- It takes two steps to use the Ctrl key on the onscreen keyboard: first, you have to tap the Ctrl key, and then touch another key.
- Some of the Ctrl-key combinations in Word can't be made by using the on-screen keyboard.

Figure 2: An Onscreen Keyboard

2. The Mouse

The mouse is another input device that can be used for typing or inputting different commands on Ms word. With a mouse, you may move the cursor or pointer on a computer screen by simply dragging it across a flat surface, such as the surface of your desk or table. Because it looks like a small, corded, and oval-shaped device, the term "mouse" came to be known as "mouse." Some mouse devices have built-in features, like extra buttons that can be programmed and used for different things. What a mouse looks like is shown in figure 3.

Early mouse devices were connected to computers by a cable or cord and had a roller ball built-in as a movement sensor on the bottom of the device. While modern mouse devices are now optical technology, this signifies that a visible or invisible light beam is used to move the cursor. Many models have wireless connectivity through radio frequency (RF) and Bluetooth, among other technologies.

The three main types of the mouse are:

- **Mechanical:** The mouse has a trackball under it and mechanical sensors that make it easy to move in all directions.
- **Optomechanical**: The same as mechanical, but optical sensors instead of mechanical ones are used to detect the movement of the trackball.
- **Optical:** The most pricey. Uses a laser to see when the mouse moves, has no moving parts, and reacts more quickly than other types.

Figure 3: A Mouse

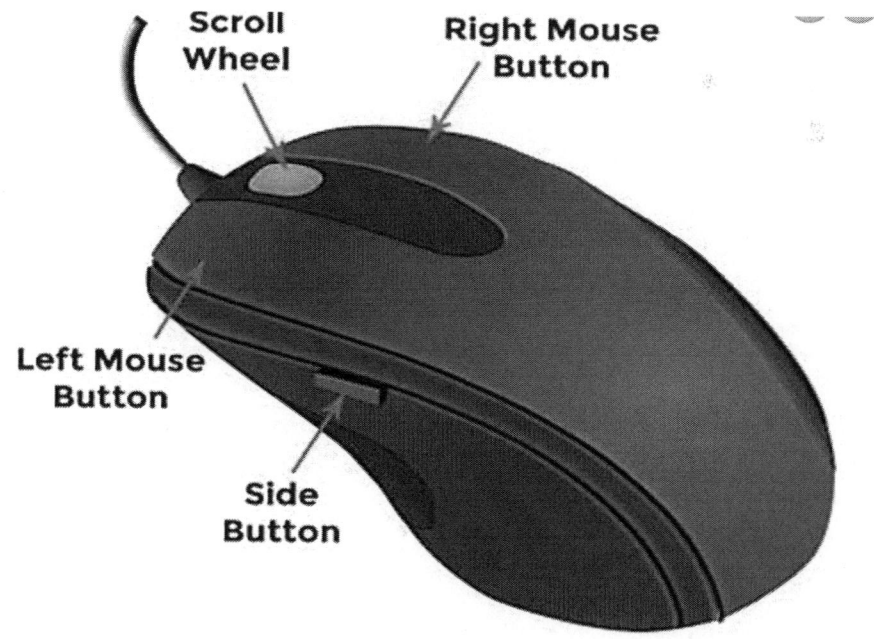

Understanding How The Mouse Pointer Works

A mouse pointer, also called a cursor, is a visible item that shows up on a computer screen. Computer users can move the mouse pointer around the screen by moving the mouse, which moves the mouse pointer. You can move around the document and select text with it too.

In most cases, the mouse pointer on a computer is in the shape of either an arrow or a hand. Often, the arrow points toward the screen's top and tilts a little to the left. Graphical user interfaces use arrows to show where the mouse is on the screen and a line-like pointer to show where text can be added. Text-based interfaces can use a rectangle instead of arrows or hands to show where things are.

Cursors often change how they look on a screen because of how they are being used and manipulated on the screen as shown in figure 4

- If you want to edit any text, the mouse pointer turns into an I-beam.
- In some documents, users might see hand cursors.
- Mouse pointer 11 o'clock is used to choose items.
- When you want to select lines of text, you use the mouse pointer at 1 o'clock to do it.
- In some document types, users might be able to press a mouse button and see that the pointer responds by "grabbing" the document page or an object in it.
- When the user is working with graphical editing software, the cursor might change to match the function that he or she is using.

Figure 4: Different Suggestions cursor on Microsoft Word

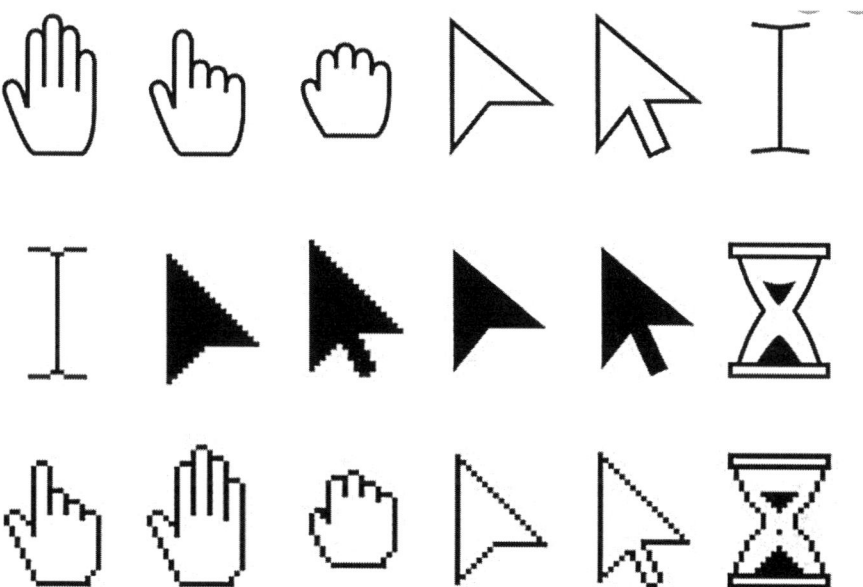

Note: When the click-and-type feature is on, the mouse pointer looks different. Lines appear below, to the left and right of the I-beam mouse pointer and they're very small. This is what happens when you point your mouse at a word tool - a pop-up information bubble comes up. You might be able to get a sense of how to use the command from the text in the bubble.

Also, in addition, As a person moves the mouse, the mouse pointer will move around the screen in the same way. When the mouse pointer is over a place where text can be typed, the pointer can blink as it thinks about typing. If a user wants to stop the cursor from blinking, he might be able to change the pointer's settings, such as how visible it is and how quickly it blinks. This will depend on the interface.

Keyboard "Do's and Don'ts."

It is important to know how to type with the keyboard as it will help you to know a few things about typing that are unique to word processing. Although, it's not necessarily compulsory to learn how to type but to save yourself some stress you should learn it.

i. Following the Insertion Pointer

The text you write in Word shows up where the insertion pointer is. As soon as you move the pointer, it looks like a moving vertical bar: When you move the insertion pointer, a character comes up in front of it one by one. It moves to the right after a character is added, making room for more text.

Note: The Insertion Point can be moved to a new place and the key moves the insertion point to where you want it to be.

ii. Pressing the Space Bar

The space bar is what you use to type in space on your text. On a keyboard, the space bar is a key that looks like a long horizontal bar. It is in the lowermost row, and it is much bigger than all of the other keys on the keyboard. When you're typing, you can use it to quickly enter a space between words.

The most important thing to remember about the space bar is that you only need to hit it once when you're typing. Between words and after punctuation, there is only one space between them. That's all!

Note: Any time you think you need two or more spaces in a document, use a tab instead. Tabs are the best way to indent text and to line up text in columns, so they are good for both.

Figure 5: The Spacebar Key

iii. BackSpace and Delete Key

Backspace is the button on the keyboard that you press when you make a mistake while typing. It moves the insertion pointer back with one character and deletes that character. The Delete key also deletes text, but it deletes characters to the right of the insertion pointer, so it doesn't erase everything.

Figure 6: The Backspace and Delete Key

iv. Pressing The Enter Key

It is also referred to as the Return key. It is the keyboard key that is used to instruct the computer to input the line of data or instruction that has just been written into the computer. In word processing, you only use the Enter key when you reach the end of a sentence.

Note: In Word, if your text gets too close to the right margin, it automatically moves all of your last words down to the next line. This word-wrap feature doesn't make you have to press Enter at the end of a line.

Figure 7: The Enter Key

During The Time You Type, Things Happen.

As you type your text quickly, with your fingers pounding the keys on the keyboard, you might see a few things on the screen. You may see spots. lines and boxes that may appear. We are going to look at some major stuff that happens when you type

i. Text Prediction

As you type, Microsoft helps you write faster in Word. The application anticipates your next words as you type and displays them for you to accept and proceed through your manuscript faster than ever before. Accept the suggested text by using the Tab or Right-arrow key on your keyboard and continue to type. Simply continue typing or hit Esc, and the suggestion will be removed.

ii. Keep an Eye on the Status Bar.

A status bar is a type of graphical control element that shows a section of information at the bottom of a window. As you type, it shows you how your document is doing. The status bar shows a collection of information that starts at the left end and moves right.

The information that shows up on the status bar can be changed. It talks about how to control what shows up on the status bar and how to hide things.

It can be broken up into sections so that you can group information. Its main job is to show information about the current state of its window, but some status bars have extra features. For example, many web browsers have sections that can be clicked on to show security or privacy information.

Some good things about status bars: They let you see messages and the whole screen at the same time, they let you write while you look at your status data, status data is shown in a way that lets you see other menu options at the same time and they show how things are going at all times.

iii. Notice the Page Breaks.

If you put a page break in your text, it will show where the current page end and start the next one. Then you can click on anywhere you wish to start a new page. To insert a page break, click on the Insert tab is at the top of the screen. On the Pages group, the Page Break button is on the right of the screen, click on it and the page break becomes visible.

Inserting page breaks Manually

It's best to put your insertion point where you want the page break to be. To change the layout of your page, click on the Page Layout ribbon. Then click on Breaks and then choose Page. Page break becomes visible.

Note: The Pages group has a button called "Blank Page." If you want to add a blank page at the break, click on that button.

Remove the Page Break

A page break you put in now can be taken out at any time if you change your mind.

To find and remove page breaks quickly, you should first show the formatting marks.

- Click the **Home button.**
- The **Show/Hide button i**s on the right.
- This shows punctuation characters like spaces, paragraph markers, and the most important for this lesson, page and section breaks.
- Double-click the **page brea**k to pick it up.
- Press the **delete key.**
- The page break is gone.

iv. Collapsible Headers

While typing, you might see a small triangle on the left of some of the headings in your documents. These triangles let you change the size of all the text in the header's section. Click once to hide the text; click again to show it.

The collapsed sections don't make the page look like it's empty. They do a good job of cutting down the size of the page in a way that is easy for people to read.

vi. Getting Rid of Spots and Clutter in the Text

Seeing dots or spots in the text you write doesn't mean anything bad is going on. What you're seeing are characters that can't be read. Word uses a lot of symbols to show things you usually don't see, like spaces, tabs, the Enter key, and more. These dots and tittles show up when the Show/Hide feature is on. If you want to get rid of them again, click the Show/Hide button again.

vi. Understanding the Colors of the Underlines

When Word underlines your text without your permission, it's alerting you to something that's not right with the way things are going. These underlines are not text styles. At times, you might see these:

- **Red zigzag**: This indicate there is a mistake in the word
- **Blue zigzag**: It indicates errors in grammar and word choice
- **Blue single line**: When you write a document, Word adds blue underlined text to show where web page addresses are. You can press Ctrl+click the blue text to go to the web page.
- **Red lines:** You might see red lines in the margin, below text, or even through text. It means that you're using Track Changes in Word.

CHAPTER 3

BASIC THINGS ABOUT WORD 365 THAT YOU SHOULD KNOW

Here, we will show you basic things about word focusing on scroll bars, how to move the insertion pointer, and how to use keyboard shortcuts to get around. It also talked about how to remove characters, lines, sentences, paragraphs, and pages from the text. You'll also learn how to use the Undo command, which can help save your document.

Moving To and Fro in a Document

Using Microsoft Word is a very common way to do word processing. While it can be used to write letters and simple documents, a Word document can also include pictures and graphics that can be used to make posters, birthday cards, or other things. Most times you need a larger screen to perform these operations. Your Word document could be a lot bigger than the computer screen and you might need a lot of screens to see it all at once. In the real sense, this cannot be possible that is why some word has ways for you to move to and fro around your document. This is what we will discuss

Document Scrolling and Scanning Through a File

When a document is long enough, it can be hard to move around the whole document with just the keys but when you use a scrollbar, you can continuously move text or other content in a specific direction on a computer screen so that all of the content is visible. The fastest way to move through a document is to click and drag a scroll bar. The process of scrolling on a computer is when you look at a small part of a big document in a small window.

Therefore, there are two scroll bars on the right and bottom of the window. You can use them to quickly move through the document. Also, the arrow buttons on the top, bottom, and sides of the scroll bar can be used to scroll one line at a time. Let's discuss each of them separately.

i. Making Use of a Vertical Scroll Bar

On the right side of the computer screen, there is a vertical scroll bar and it's used to scroll between the top and bottom of the page. To make the vertical scrollbar show up, do the following:

- Get to **File** and click on the **Options** tab
- The Word options dialogue box will now show up on the screen.
- Select the **Advanced** tab.
- Then, scroll down and click on the **Display button.**
- Now, choose the option to show **vertical scroll bars.**
- Click the **OK** button to finish. The **vertical scroll bar** becomes visible.

Note: The scroll bar works the same way as the scroll bar in any Windows program.

One of the most important parts of the scroll bar is the button that takes you up. Use the mouse to move this button up or down to move the document around on the screen. Its position on the scroll bar shows where the text you see is. Also, when you move the button up or down, you see a page number on the screen. This works when a document has been formatted with heading styles.

Move your mouse pointer over your text, and the vertical scroll bar comes back to the top of your text. It gets smaller as your document gets longer because the button's size is based on how much of it is in the window, so the button gets smaller as your document gets longer.

Figure 1: The Vertical Scroll Bar

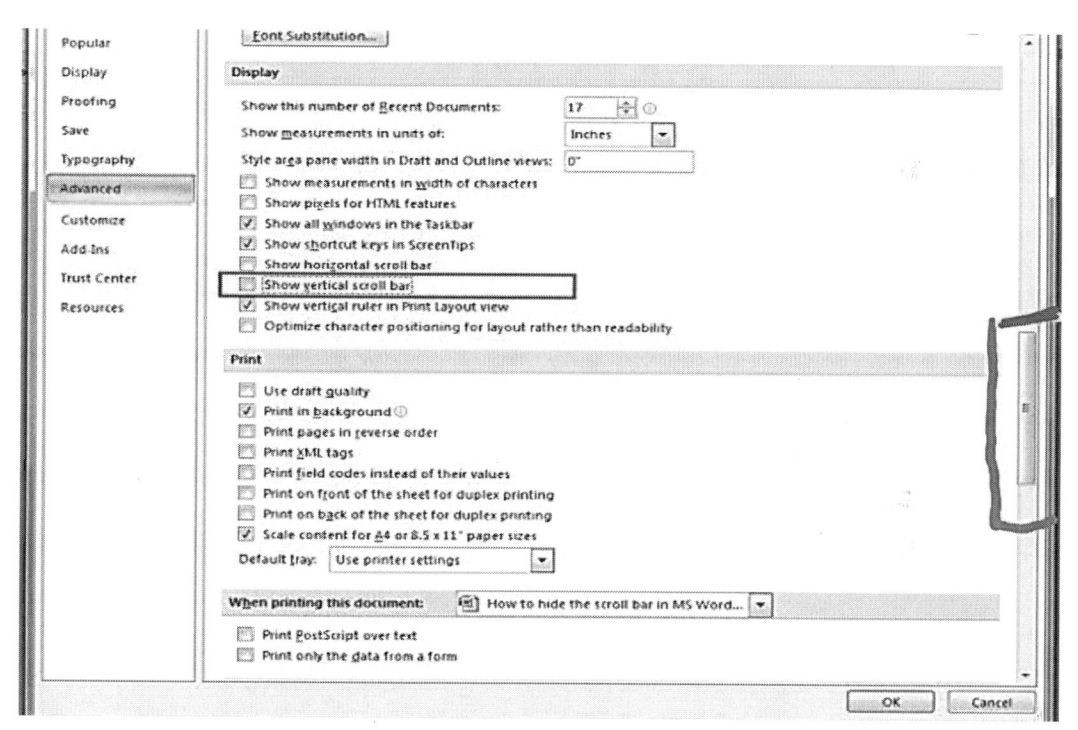

ii. Making Use of Horizontal Scroll Bar

When your document is bigger than the window can show, a horizontal scroll bar shows up to help you move it. It shows up at the bottom of the window, just above the status bar. You can use it to move the page around in any direction.

To make the horizontal scrollbar show up, do the following:

- Get to **File** and click on the **Options tab**
- The Word options dialogue box will now show up on the screen.
- Select the **Advanced tab.**
- Then, scroll down to the **Display** menu and click on the button.
- Now, choose the option to show horizontal scroll bars. (Same place as the Vertical scroll bar. Check figure 1)
- Click the **OK** button to finish. The horizontal bar becomes visible? How the horizontal scroll bar looks is displayed in figure 2

You can't stop word from moving the document to the left and right as you type, but you can try to move the horizontal scroll bar so that as much of the text as possible is shown.

Note: Use the Zoom tool to change the size of your document on the screen if the horizontal scroll bar bothers you.

Figure 2: The Horizontal Scroll Bar

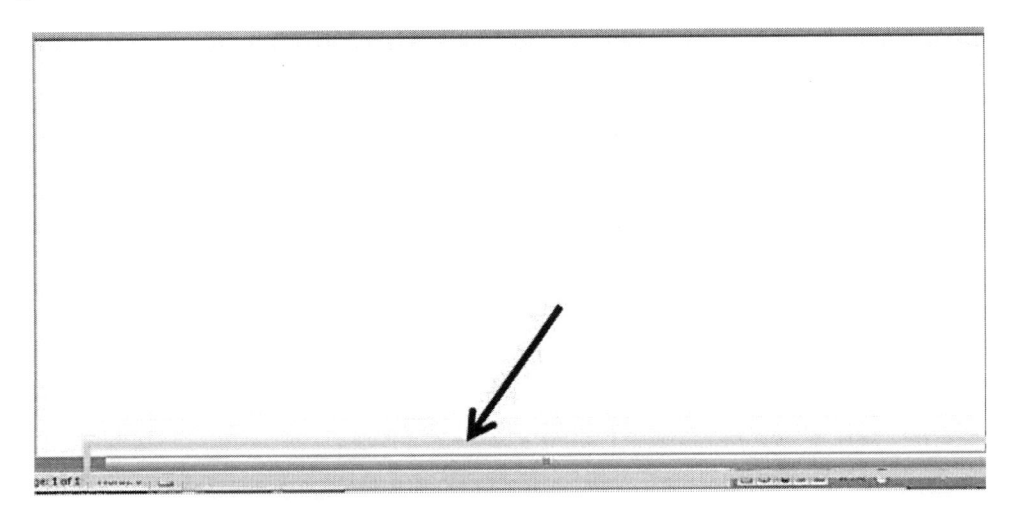

iii. Making Use of The Mouse Wheel to Scroll.

You can use the wheel on your mouse to help you move around in a Word file. Use the mouse wheel to scroll and do the following:

- To scroll up, roll the mouse wheel upward
- To scroll down, roll it the other way.

Also, keep in mind that when you use the mouse wheel to scroll the document, the insertion pointer moves with your view.

Figure 3: The Mouse Wheel for Scrolling

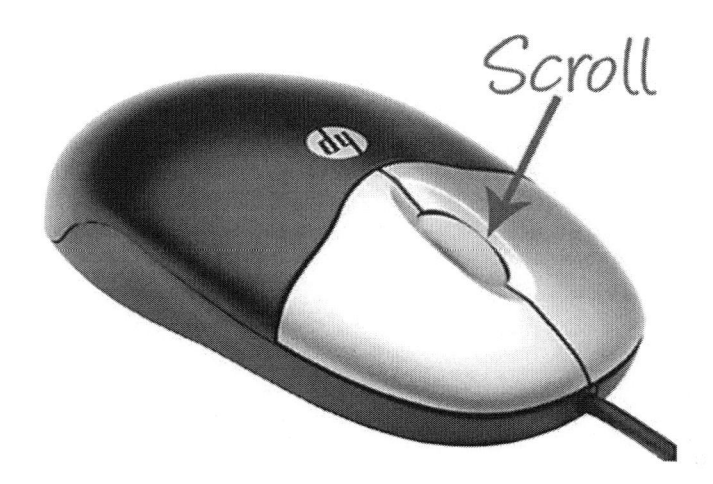

iv: Using the Navigation Pane

You can use the Navigation Pane to swiftly navigate across parts and pages in your document especially when you have a larger document with several pages or if you've divided your text into sections using headers. To do this:

- Click the **View** tab on the ribbon.
- On Show group, so choose "Navigation Pane."
- The Navigation Pane is on the left side of the screen, and it shows the headings that are used in the document.

- Click on **pages** as shown in figure 4
- The Navigation Pane will display all the pages in that document, represented by a thumbnail.
- When you click on a page in the Navigation Pane, you can see that page on your screen.

Figure 4: The Navigation Pane

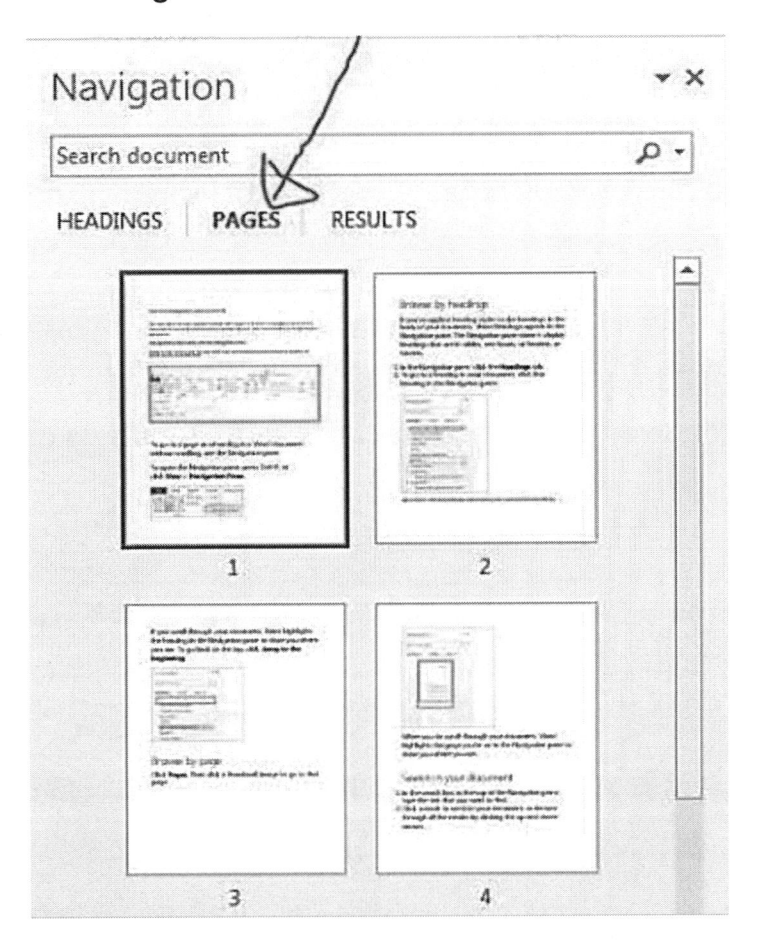

Moving the Insertion Pointer

The insertion point is the vertical bar that blinks as you type. It shows where text will be added as you type. In Word, you can make changes to any part of your document. You don't always have to work at the end of your document. Moving the pointer is very important! New text only shows up where the insertion pointer is. Text is deleted at the point where the insertion pointer is. Text is put where the insertion pointer is. The main thing you can do to get this to work is to know how to move the insertion pointer to the exact spot where you want it to be.

Note: You can also move the insertion point around with your keyboard.

Taking Control of the Insertion Pointer

Click the mouse on the spot where you want the insertion pointer to be. If your computer or laptop has a touchscreen, you can tap the screen with your finger to move the pointer.

i. Moving in Small Step

Use the keyboard's cursor keys to move a document's insertion pointer quickly. To move the pointer up, down, to the right and the left: The four arrow keys do this.

- ↑: To move the Insertion Pointer, you can move it up to the previous line of text
- ↓: Down to the next line of text
- →: You can also move it right to the next character
- ←: Left to the previous character.

Note: Moving the cursor doesn't change the text.

Also, if you hold down the Ctrl (Control) key and then press an arrow key, the insertion pointer moves in bigger steps. When you want to move the Insertion Pointer, you do this.

33

- **Ctrl+↑** : Up to the start of the previous paragraph
- **Ctrl+↓** : Down to the start of the next paragraph
- **Ctrl + →**: Right to the start of the next word
- **Ctrl + ←**: Left to the start of the previous word

Note: There are two sets of arrow keys on the computer keyboard. Make sure the Num Lock light is not on when you use the numeric keypad. If it's on, press the Num Lock key again to out it off.

ii. Moving From Beginning to End

Some cursor keys have no arrows on them that make the insertion pointer move when they are used. Depending on how you use End and Home buttons, you can move the pointer to the start or end of something.

- **Home**: The beginning of a line of text
- **End**: The end of a line of text
- **Ctrl+End**: To the end of the document
- **Ctr +Home**: To the very top of the document

There are two last cursor keys. They are the Page Up key and Page Down key. As you might have guessed, these keys don't move up or down a page in the text. They slide through the document based on the amount of text that can be seen in the window.

This is the Key or Combination that you need to use.

- **Page Up:** Up to one window full of text, or the top of the document if you're close enough.
- **Page Down:** Down to one window of text or the end of the document if you're near the end.

- **Ctrl+Alt+Page Up:** To the top of the text in the current window.
- **Ctrl+Alt+Page Down:** To move down to the bottom of the text in the current window.

Return to The Last Edit

Because there are so many different commands for moving the insertion pointer, it's very easy to make a mistake and not know where you are in a text file. There is no doubt about it, the insertion pointer has gone where no insertion pointer has gone before.

To get back to where you last changed something in Word, press Shift+F5 on your keyboard. Before the cycle starts again, you can use this keyboard shortcut three times. The first time should get you back to where you were before you went off the trail.

Auto-Scrolling in Microsoft Word: How to Make It Happen

To save yourself some stress, there is what is called auto-scrolling. This is a simple guide on how to activate it

- On the top left, click **File** and click **Options** in the bottom left corner.
- You'll see the Word Options dialogue box when you open it.
- Go to **Customize Ribbon** and click "Commands" in Ribbon.
- Then click "New Group"
- Auto-scroll is in the drop-down list, so choose it and hit **Add.** You'll see it in the Main Tabs.
- Click **OK,** and the Auto-Scroll button has been added to the Home tab

The Go-To Command

If you want to move the pointer to a specific page or line, you can use Word's Go To command. You can also send the pointer to the location of a lot of interesting things that Word could put in your document. The Go-To command is your word processor's way to get to any place.

Follow these steps when using the Go To command:

- Click the **Home ta**b.
- In the Editing group, choose the **Go To** command.
- When the **Find and Replace dialogue box** opens, the Go-To tab is moved to the front of the dialogue box.

However, for shortcuts: Press **Ctrl+G** to quickly get to the Find and Replace dialogue box which opens up quickly.

When you want to move the pointer to a specific place, choose it in a list called the "Go to What" button. For example, you can choose Page to go to a certain page. In the Enter Page Number box, type the page number. Then, click the Go To button to go to that page in your text.

It's important to note that the Enter Page Number box can also accept relative pages as input. Suppose you want to move five pages forward. To do this, type +5. To go back ten pages, type – 10.

On a final note, this chapter has covered the basic word you need to know about moving to and fro your document making it easy and fun to type faster.

CHAPTER 4

EDITING OF TEXT ON MICROSOFT WORD 365

Typing is all about making text. Part of the process is also going over and editing your words. To help you with text editing, Word has a lot of commands that can cut, slice, stitch, and so on. The commands are an important part of word processing, and they work best when you have a lot of text to work with. It's a good idea to write first and then edit it.

Therefore, this chapter will cover how to edit text, how to delete lines and sentences, splitting and joining paragraphs, how to use the Redo command to undo what you did, etc will all be discussed in this chapter.

Deleting a Single Character

When you write in Word, you can use the keyboard to both add and remove text. There are a lot of keys that make text but Backspace and Delete are the only keys that can delete text. These keys become more powerful when they are used with other keys, or even the mouse, that help them delete large amounts of text.

- **The Delete key** deletes characters to the **righ**t of the insertion pointer
- **The backspace key** deletes characters to the **le**ft of the insertion pointer.

Deleting a Word

You can delete an entire world with the Ctrl and Backspace or Delete keys. There are two ways to use these keyboard shortcuts. They work best when the insertion pointer is at the start or end of a word. Delete commands are only used when the pointer is in the middle of a word. These commands only delete from that middle point to the start or end of the word. The shortcut to delete is illustrated as;

- The word to the left of the insertion pointer is deleted when you press **Ctrl+Backspace.**
- The word to the right of the insertion pointer is deleted when you press **Ctrl + Delete.**

Note: When you use Ctrl+Backspace to delete a word to the left. The pointer is at the end of what comes before it. When you use Ctrl+Delete to remove a word, the cursor moves to the start of the next word. This is done to make it easier to quickly remove several words in a row.

Deleting More Than a Word

The keyboard and mouse must work together to remove chunks of text that are bigger than a single letter or single word. The first step is to choose a chunk of text and then delete that chunk of text.

Remove a Line of Text

A line of text starts on one side of the page and goes to the other. If you want to remove the line, you can:

- Make sure the mouse pointer is next to a line of text by moving it to the left.
- Then click on the mouse.
- The line of text is chosen and is shown in a different color on the screen.
- Press the delete key to delete that line.

Delete a Sentence

A sentence is a group of text that is made up of words that starts with a capital letter and end with a period, a question mark, or an exclamation point, depending on what you want to say. To do this;

- Place the mouse pointer where the sentence you want to delete lies.
- Press and hold down the Ctrl key at the same time as you click the mouse.
- Using Ctrl and a mouse click together, you can choose a sentence of text that you want to delete.
- The Ctrl key can be let go of, and then you can hit delete.

Deleting a Paragraph

A Paragraph is a group of sentences formed when you press the Enter key. If you want to delete a whole paragraph quickly, here's how to do it:

- Click the mouse **three times.** In this case, the triple-click selects the whole paragraph of the text.
- Press the **Delete button.**

Another way to select a paragraph is to click the mouse two times in the left margin, next to the paragraph, to make it select and then click on delete.

Deleting a Page

Page of text is everything on a page from top to bottom. This part of the document isn't one that Word directly addresses with keyboard commands. To get rid of a whole page of text, you'll need some sleight of hand. Take these steps:

- Press the keys **Ctrl+G.**
- The Find and Replace dialogue box comes up, with the Go To tab at the top of the list of tabs.
- On the Go to What list, choose Page and then type the number of the page you want to remove.
- Click the Go To button, then the Close button. And the page shows up.
- Press the **Delete** button.
- All of the text on the page is taken off.

Split and Join Paragraphs

A paragraph as earlier defined is a group of sentences that all say the same thing about a thought, idea, or theme. In Word, a paragraph is a chunk of text that ends when you press the Enter key. In a document, you can change a paragraph by splitting or joining text.

To split a single paragraph in two;

When you want to start a new paragraph, click the mouse where you want it to start. That point should be at the beginning of a sentence. Press the Enter button. During this process, Word breaks the paragraph in two. The text above the insertion pointer becomes its paragraph, and the text below it becomes the next paragraph.

Making a single paragraph out of two separate ones

To join two paragraphs together and make them one, simply do this; When you place the insertion pointer at the start of the second paragraph or use the keyboard or click the mouse to move the insertion pointer where you want it to be then press the Backspace button.

This implies that you have removed the entered character from the paragraph before this one thus making two paragraphs into one.

Soft and Hard Return

The **Return or Enter key** is pressed at the end of each line when typing on a keyboard. This indicates that you've finished one paragraph and are ready to go on to the next. However. When you set your page margins, Word knows that when you get to the right margin, your text should wrap to the next line automatically.

However, there may be situations when you want to stop writing a line before reaching the right margin. You can terminate a line in one of two ways in these circumstances. The first method is to enter where you want the line to terminate and then hit Enter. As a result, the document is filled with a **hard return.** This action (hitting Enter) signifies that you have reached the end of the paragraph and wish to begin a new one.

Another approach to end a line is to hit **Shift+Enter,** which will insert a soft return, also known as a line break or newline character, into the document. The end of a paragraph is indicated by hard returns, whereas the end of a line is indicated by **soft returns.**

A hard return displays on your screen as a paragraph mark (a backward P), while a soft return appears as a down-and-left pointing arrow.

The Undo Command

The Undo command can undo anything you do in Word, like changing text, moving blocks, typing, and deleting text. It does this for everything you do in the program. If you want to use the Undo command, you have two ways to do it:

- The shortcut method is to Press **Ctrl+Z.**
- Alternatively, you can click the Undo command button on the Quick Access toolbar to get back to where your previous work is.

Note: In some cases, you can't use the Undo command because there's nothing to undo. For example, you can't go back and undo a file save.

The Redo Command

If you make a mistake and undo something you didn't mean to, use the Redo command to get things back to the way they used to be. Suppose you write some text and then use Undo to remove the text. Then, you can use the Redo command to go back and type again. It's your choice. You can choose

- The shortcut method is to press **Ctrl+Y**.
- Alternatively, take a look at the **Quick Access toolbar** and click the **Redo button.**

Note: The Undo command does the opposite of what the Redo command does. So, if you write text, Undo removes the text, and Redo puts the text back.

The Repeat Command

To repeat what you did in Word last time, use the Repeat command to do the same thing again. This could be typing new text, formatting it, or doing a lot of other things.

Using the Repeat command, you can keep the same picture. Whenever there is no more to redo, the Redo command turns into the Repeat command.

To do this:

- The shortcut method is to Press **Ctrl+Y**, which is the same keyboard shortcut as to redo something.

Figure 1: The Undo and Repeat Button

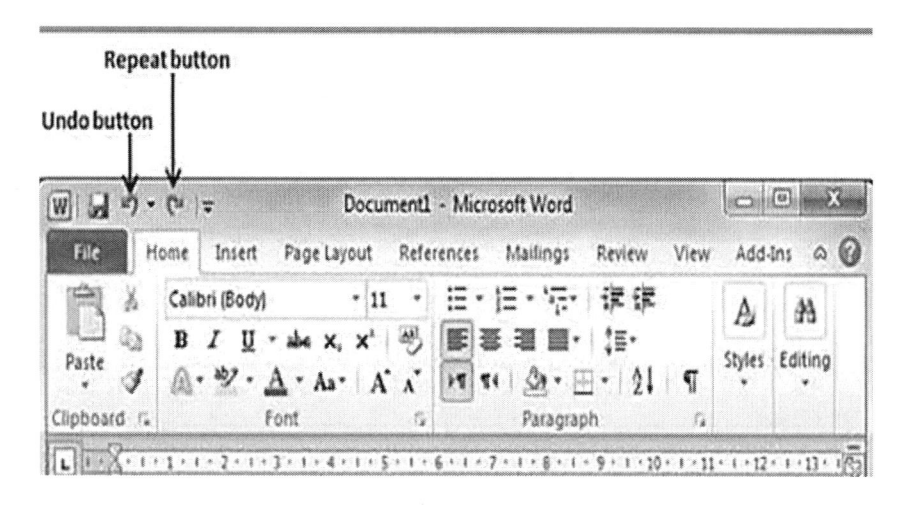

43

Finally, now that you know how to use the basic tools in Word to make a document, this chapter has covered some more editing tools and simple formatting effects to make a document look better. More editing tools will be discussed in other chapters.

CHAPTER 5

SEARCH FOR WORDS ON MICROSOFT 365

Introduction

In this chapter, we'll talk about how to find text in your document, how to use special text-finding options, how to find whole words, how to look for text that can't be typed at the keyboard, and how to replace found text with other text. Microsoft Word's Find and Replace tool has been made to help us change as many words as we want in a matter of seconds.

How to Search for Word on Microsoft Word 365

To find a text in your document, press Ctrl+F, which is a well-known keyboard shortcut for Find. The Find command can look for a single character, a word, or a group of words. It can also look for a whole group of words. To make it easier to find things in a document, Word lets you search for things like headings or pages as well as words.

These are the steps to search for a word on Microsoft Word 365

- Click the **Home** button.
- In the Editing group, click the **Find icon** to search for things to do.
- On the left side of the screen, the Navigation pane shows up. You can see it.

- When you're in the **Navigation pane,** type in the text you want to look for, then press Enter.

Note: If you click the arrow to the right of the Find icon, a menu comes up that lets you choose whether you want to Find or Go To.

- It shows all the text that is similar to what you typed.

Note: When text can't be found, the navigation pane tells you that it can't find the word in the text. To remove text from the search box, click the X button at the right end of the box.

How to Find and Replace Text in Microsoft Word 365

You can use the "find and replace tool" to find words in your file and then change them if there are needs for changes. There are times when you make mistakes while typing or need to change some text quickly. This tool can be useful. Here's a quick guide to how to use this feature in MS Word:

- Click on the **Home ta**b on the top menu bar
- Select the **Replace** option at the top-right corner of your screen.

Alternatively, you can also press Ctrl + H to do this faster. The Find and Replace pop-up box will show up

- **Find what:** Type in the phrase or word you want to find in your Word document in the Find what field under the Find tab.
- **To Replace**: On the top menu bar, click on the Replace tab and then click on the button that says Replace. In the

Replace with a field, type the word you want to change and then click Replace with.

Note: In Word, when you click Replace, the changes you want will be made one by one. However, if you want to change all of the fittings at once, you can choose to Replace All.

The image below shows the find, replace and replace all icons on Word.

Figure 1: Microsoft Word showing the Find and Replace Icon

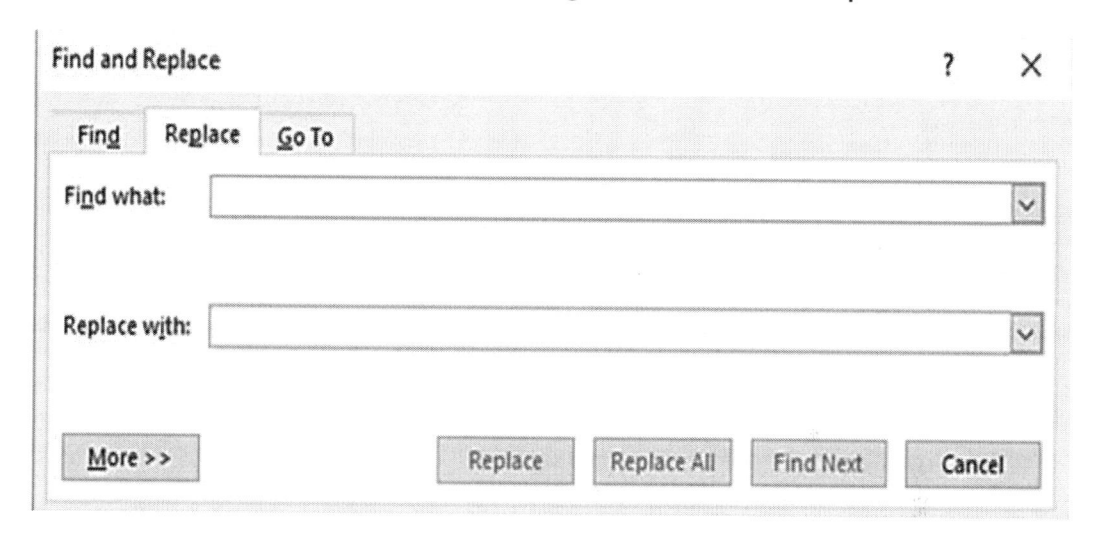

Advanced Find and Replace Features

With Microsoft Word's Advanced Find and Replace option, the process becomes even easier and the results even more accurate, you can use the Advanced settings to do this even faster and better.

There are a lot of ways you can use this feature.

- Go to the "Editing" group of the "Home tab",

- Click on the arrow next to "Find," and choose "Advanced Find."
- In the "Find and Replace" window, you will be able to search for and replace things at the same time. This is shown in figure 2

Figure 2: The Advanced Find and Replace Icon

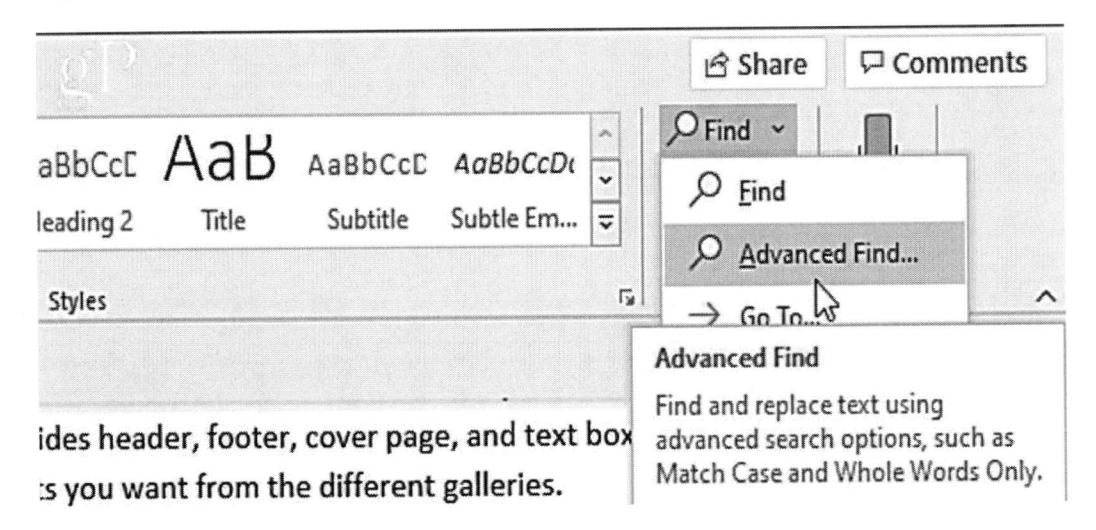

You can choose "**More**." You'll see a lot of new options right away as shown in figure 3 like Match case, Use wildcard, Match prefix, Match suffix, and so on, as well as a lot more. Each of these has a different job. We'll talk about them in more detail below.

    i. A tool called "**Match Case**" helps you find text that is exactly like the uppercase and lowercase letters you type.
    ii. There is a tool called "**Find Whole Words Only**." It only finds text that is not part of another word.
    iii. Use wildcat: A wildcat is a short string of characters that represents multiple characters in a search.
    iv. **Sounds Like:** It looks for words based on their phonetic pronunciation.

v. **Find All Word Forms:** Finds all forms of a word, like run, ran, and running.

vi. **Highlight All:** Highlights all of the matches in the text.

vii. **Incremental Find:** Highlights words as you type. It does this all the time. If you choose to turn off this option, Word will only highlight words in a document when you finish typing and press the Enter key.

viii. **Match Prefix:** This type of search looks for the prefix of words.

ix. **Match Suffix**: This type of search looks for the suffix of words, like runner or keeper, by looking for er. This type of search looks for the suffix of words.

After the Find command has looked through the whole document, you see an information box that says the search is over.

- When you're done, click **OK** and then click Cancel to close the Find and Replace window.

Note: Unless you turn off the Find and Replace dialogue box, the options you see there will stay in place until you turn it off again.

Figure 3: The More Options

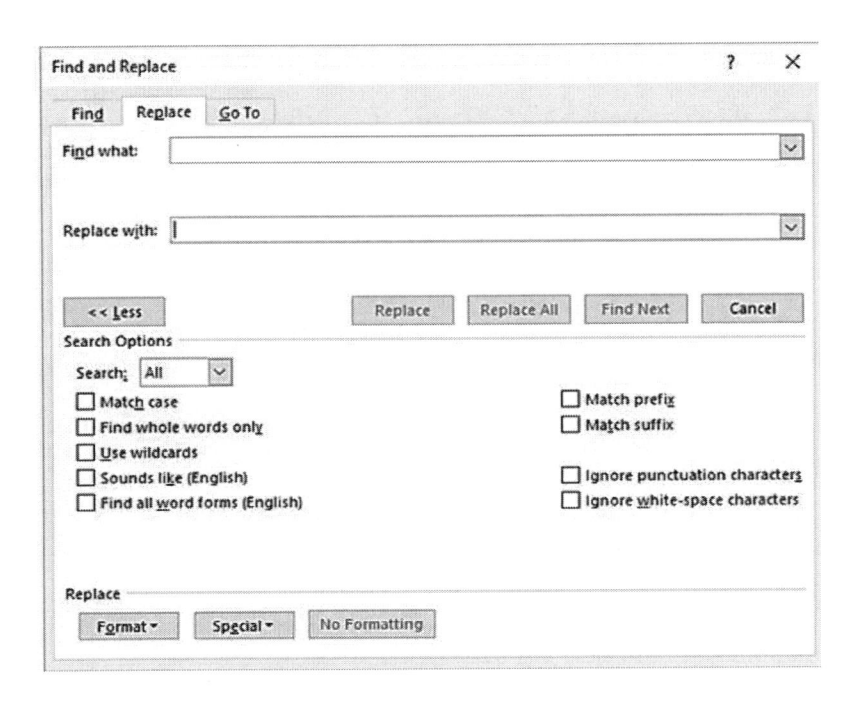

CHAPTER 6

BLOCK OF TEXT

In this chapter, we'll understand blocks of text, how to mark a block of text using the keyboard, the mouse, and the F8 key. It will also cover how to manipulate a block of text by copying a block, moving a block, using the mouse to copy and move a text and finally discuss on the clipboard.

What Does Block Mean in Microsoft Word 365?

In Word, blocks are groups of text in a document that have been selected in which you can choose to do anything with the selected word. When you select a block of text, you can do things that only affect the text in that block. You can move, copy, or remove the block. Hence, to move or copy a text, you first need to block it. This can be done with various special keys on the keyboard or with a mouse. It's possible to use both at the same time, or you can use some of Word's more complicated text-selection commands.

How To Mark a Block of Text

A block of text must show where it starts and where it ends before you can use it. A way to do this is to mark or select a piece of text.

i. Using the Keyboard

You can use the keys on your keyboard to mark a block of text. One of the simplest ways to do this is to hold down the Shift key as you move the cursor. When the Shift key is down, Word's standard cursor-key commands not only move the insertion pointer but also select chunks of text, making it easier to find what you want to write. Some common key combinations that people use.

- To select a character at a time to the right of the insertion pointer, press Shift+→
- To select a character at a time to the left of the insertion pointer Press **Shift+←**
- Shift+End will move a block of text from where you're typing to the end of the line.
- You can press **Shift+Home** to move a block from where you're typing to the beginning of a line.
- To select a block of text from the insertion pointer to a line above press **Shift+↑**
- To select a block of text from the insertion pointer to a line below press **Shift+↓**

ii. Using the Mouse

To use the mouse to mark a block of text on Word, the mouse pointer should be at the beginning of the text block. Then, drag the mouse over the text you want to select. As you move the mouse, the text gets highlighted or selected. For more clarity,

- **To select a single word or phrase: Double-click it.**
- **To select a line:** Move your mouse pointer to the left margin next to the line you want to select. Then click on the line. The mouse pointer changes to an arrow that points northeast. Mouse click on a line of text. Drag the mouse up or down to choose a group of lines.
- **To select a sentence:** Place the insertion pointer over the sentence and press Ctrl+click. (Press the Ctrl key and click the mouse.) The mouse will move.

iii. Using the F8 Key

Another way to mark a block of text is using the **F8** key. When you press the F8 key, the word's **Extend Selection command** comes up, and "drop anchor" will be placed where the insertion pointer is. Then, you can use the mouse or the cursor keys to choose text that you want to copy.

Note: When Extend Selection mode is on, you can't do anything else but select text. To put off the Extend Selection mode, you can either do something with the block of text or press Esc to get out of it. Also keep in mind that to use the F8 key and Extend Selection mode effectively, you can right-click the status bar and choose the Selection Mode item from the drop-down menu. When this mode is on, the text Extend Selection shows up on the status bar.

Blocking a Whole Document

To block a whole document, follow these steps:

- Click the **Home** button.
- In the **Editing** group, choose Select All to choose all of the items.
- The whole document is marked as one big piece of text.
- Alternatively, press **Ctrl+A** to select the whole document as a single block.
- The whole document has been successfully copied as a single block

How to Deselect A block

When you select a block of text and then change your mind, you must unmark or remove the text by any of the steps below;

> i. To get the block to un-select, you can move your insertion pointer with your keyboard or with the mouse and then press the Esc key.

Note: This trick doesn't work if you use the F8, Extend Selection key to select text.

> ii. Press **Shift+F5.** The Shift+F5 also deselects a block of text and moves back to the text that was already being edited before you made a selection.

> iii. To get rid of a block, press the Delete or Backspace button. The block is gone now.

iv. Formatting commands can be used on any text that has been marked. For example, character and paragraph formatting can be used.

Manipulating a Block of Text

It's possible to manipulate a block of text after you have marked it. Let's consider some ways to do this below;

i. Copying a Block

After you have marked a block, you can copy it to another part of your document and paste it. This operation doesn't change the original block in any way. You can copy text from one place to another in the following ways

a. Click the **Home** button.

- Then click **Clipboard** group, click the Copy command button in the group.
- Select the text you want to copy and click on copy
- Click to move the insertion pointer to where you want to put the copied block of text
- Make sure you pick the Paste tool from the Clipboard area, then click on it

b. Using the keyboard shortcut method. Use **Ctrl + C** to copy and **Ctrl+V** to paste.

Note: It's possible to paste the same block again after you've copied it. Whenever a piece of text is cut or copied, Word stores it. The copy and paste icon is indicated with an arrow in figure 1 below

Figure 1: The cut and Paste icon on Word

ii. Deleting a Block

Select the block and click Delete selected text, you can delete the text in the block that you've chosen.

iii. Moving a Block

a. To move a block of text, you first select the text, then cut and paste. Almost everything about this process is the same as copying a block. However, you can choose the Cut command button or press **Ctrl+X** on your keyboard to cut the block. When it comes to other things, they are all the same and then **Ctrl + V** to paste. The cut icon is shown in figure 2 below

b. Select any text and press **F2**. It says "Move to where" in the status bar at the bottom of your screen. Right-click on the text you want to move and choose "Move." It will be moved if you press Enter.

Figure 2: Word Showing the cut icon

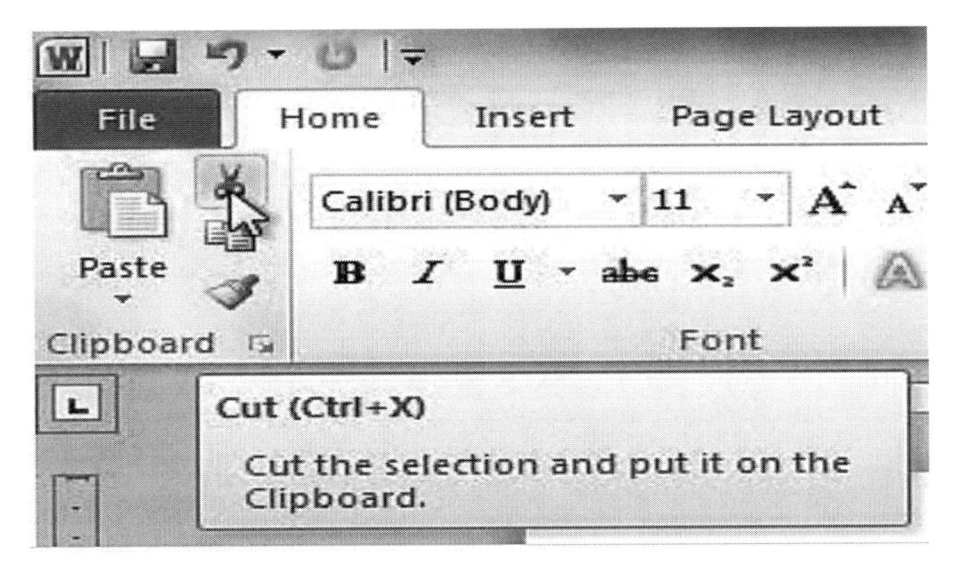

iv. The Mouse Can Be Used to Move or Copy a Block.

- When you only need to move a block to a short distance, you can use the mouse to move or copy the block. To do this, make sure that the mouse pointer is anywhere in the blocked text and drag the block to its new location. As you move the block, the mouse pointer changes, which means you're moving some text.
- Drag the mouse while holding down the Shift and Ctrl keys. This will make a copy of the block that is linked together. Release the mouse button, and the copied block falls into your document with a dark highlight on it when you do that.

v. Setting Pasted Text Format

When you paste text in Word, the **Paste Options icon ap**pears next to the text you've pasted. The Paste Option Icon allows you to choose how the pasted block will look after it's been put in.

- If you want to use the Paste Options button, you can click it with the mouse or press and release the Ctrl key on the keyboard to do so. How it looks it's illustrated in figure 3.
- If you click on the icon K which stands for "**Keep the formatting**" of the source code the same. In this case, don't do anything the formatting is fine.
- If you press the icon M which stands for **"Merge formatting".** It makes the text look the same.

Figure 3: Word showing paste options icon

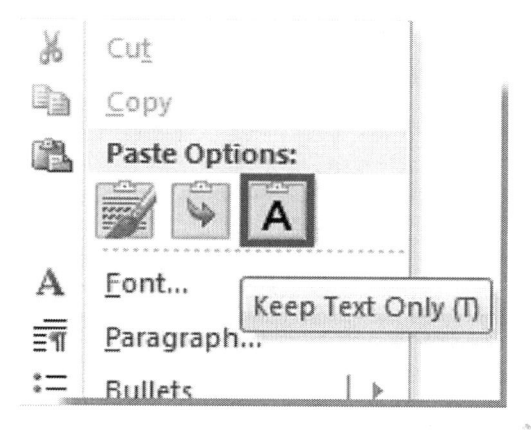

Figure 4: Labelled Diagram of the Paste Option

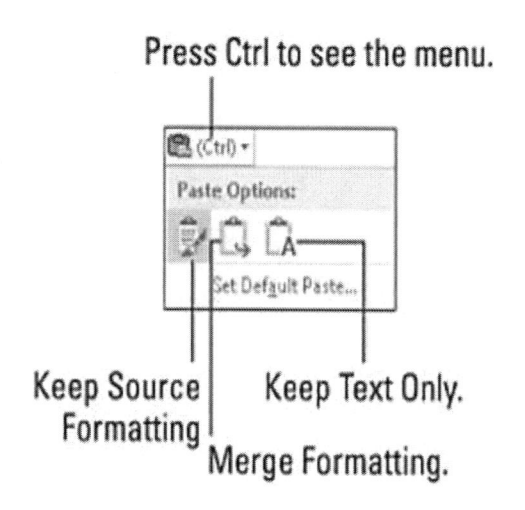

57

If you choose the icon T which means **"Keep Text Only"**. It means you shouldn't format, just copy and paste the text. You can press the Ctrl key and then the T key (Two separate keys, not Ctrl + T) after you paste to keep the only text that was copied or cut.

Note: It's possible to choose the Set Default Paste command after you click the Paste Options icon. This command tells Word how to deal with pasted text for good. It's a good idea if you keep picking the same Paste Options format over and over again.

Figure 5: Paste Option

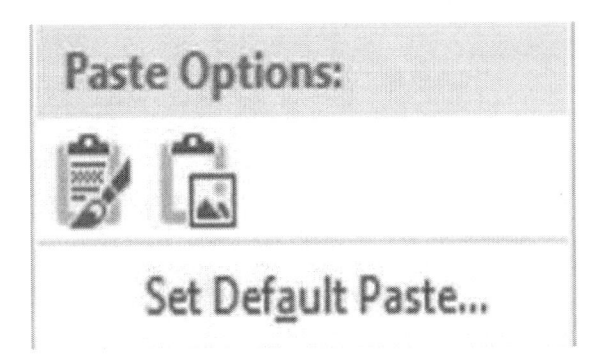

vi. **Viewing The Clipboard**

The Clipboard stores all of the content that you copy or cut. The Clipboard task pane contains items or text that you've cut or copied, and then paste them back into your document in any order. To do this follow these steps:

- Choose where you want the pasted text to go in your document.
- Click the **Home** button.
- In the **Clipboard** group, click the button that opens a dialogue box.

- If you open Word, you'll see the Clipboard task pane, which shows all of the text that you've cut or copied since you opened the program.
- Click on an item in the task pane with your mouse. The item has a menu button on the right.
- When you press the menu button, choose "Paste."
- The text has been added to your document. This is illustrated in figure 6 below

To remove the items from the Clipboard that you don't need.

- Click on the cl**ipboard group**
- Click the arrow on the right side of the item, and then click Delete to remove it.
- Click the Clear All button to remove everything from the Clipboard and to start over from scratch.

Alternatively, click the **X** in the upper-right corner of the Clipboard pane to get rid of it.

On a final note, It's possible to apply a format to all text in a block, copy a block, move a block, search for text in a block, proofread a block, print a block, and even delete a block from the document. Also, note that blocks must be chosen before you can do anything with them.

Figure 6: The Clipboard

Clipboard

[Paste All]   [Clear All]

Click an Item to Paste:

> their level of investments in accessibility. In order

- Paste
- Delete

CHAPTER 7

CHECK YOUR SPELLING ON MICROSOFT WORD 365

In this chapter, we are going to discuss how to check your work for typing and spelling mistakes. We will go further to discuss AutoCorrect settings, how to adjust, add and undo AutoCorrect correction. Also, we will look at how to get rid of grammatical mistakes to make sure that everything is correct and finally on document proofing.

Introduction

It is said that one of the most important parts of writing well is spelling, which is the art of putting words together correctly from their letters and helps people read better. Hence, it is very important in Microsoft Word.

Checking Your Spelling

To start a check of your document spelling and grammar, use the shortcut F7, or follow these steps:

- Click on the **Review tab** is on the ribbon.
- Then Click on S**pelling or Spelling and Grammar** as shown in figure 1 below.
- The program finds spelling mistakes and a dialogue box shows all the words that are wrongly spelt.

- You can use Word's Spell Check right away. The red zigzag line on any word indicates wrongly spelt words and mistakes as shown in figure 2. In figure 2, the word 'Content' was wrongly spelt as 'contrent' hence a red zigzag line is displayed on the word. The spell-check feature also tells you if you've used the same words over and over again by underlining them with a red zigzag. You can either delete the word that is repeated or you can choose not to pay attention to it.

Note: You can choose to correct the word, delete the word, leave it if it's correct and add it to the dictionary if it doesn't recognize that word.

Figure 1: The Spelling and Grammar icon on Microsoft Word

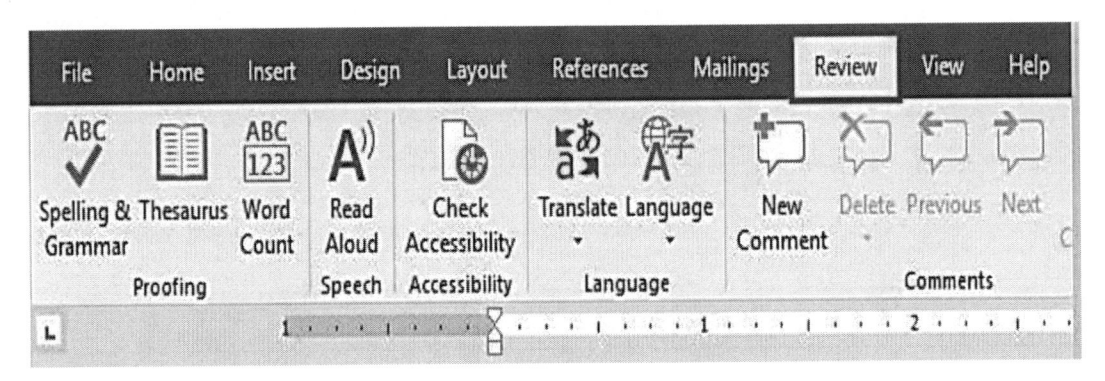

Figure 2: Microsoft Word showing a Red Zigzag line

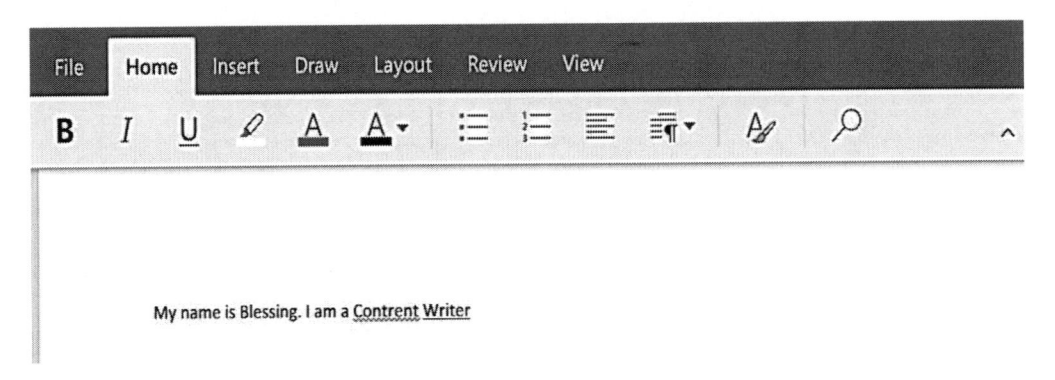

Turning On or Off Spell Check on Microsoft Word

- Click on **File**
- Click on **Options**
- Next, click on **Proofing**
- Clear the Check spelling as you type box, and then click **OK.**

To Turn Spell Check Back on, all you have to do is repeat the same process and select the Check spelling as you type box.

Fixing Words That Aren't Spelled Right

- Choose Check Spelling from the Edit menu to make sure your words are correct.
- Select the misspelt words that you want to find, then press the Enter key
- The spelling submenu is displayed
- From the submenu, type the correct and click Ok

Words That Have Been Mistakenly Flagged.

You might have typed a name that Microsoft Word doesn't know. To correct a word that has been falsely accused, you can do any of the following:

- Right-click it and choose the correct word from the list.
- **Add to the Dictionary:** click on add the word to the dictionary. The word will no longer be marked as spelled incorrectly in this or any other document because it is now correct.
- **Ignore** This command tells Word to ignore the word and accept it as spelt correctly through the whole document.

AutoCorrect in Microsoft Word 365

AutoCorrect is a useful feature in Microsoft Word that checks your spelling and corrects it for you automatically. Word quickly fixes a lot of common typos and spelling mistakes on the spot, so you may not even notice the red zigzag when the AutoCorrect feature is on. AutoCorrect fixes that typo as soon as you hit the spacebar or punctuation marks at the end of a word. It also turns common text shortcuts into the single characters they should be. It corrects common punctuation mistakes, when you start a sentence, it capitalizes the first letter of it. When you forget to capitalize your name, AutoCorrect corrects it, it fixes the inverse caps lock problem and other common typos, as well as a lot of other mistakes that can be made when typing.

How To Turn On and Off AutoCorrect on Microsoft Word

- Go to **File** and click on **Options**
- Click on **Proofing** and choose AutoCorrect Options from the drop-down menu on the right.
- Click on the **AutoCorrect button.** This is shown in figure 3
- On the AutoCorrect tab, you can choose or choose not to replace text as you type.

For AutoCorrect to work, make sure that the Replace text as you type box is checked or unchecked.

Figure 3: The AutoCorrect Feature on Microsoft Word

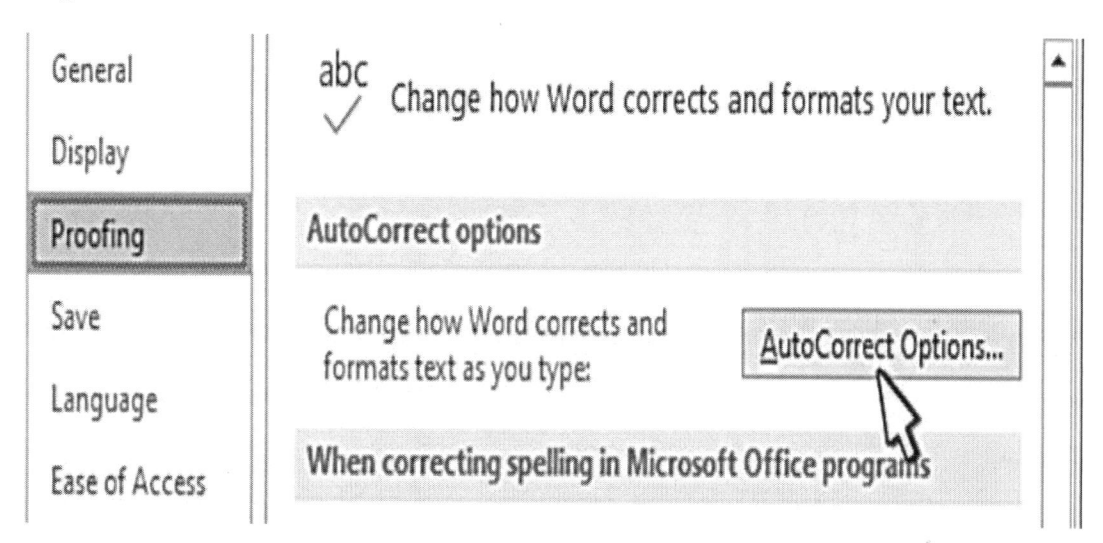

Undoing a Correction Made by AutoCorrect

You can easily undo a correction made by AutoCorrect. To do this, click on Ctrl+Z (the Undo command).

Note: You need to press it right after AutoCorrect makes its correction.

Adding a New AutoCorrect Entry

To do this follow the steps below:

- Right-click a word that you want to add to your AutoCorrect list.
- Type a word or phrase that you often misspell in the Replace column, and then click Replace.
- In that column, type the correct word.
- Then, click **Add**.

Note: If you want more information about the AutoCorrect tab, check out the AutoCorrect options page and you can add as many entries as you want. Add a new entry for each new thing that you do and click add.

Adjusting AutoCorrect Settings

To change how AutoCorrect works and the words it corrects, follow these steps:

- Click on the **File** tab.
- Then, choose Options and the Word Options dialogue box appears
- Choose the **Proofing** category on the left side of the window.
- Then click on the **AutoCorrect** Options button on the right. When you open the AutoCorrect tab, you can see all of the things that AutoCorrect can do, like capitalize the first letter of a sentence, change words that don't follow the rules, click the Exceptions button and so on

To remove an entry from the AutoCorrect list, scroll down until you find the item you want to remove, click on it, and then click the **Delete** button on the right.

Grammar Check

Microsoft word grammar checker works the same way as to spell check. The main difference is that offenses are marked with a frigid blue zigzag. When you right-click the blue-underlined text the pop-up menu shows to find out what's wrong. You can also choose to ignore it if you wish.

The grammar proofing tool looks at the text and thinks about how the actions and the people or things that are doing them are linked together. When the subject and verb don't match, this is the most common cause of grammatical mishaps in the English language. The grammar checker is very good at spotting when there are two spaces between words when there should only be one space between the words.

Turning on Grammar Check

- First, put on Microsoft Word
- Click on the Tools menu, then click on **Options**.
- When you're on the Spelling and Grammar tab, change the Writing style box to Grammar and Style.
- Then click **OK**.

An All-in-One Document Proofing

There is an all in one process for spelling and grammar checker if you don't want to look at the red zigzag underline or if you don't have that feature turned on, you can just simply do a final document proof with these steps:

- Click the **"Review"** button.
- The "**Spelling & Grammar button**" is on the Proofing group. To get to it, click it.
- The **Editor** pane shows up. Errors are shown one at a time as they happen in your text. You must check each of them one after the other.
- And then correct each of them.

Note: The Spelling pane or the Grammar pane shows up depending on what the person did. You can choose to ignore, ignore all, however, If you make the same spelling mistake or similar grammatical mistakes again, you'll be reminded of them. You can choose to delete repeated words, add to dictionary etc. You can choose to select the correct answer from the list that's shown and then click the Change button to change the text. You can also click the correct word, then click Change All to change all of the places where you made that spelling mistake.

- Afterwards, click the **OK** button.

Note: Another way to go through spelling and grammar mistakes one by one is to use the Spelling and Grammar Check button on the status bar. You can use that button to jump from one spelling or grammar mistake to the next.

Checking a Document Again

The Ignore or Ignore All button has consequences. If you've used the ignore all options too many times, you can tell Word to recheck your document, which brings forgotten misspellings and grammatical mistakes back into the word document proofing, so you can fix them again, too. Follow these steps:

- Click the **File** button.
- Choose **Options** to open the Word Options window.
- Then choose the Proofing option on the list.
- To check the document again, click the Recheck Document button on the toolbar. It's under the title **"When Correcting Spelling and Grammar,"** and it says "When."

- Click the Yes button to say that you want to un-ignore things you've chosen to ignore in the past.
- Click the OK button to close the Word Options window.
- Then the document shows itself again, highlighting all the words and things you've chosen to not read before.

Note: Rechecking a document doesn't erase any changes you made to Word's dictionary. If spelling and grammar errors don't show up when you recheck them, it might be because the option to hide them has been turned on, that is "Hiding all proofing errors in a document" is turned on.

Settings for Document Proofing

There are a lot of settings and options you can use to control Word's document-proofing tools.

i. Making Changes to the Custom Dictionary

You build the custom dictionary by adding words that are correctly spelt but have been marked as misspelled to the list of words. If you want, you can also manually add words, remove words, or just look at the dictionary to see if you're making any mistakes. Take these steps:

- Click the **File** button.
- Choose Options to open the Word Options window.
- Then, choose **proofing.**
- Click the button that says "**Custom Dictionaries**" to make your own.
- The Custom Dictionaries dialogue box comes so you can add words to it.

- Make sure you put the words you want in a custom dictionary in the text box that says Word(s). When you're done, click "**Add**."

To remove a word from the custom dictionary: click on the word in the scrolling list and then click Remove from the custom dictionary. To delete, click the Delete button.

Note: Click OK when you're done with your dictionary. Then, click the OK buttons on the open dialogue boxes to close them and go back to your text.

ii. **Putting an end to automatic proofing**

To get rid of the red zigzag underlines and blue underlines from your document, while typing follow these steps:

- Click on the File tab and then choose Options. The Word Options dialogue box comes up
- On the left side of the dialogue box, click on Proofing and then click on the button.
- You can uncheck the box that says, "Check Spelling as You Type."
- Remove the checkmark from the item while you're at it. Mark Grammar Errors as You Type, then Check Your Work.
- Choose "OK."

iii. **Cutting back on grammar-checking**

To change grammar settings, do the following:

- Click the **File** button.
- Choose **Options** to open the Word Options window.
- Then, choose proofing.

People who use Word to correct their spelling and grammar should look for the Writing Style item below the title. Here you can choose what kind of grammar to use, and how you want things to look. To the right, there is a button that says "Setting."

Click the Settings button to go to the next step.

The Grammar Settings dialogue box comes up.

In Word, you can uncheck the boxes for things that you no longer want to be marked as offensive.

iv. All proofing mistakes in a document can be hidden.

The **red zigzag** and the chilling **blue underlines** can be hidden if you tell Word to keep checking your spelling, but you can also tell it to hide them. Words are still marked as misspelled, but they don't show up in the text. Make sure you follow these steps:

- When you open the Word Options dialogue box, look for the Proofing area.
- There are options in Word called **"Options"** that let you hide spelling and grammar mistakes only in the document you're working on.
- To turn them off, check the boxes next to them and uncheck them.
- The proofing flags disappear all over your document.

This is how to hide spelling and grammar mistakes in a paper.

How to Hide a Word Document That Has No Spelling or Grammar Errors.

If you only want to hide spelling and grammar mistakes in one Word document and not all of your other documents, follow these steps:

- Click on the "**File**" tab.
- When you get to the bottom of the left-hand pane, click on "**Options**"
- The "**Word Options**" window will show up, so you can make changes.
- Click on the **"Proofing" tab. T**he proofing tab is where you go to make sure everything is
- Make sure the "Hide spelling errors in this document only" and "Hide grammar errors in this document only" boxes are checked at the bottom of the window. Click "Yes." This is shown in figure 4 below.

Figure 4: The 'Hide All Error in a Document only' icon

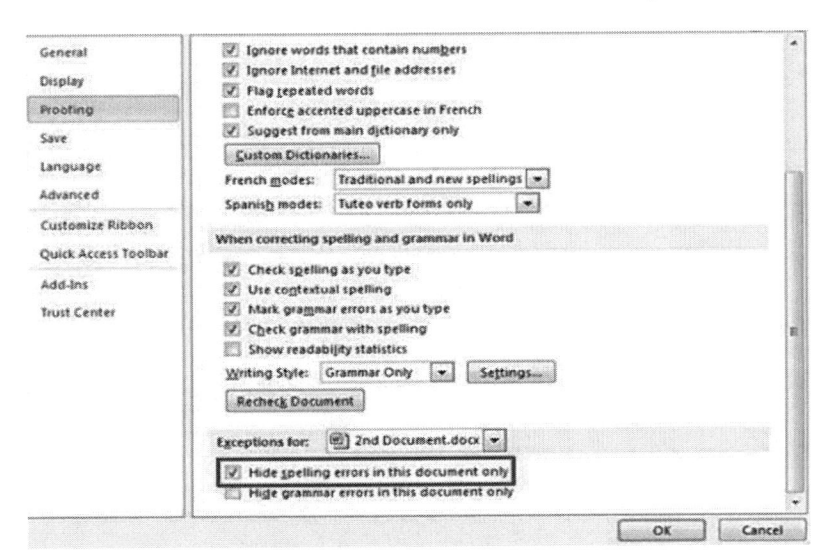

Finally, In Word, when you check your document for spelling and grammar, it keeps track of which mistakes you choose not to fix. And with all mistakes corrected, the document is ready.

CHAPTER 8

NEW, SAVED, AND OPENED DOCUMENT

In this chapter, we are going to discuss the document. We will discuss how to save and open a new document and recover a lost document.

What a Document is All About

In general, a document is a record or a file that holds a piece of information so that it won't be lost. A document can be made up of write-ups, pictures and sound. Sales invoices, wills and deeds, newspaper, individual newspaper stories, oral history recordings, executive orders, product specifications or descriptions etc are all examples of documents. You can make new documents, save them, open old documents, and close old documents.

In word processing, a document is the unit of work that you can save. Each document is saved as a unique file with a different name as shown in figure 1 below. If you want to get the most out of your word processing, you need to know a little about files and storage.

- **File**: When you write something in Word, it's called a file. A file on a computer is a piece of information that is kept for a long time and can be used again and shared with other people.
- **Folder**: A folder holds files and other folders, which creates a hierarchical way to store data.
- **Local Storage:** If you have a hard drive or a solid-state drive, you can keep files for the long run on this file.

- **Cloud Storage:** Files kept on the Internet for a long time. This storage is called "cloud storage."

When it comes to Word and the rest of Microsoft Office, **Microsoft One Drive** is the best cloud storage service out there. The advantage is that you can access your cloud storage from any computer that has an Internet connection. Cloud storage services like Dropbox and Google Drive work with Word as well, so you can store your files there.

Figure 1: An image of documents saved on Word

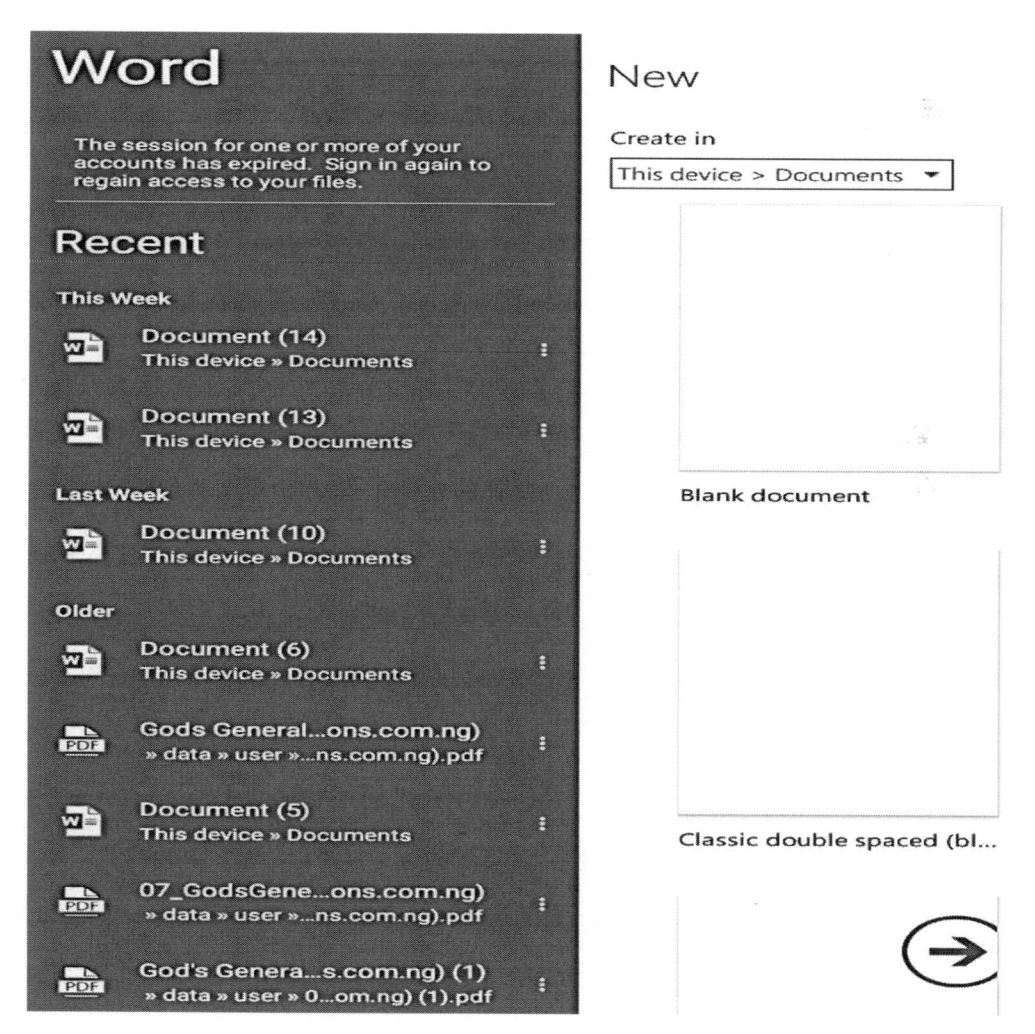

A New Document

To start a new document on Microsoft word, choose a blank document or template, and start typing. Word has a lot of professionally-designed templates that you can use to make letters, resumes, reports, and more.

Setting up a New Blank Document

- Go to **Word** on your PC or laptop
- Click on **File**
- Then tap on **New.**
- To choose a blank document as shown in figure 2 click on the blank document and start typing.

If you want to open a template, a list of Word templates that can be used is shown. Then, double-click the template you want to open and it will open. Some templates are also shown in figure 2 below.

Note: Pin the templates you like. This way, you can always see them. Select the template and then click on the pin icon next to the name of the template. You can make as many new documents as you need. Word lets you work on a lot of different things at once.

But here's a quick way: To start a new document, press **Ctrl+N**. It's faster.

Figure 2: How to Create a New Document

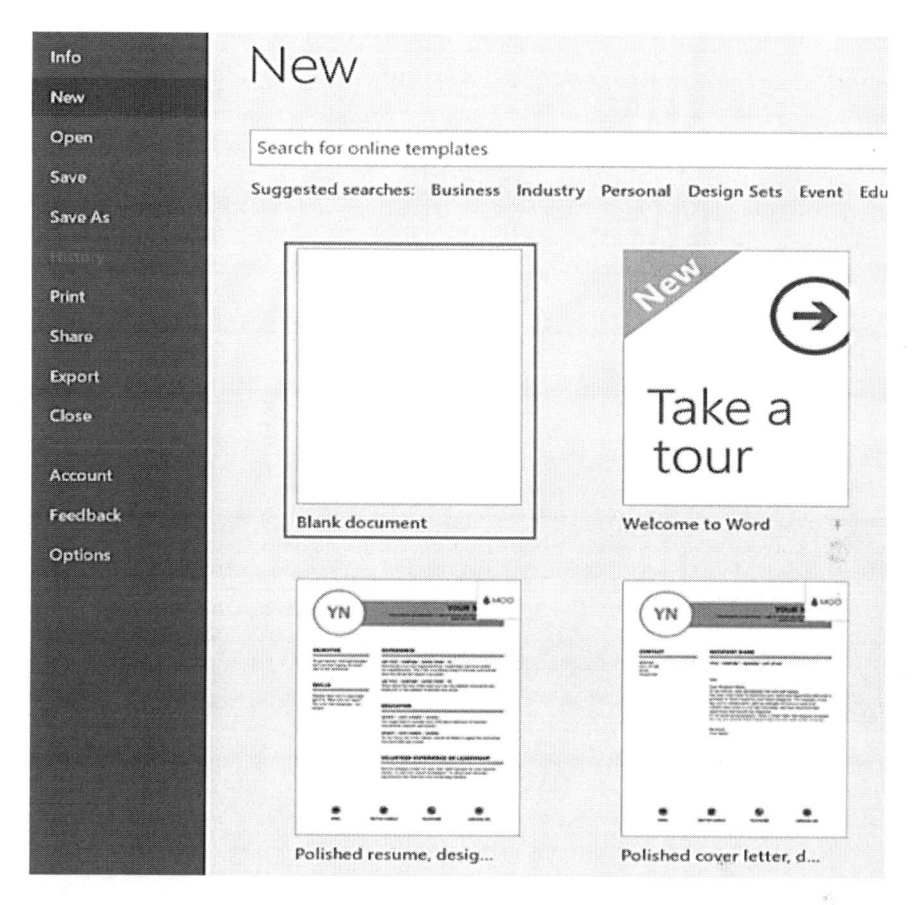

Save Your Document

In Microsoft Word, the content you type is stored in the computer's memory as you type. However, this memory is only for a short time. When you close Microsoft word or shut down your computer, everything that is in memory is thrown away. Unless you save it, it will be gone for good. Hence, you must save your document. To save your document below:

- Click on **File**
- Then click on the Save icon on the **Quick Access Tool Bar**
- Choose a folder to save your document

- Type a name for your document in the **File** name box
- Then click **Save as** circles in figure 3 below to save your document.

Another easy way to save your work is to click on Ctrl+S. Do this often while you type.

Figure 3: The Save Button

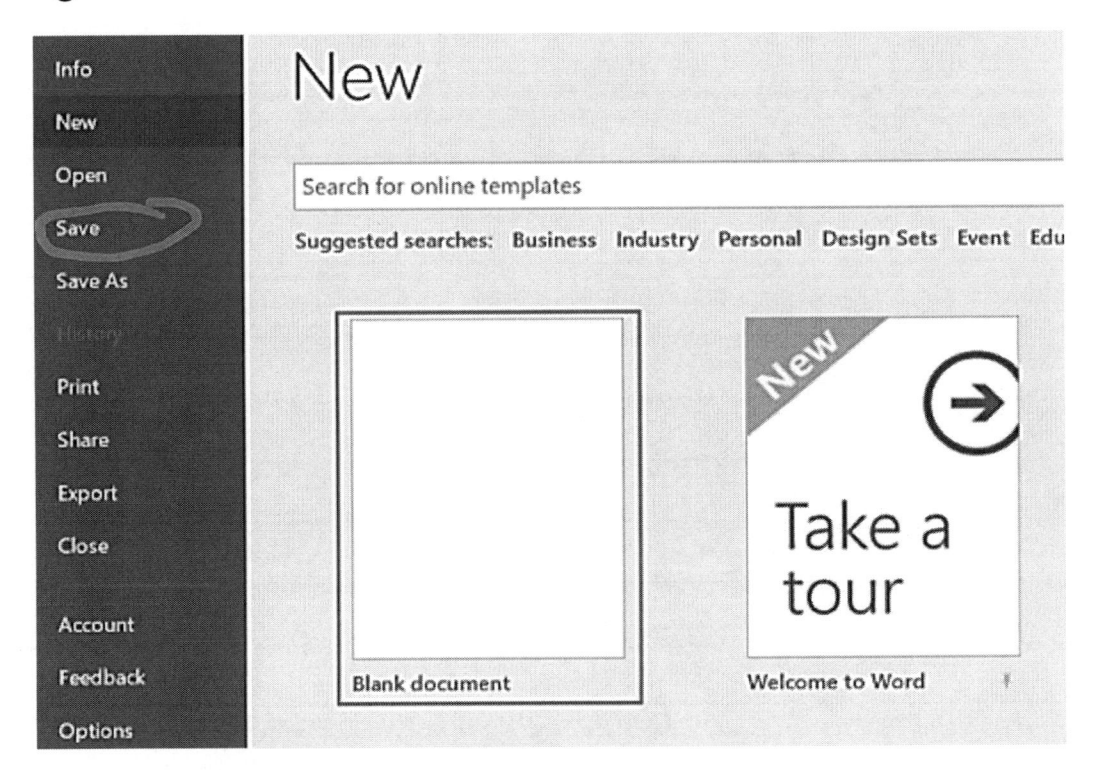

Saving a File for the First Time

To save a document, you don't have to finish writing all of the words. No! You should save as soon as you finish writing a few sentences or paragraphs so that you don't lose your work.

Follow these steps:

- Press the key**s Ctrl+S.**

Note: The **Save As** the screen is on the File tab as shown in figure 4 below. You could also go to the File tab and choose Save As, but Ctrl+S is a universal keyboard shortcut and it's faster to use.

Choose a place for the document. There are folders where all documents (files) are kept as shown in figure 4 below. Your job is to choose one that is right for your needs. You can choose to store your files on your computer or in the cloud. You can also choose a pinned or recently used folder.

- Then click on **save**

Note: When you re-save a file that has already been saved, the Save As screen doesn't show up again. The file saves itself with the most recent settings either by clicking ctrl+save or clicking on the save icon on the top left corner of your screen.

Figure 4: The "Save As" icon

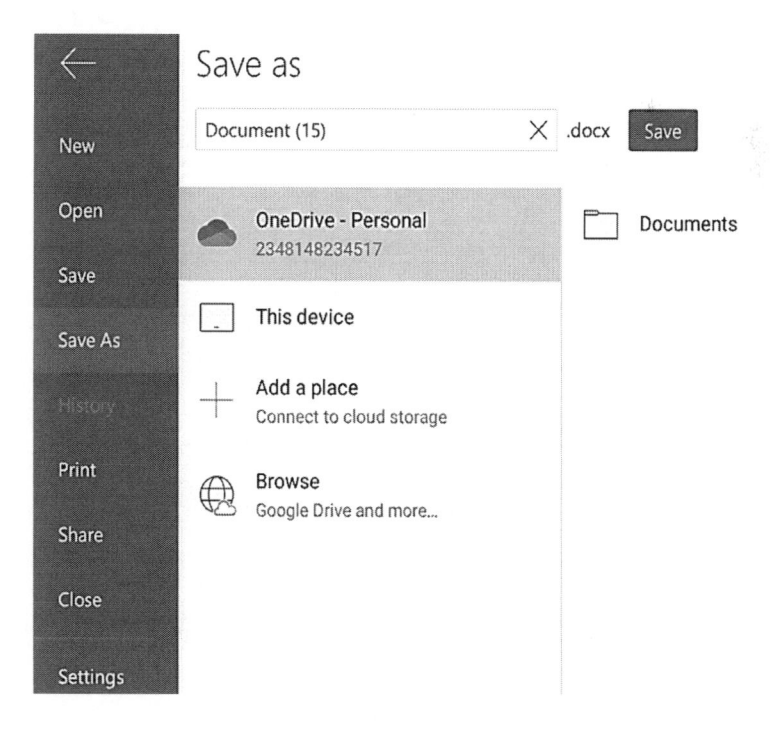

Changing Where The Saved Document Are Kept

If the current folder doesn't meet your needs, you can click the New Folder button to make a new folder. Word then saves your document in the new folder.

The Save As command can also be used to save a document with a new name, move it to a different place, or save it differently. To open the save as icon, click the "Browse" button. With the Save As dialogue box opens, you can then change where the file will be saved as shown in figure 5 below

When you open the Save As dialogue box, the parts of a path are separated by right-facing triangles instead of slashes at the top. Because there are so many subfolders inside each folder, you can click any triangle to open a drop-down list of all of them. Then, you can quickly switch to one of those subfolders by clicking it.

Figure 5: Where to Save your document

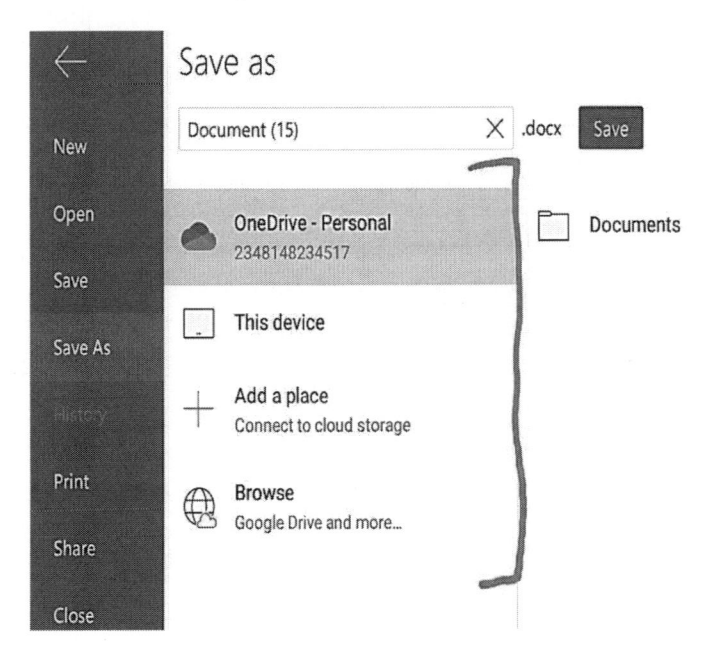

80

Document-save errors: How to fix them

Word and Windows must work together to save a document. This makes it more likely that something will go wrong, so it's time for an error message.

Some Error Messages you can get include:

i. "**The file already exists.**" In this case, do not Replace otherwise you will be lost the document saved with that name placement. The best way to solve this is to use a different name. You can change the name of the file you want to save in the Save As dialogue box

ii. Another common error is when you want to save a document and it says a"**the name of the file is not valid**" That's how Word tells you that the filename has an illegal character in it.

Note: When you are naming your files make sure is short and descriptive. Letters, numbers, and spaces can be used in a file name. It can have periods, commas, hyphens and even underlines in the name of a file.

Also note You should save your work as you go along: Changes you've made since you last saved are caught by the frequent re-save. This keeps your work fresh. It's never a bad idea to save a document again and again.

To make sure that AutoSave is on, look for the AutoSave item on the **Quick Access toolbar.** If the switch doesn't work, click it. In a game, AutoSave is on when you see the word "On" as shown in figure 6. When the Autosave item is turned off, the document has been saved to a place other than One Drive.

Figure 6: The Autosave icon

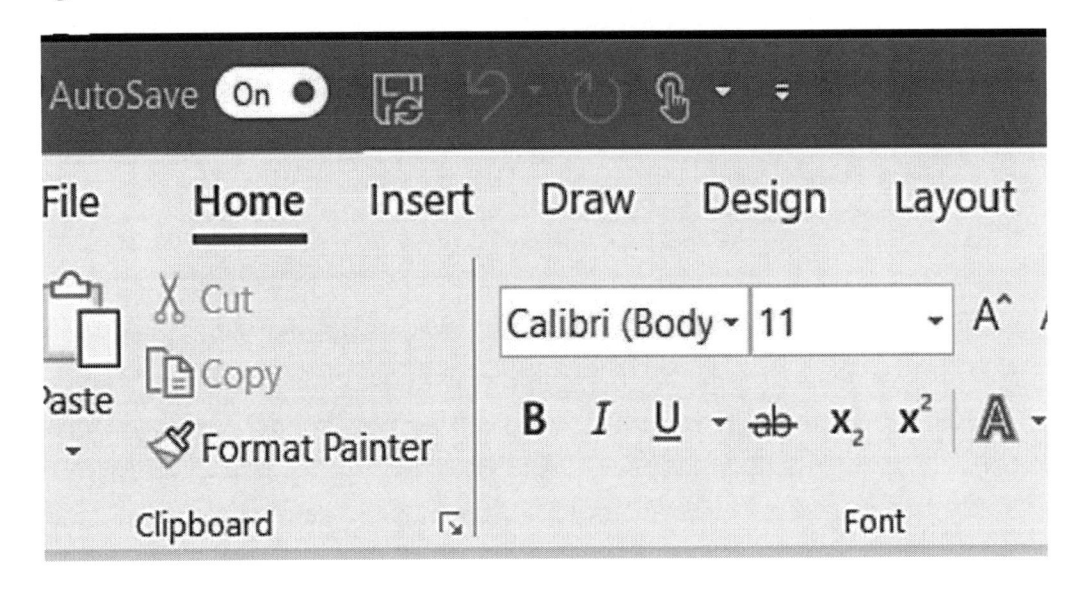

Making a mistake and not saving your work before you quit

To stop writing in Word, you either shut down or quit it. You do this when you're done with a document, a window, or Word itself. If your document hasn't been saved yet or has changed since the last save, you're asked to save one last time before leaving.

The warning box that appears when you try to leave before saving has three options as shown in figure 7 below:

- **Save**: Click this button to save the document and then close it, and then you can finish.
- **Don't save**: It doesn't save when you click this button. Later, it might be possible to get it back.
- **Cancel**: This button lets you forget about saving and go back to the document to do more editing and things like that.

Figure 7: Quitting a Document without Saving it

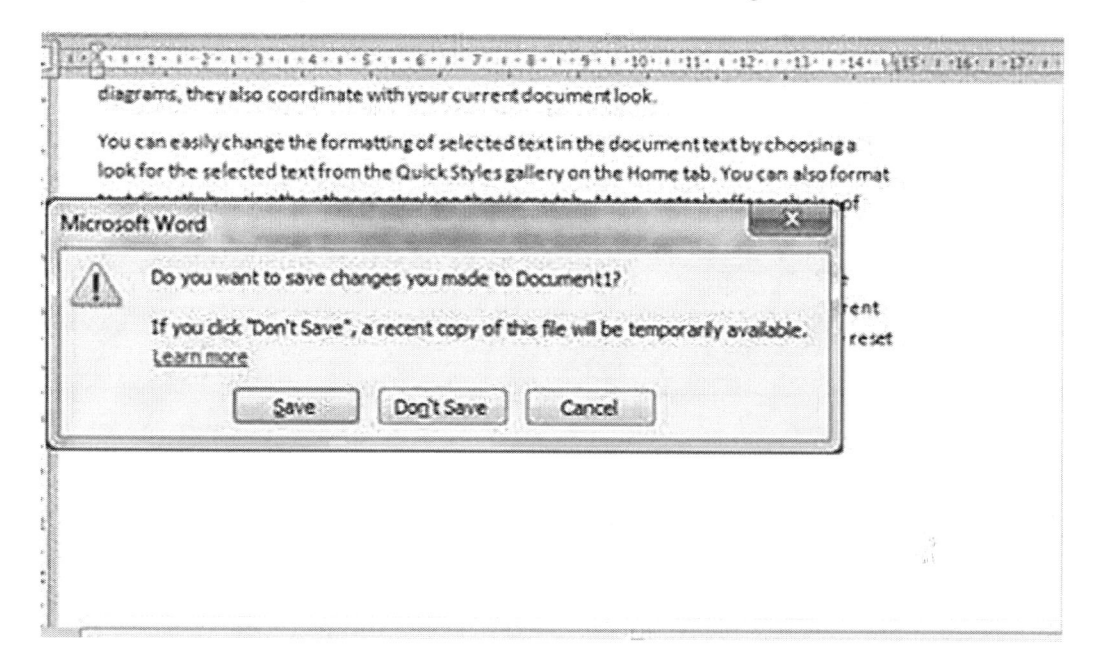

Open a Document

These are the steps you need to take to open a document in Word:

- Go to **"Files."**
- Choose the "**Open**" button which is circled in figure 8 below
- Choose a place where the document could be found.
- Choose from Recent Documents, one drive cloud storage, or local storage called "This PC" to store your files.

Alternatively, If you see the document you want on the Recent list, click it. The document comes up on the screen and you can read it now. The good news is that you're done.

Note: It's possible to do anything you want with the document after you open it. You can change it, look at it, print it, or do anything else. Also, keep in mind that the fact that you open a file does not remove it from storage. The file is still on the storage system except you use the Save As command to update the document with any changes that you make to the document.

Figure 8: An image showing the open icon

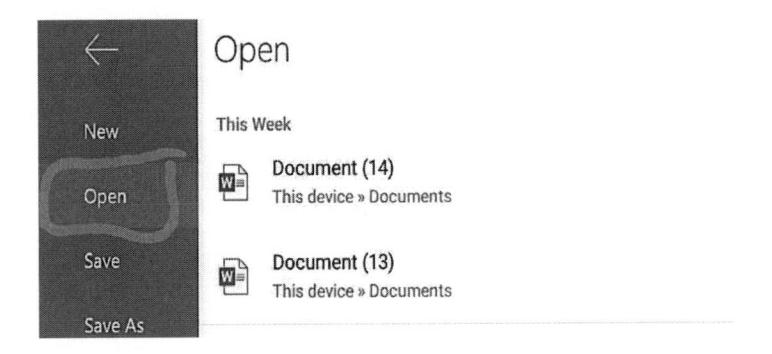

How to Insert a Document into another Document

When you open a document in Word, you can insert another document inside of it. To give an example, you might be writing a letter asking for a new job and want to add your résumé, CV, or biography at the end. If so, or in any other case, follow these steps:

- Place the insertion pointer where you want the other document's content to show up.
- Click on the **Insert tab** and the **Insert File d**ialogue box comes up.
- Find and choose the document you want to add.
- Click on Insert after selecting the document. It is automatically added to your document

Note: The name of the first document is kept when the two documents are combined and you can put as many documents as you want into another document. This is called "boiler plating." It's when you copy and paste text from one document into another.

To Get Back a Draft

Whether your computer crashes or the power goes out, you can sometimes get back some of the documents that you didn't save. Follow the steps below:

- Click on **Open** on your screen (Refer to open a document on this chapter)
- Make sure that the file location is set to Recent as shown in figure 9 below
- The Recover Unsaved Documents button is at the bottom of the list of recently opened files. You can find it there as shown in figure 10.
- The Open dialogue box comes up, and it shows the contents of a special folder called Unsaved Files.
- Select a file to recover.

Figure 9: An image showing the Recent icon on Word

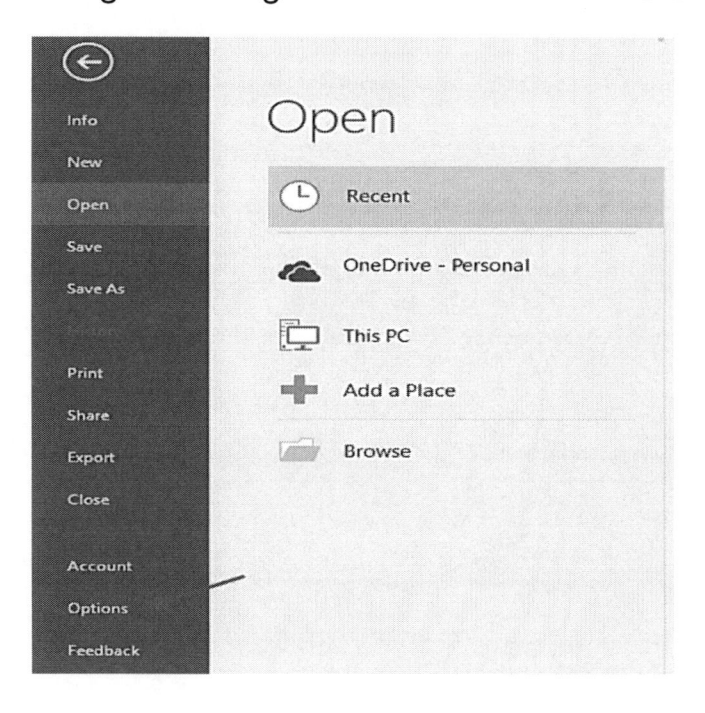

Figure 10: Recover unsaved Document

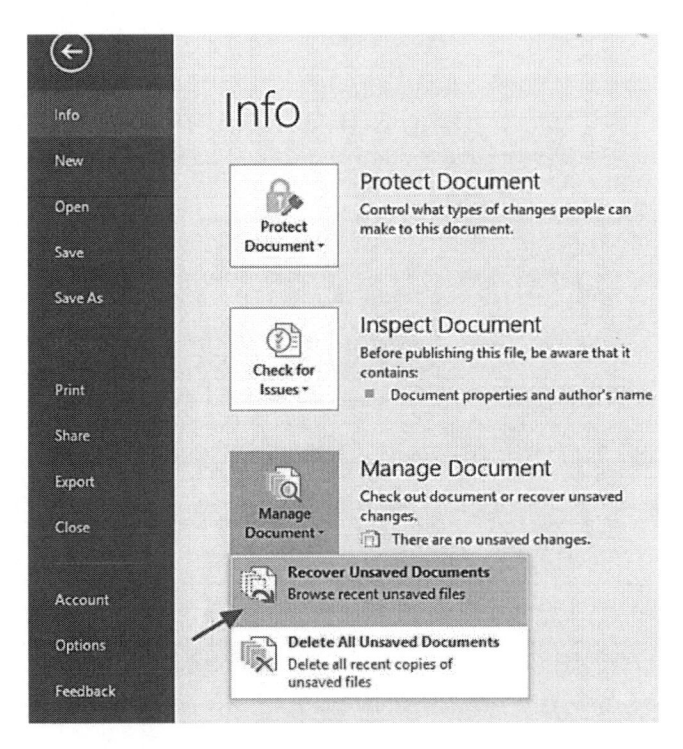

To find a document that has been lost

You can search for Word documents. Try looking for the file in Windows:

- Select "Start," type the name of the document (type the name in the search box), and then hit Enter.
- Documents are shown in the "Files" or "Documents" list. If the document is there, double-click the document to open it in Word.
- It doesn't show up in the search results. Then, the document is lost.
- To open Auto Recover files, you have to restart Word.

Every time Word starts, it looks for Auto Recover files and finds them. So, you can try the Auto Recover feature by shutting down and then opening Word again. The Document Recovery task pane opens when Word finds a file that was automatically recovered. The missing document should be shown as "document name [Original]" or "document name [Recovered]." If this happens, double-click the file name in the Document Recovery pane, choose File and then Save As, and then save the document as a.docx file. You can thereafter open the file in Word.

CHAPTER 9

PUBLISH YOUR DOCUMENT ON MICROSOFT WORD 365

In this chapter, we are going to learn how to publish and print a document. Before you print a document, you must look at it and make sure that everything is in order. This chapter will also cover how to export a document and create a PDF

Introduction

After writing, editing, formatting, and proofreading, the last step in document preparation is to put it on the Internet. Publishing is a broad term that includes printing a document on paper and making an electronic document that you can share on the web.

Document On Paper

When you finish your document on Microsoft Word, you can choose whether to make a paper copy of the document, which is also called a printout or a hard copy.

Previewing Before You Print

Before you print, look at what the document will look like. Even if your document is supposed to look the same on the screen as it does on paper, you might find little mistakes like missing page numbers, blank pages that don't belong there, and so on. Therefore, you must get a look at things before you print.

To see your document, first, you have to save your work. Then click on the **Ctrl+P** key (The Ctrl+P keyboard shortcut is the most common way to print). Another way to do this is to click the File tab and choose Print from the File screen's left side. The Print screen comes up, like the one shown in Figure 1.

Figure 1: An image of the Print screen

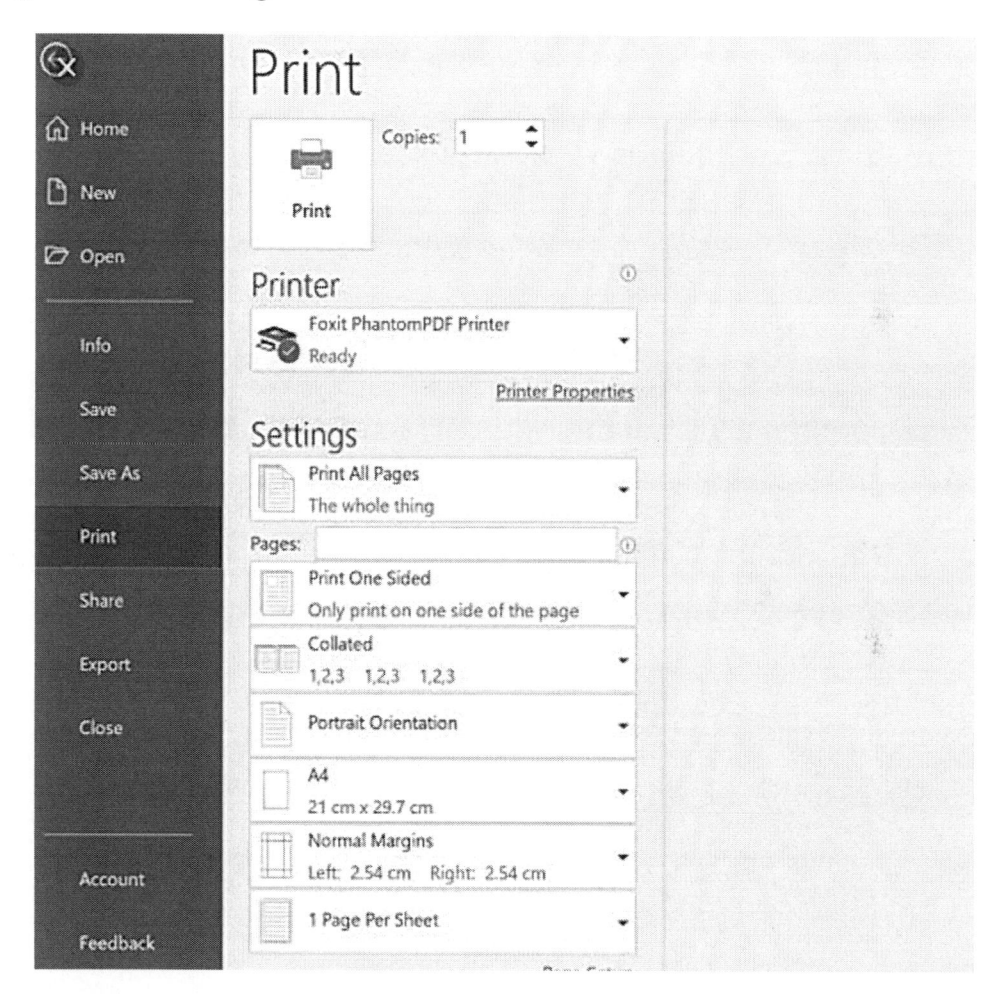

If you want to see a preview of each page, click on the forward and backward buttons at the bottom of the page. To read more text, use the zoom slider at the bottom of this page to make it bigger. The zoom slider that lets you change the size of the text is shown

89

in chapter 1, figure 5. You might want to look at the layout of footnotes, headers or footers if you're using them in your text. The goal is to find anything that's not appealing before you print. When things need to be fixed, you can click the back button or press the Esc key to get back to your text.

Printing The Whole Document on Microsoft Word 365

To print a document, ensure the printer is on and ready to print. It is faster to print when the printer is on, so make sure it is turned on.

Save your document and then click on the **Print command** on the File tab or press Ctrl+P. Choose Print from the **File tab**. The Print screen comes up. Look at Figure 1. Click the big Print button. The print screen closes and the document comes out from the printer

Note: Fortunately, you can keep working while the paper is printing. Also, you should not use the Print command again if nothing comes out. It's very likely that the computer is still thinking or sending information to the printer, and that nothing has gone wrong. It's likely that if you don't see an error message, everything will likely print out at some point.

Printing a Certain Page

To print a particular page that you want. Take these steps:

- To print, you need to move the insertion pointer so that it's sitting somewhere on the page that you want to print.

- To make sure you're on the right page, look at the page number on the status bar
- Press the keys Ctrl+P. The Print Range button is next to the Settings button on the right shown in figure 1, it says Print All Pages.
- The menu has a print option called **"Print This Page,"** which you can choose from.
- The Page Range box at the bottom of the Print screen can also help you check the page number.
- Then print.
- That single-page prints with all the formatting you put in.

Printing a Range of Pages

On Microsoft Word, you can print a range of pages including odd number pages, even number pages, or a mix of different pages from your document. To print a group of pages, go to the Print screen or press the keys Ctrl+P.

The Pages text box shows up as shown in figure 2

- To print pages 5 to 9, write 5-9.
- To print pages 3 through 9, type 3-9.
- To print pages 4 and 8, type 4,8.
- To print pages 3, 5 to 9,15 to 17 and 19, type 3, 5-9, 15-17, 19.
- Print All Pages is now turned into Custom Print if you type any value into the box.
- Print when you're ready. Only the pages you tell the printer to print come out of it.

Figure 2: An image of the Print screen with an arrow pointing at the page box

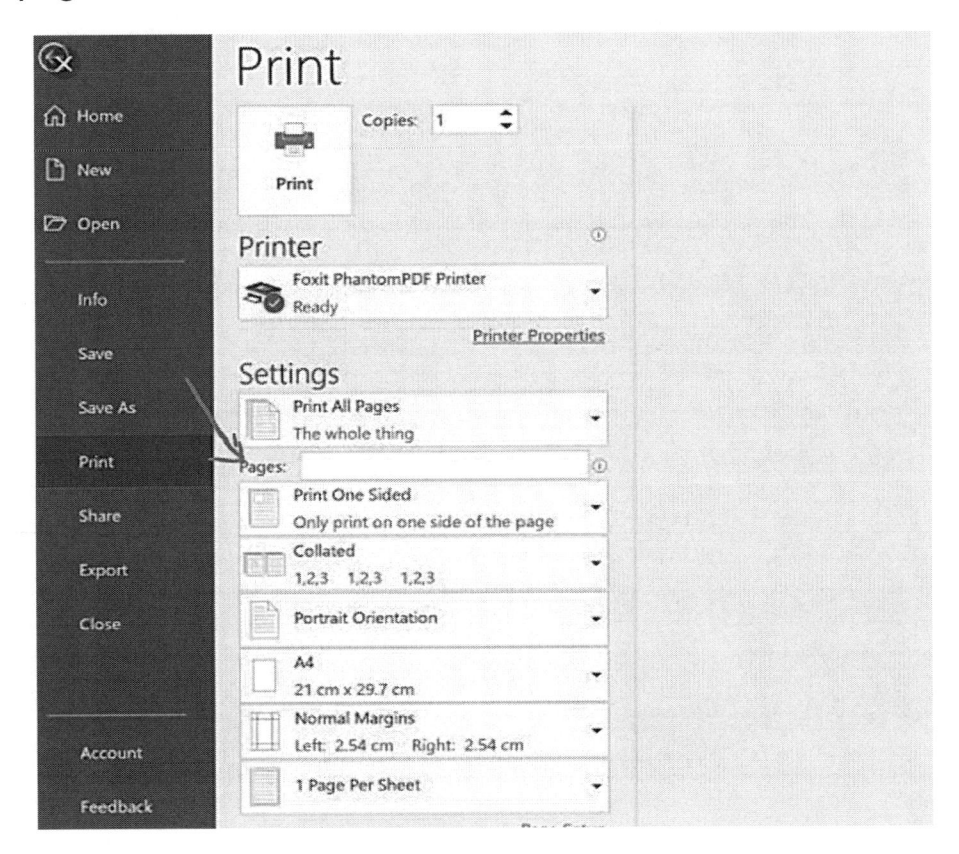

Making Copies of a Page that are Printed on Both Sides

On Microsoft Word, you can print your document on both sides of a sheet of paper. Take these steps:

- Right after you save the document, press Ctrl+P.
- Click the **Duplex Printing button** on the Print screen to make two copies of the same thing.
- Choose "Print on Both Sides, Flip Pages on Long Sides," then click "OK."

Short Sides isn't worth it if you don't plan to bind your document in that way.

Odd and Even Pages are Printed on Both Sides of the Paper

If you have a printer that doesn't print on both sides of the paper, what would happen? If that's the case, you can print all the odd pages in your paper. Turn the paper over and put it back in the printer again. In the next step, print all the even pages. This means that the text will be printed on both sides of the page.

Note: It's a good idea to print only one odd-and-even page first, to make sure that when you put the paperback in, it's in the right orientation.

Printing a Block on Microsoft Word 365

When you print a document with Word, you have a lot of different options for how it looks. Make sure you have marked a block of text on the screen. Then, ask the Print command to print only that block of text. This is how:

Mark the text you want to print

See Chapter 6 for all the instructions on how to block a text on the word document.

- Press Ctrl+P to bring up the Print screen.
- The Print Range button is next to the Settings button on the right.
- When you go to the menu, choose the Print Selection item.
- To see the Print Selection option, you need to select at least one block in your document.

It's time to print.

The block you chose prints in the same place and with the same formatting (headers and footers) as if you had printed the whole document.

Printing More Than One copy

This simply means making more than one copy. When you print a document with Word, you can choose how the paper looks. If you want to print more than one copy of your document, you can do that, too. Follow these steps to print more than one copy:

- Press the keys Ctrl+P. Word opens up the Print dialogue box as shown in figure 1.
- In the Copies box, choose how many copies you want to print.
- Click on the **Collate check box.** If the check box is selected, this indicates the copies will be collated.
- Click the Print button and click OK.

Note: As a rule, Word prints one copy of a document after the other. This is called collating, and it is how things are put together. However, if you want Word to print five copies of page 2 and then five copies of page 3 and so on, choose the option from the Collated menu button and type in the number of copies you want of each page The collated option is indicated with an arrow in figure 3 below: Then click on print.

Figure 4: The Collation Option

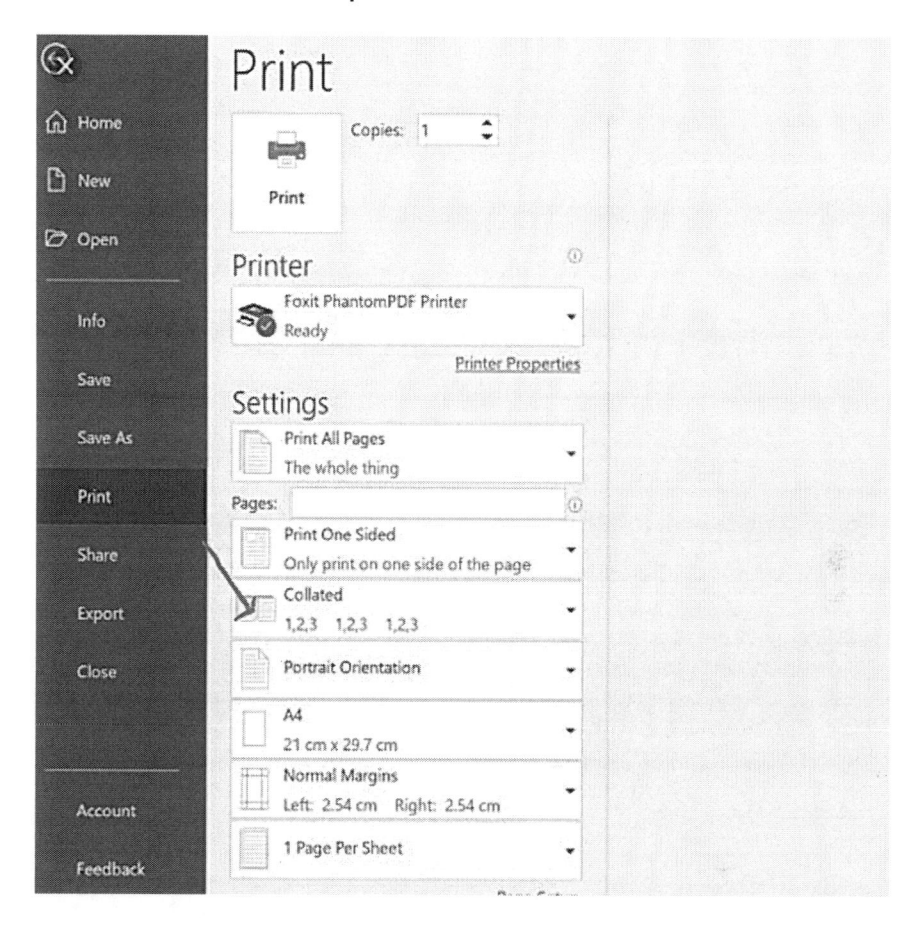

Choosing a Different Printer

Your computer may be able to use several printers, such as one that is connected directly to your computer, as well as some network or wireless printers. To choose a specific printer, such as that fancy color printer, you should follow these steps:

- Press Ctrl+P to bring up the Print screen.
- Make sure you click the "**Select Printer button**" next to the Printer title.
- The button shows the name of the printer that Windows has chosen as the default one.

- Choose a different printer from the list and click on it.

Note: Not all printers have names that are easy to understand. Also, not every printer on the list is a real printer. Several of them are printers that print documents like Microsoft Print to PDF. To add printers, change their names, or set them as the default printer,

Cancelling a Print Job

You can cancel a print job in Word by running to the printer and pressing the **Cancel** button. At times, there is an icon with a red X on it. When you touch that button, the printer will stop. The button stops the document from printing, but it might not stop the printer right away.

The Cancel button doesn't work on some slow printers. You can try to use Windows to stop a print job on a printer with slight issues. Follow these steps:

- **Double-click** the little printer icon on the right end of the taskbar to open the printer.
- Select the job that you want to delete from the list.
- Choose either the Document Cancel command or the Document Cancel Printing command to cancel the document or print job.
- Click **"Yes" or "OK"** to stop the job.
- Then shut down the printer's control window now.

Note: It may take a while for the printer to stop. This is because printers have their memory, and even though you cancel it, some pages of the document may be stored and keep printing even after you have cancelled it.

Publishing Your Document Electronically on Microsoft Word 365

Some documents don't need to be written on paper at all. They are sent to the publisher electronically, and they can be changed right on the screen. When you buy an eBook, you don't need to print it out. And sometimes, documents can be better spread by email than by paper. It's all part of putting your document online and making it public.

Convert a Document to PDF Using Microsoft Word

The best way to convert your document to PDF on Microsoft Word is as follows:

- Open the document you want to convert and then click the **"File" tab.**
- Select the "S**ave As**" option on the backstage screen
- From the Save As screen, select where you would like the PDF to be saved (OneDrive, This PC, a particular folder, or wherever).
- Choose where to save the converted PDF
- Click the drop-down arrow on the right side of the "**Save As Typ**e" box and select "PDF" from the drop-down menu.
- If you want to, you can change the filename at this time. When you're ready, click the "Save" button.
- Change the name of the file (if you wish) and then click the "Save" button

After saving the PDF, you'll be returned to your Word document, and the new PDF will open automatically in your default PDF viewer.

Other Ways to Make a PDF from a DOCX File

If you don't know how to convert a file to or from PDF, use a service like Small pdf, which has free tools for doing so. It's possible to use services like this that have some restrictions or require a fee for full access, but they can be very useful for converting PDFs when you need to do so a few times.

Close Your Document

When you're done you can close your document by simply clicking **Ctrl + W** or clicking the File button and closing the window.

Chapter 10

How to Format Characters on Microsoft Word 365

In this chapter, we will discuss how to format characters on Microsoft Word 365. We will discuss how to set the basic text formatting. How to change text size, add color to your words and all text editing tools. We will also look at the things that you should look out for paragraph formatting, how to check that paragraphs are aligned left, centre, right, and full.

Introduction

When you format text in a document, the most basic elements are letters, numbers, and characters. To make a document looks appealing, you can make text bold, small, underlined or exchange the font style. You can also make it in different sizes and colors. Word gives you a lot of control over how your text looks.

The Basic Text Formats

The "**Home**" ribbon tab has all of the basic text editing tools you need to make changes to your text. These are some of the most common ways to change how the text looks in Word. You can find these commands on the Home tab, in the Font group, as shown in figure 1.

Figure 1: The Basic Text Formatting Tools on The Home Ribbon Tab

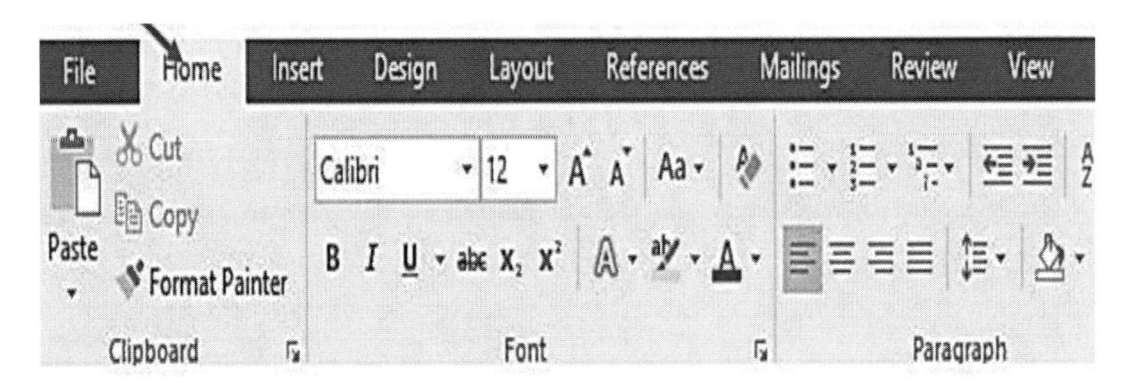

The Basic Formatting Tools

i. **Italics Button: Press Ctrl+I** to make the text in italics or Go to the home button and click on the italics icon. This is circled in figure 2 below

Figure 2: The Italics button

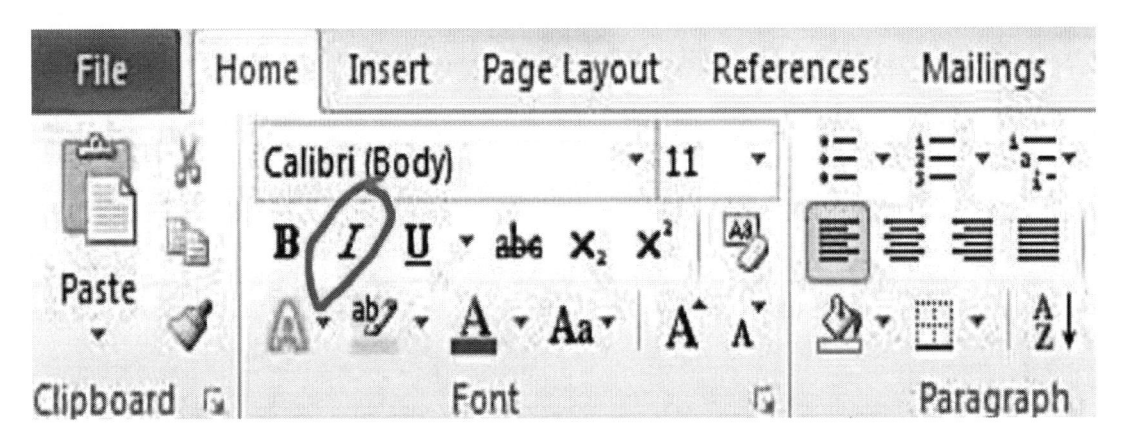

ii. **Making a font choice**: Click the **Hom**e button. The font is on the **F**ont grou**p**. Click the down arrow next to the Font item. Select a font. In figure 2 above the font is Calibri and the text size is 11.

Note: As you move your mouse pointer over a font, the text in the document changes to show you how the font looks in the document. When you click, you can choose a font and change the way the text is written. Fonts are shown in alphabetical order and in the same way that they would appear in the text.

iii. To make the text **bold, press Ctrl+B** or use the Bold command button. This is circled in figure 3

Figure 3: The Bold Button

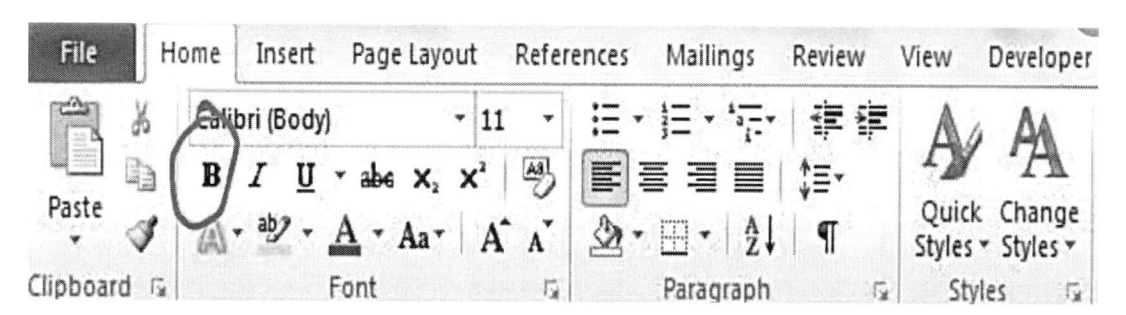

iv. **To underline a text: Click on** Ctrl+U or the Underline command button circled in figure 4. It can be used to underline text. Choose a different underline style or choose a different color by clicking on the down arrow next to the button that says "Underline."

Figure 4: The Underline Button

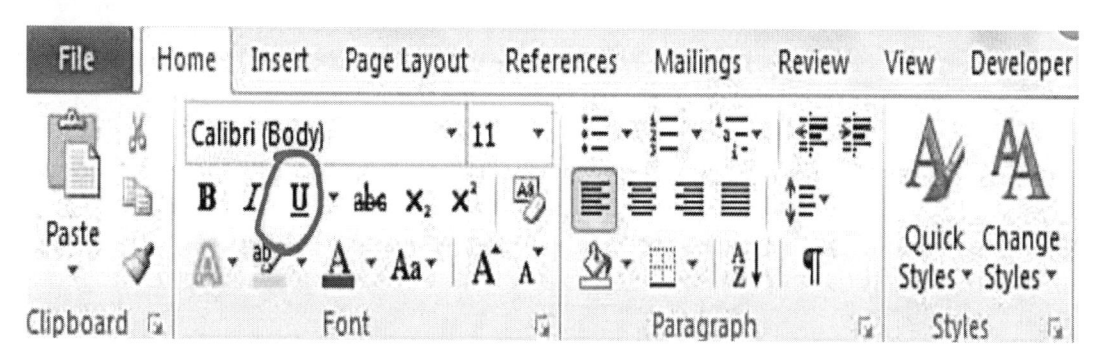

v. **The Strikethrough Butto**n: For strikethrough text, click the Strikethrough command button shown in figure 5

Figure 5: The strikethrough button

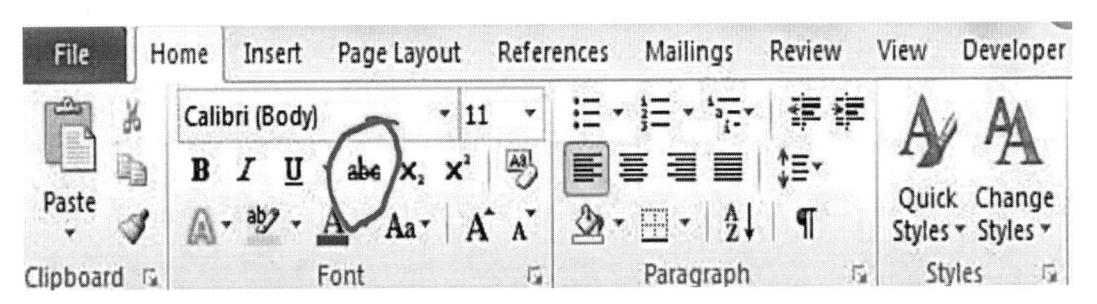

vi. **Subscript and Superscript**: When you want to make a text subscript, click the Subscript button shown in figure 6 below. It is **Ctrl+=** on the keyboard. It is used to right Words like **H20 or Al3+**

Figure 6: The superscript Button

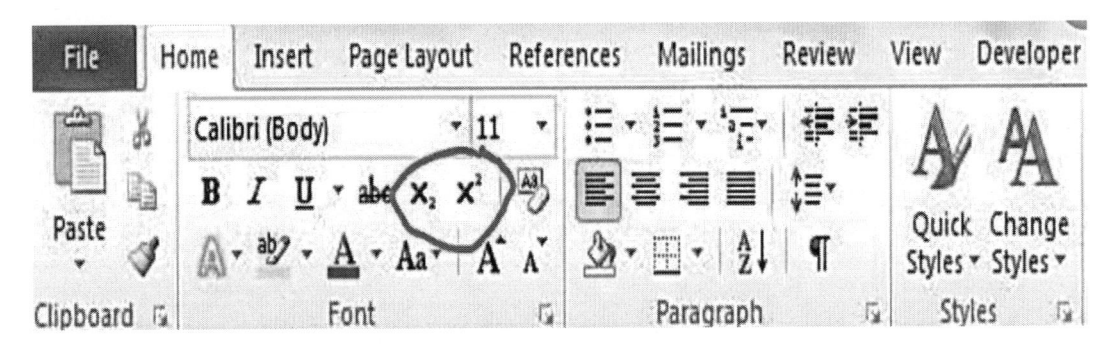

vii. **To change the color of a tex**t: Click the **Home** button, when you're in the Font group, click the Font Color button as shown in figure 7. It turns the current word into the color of the button.

Figure 7: The Color Font Button

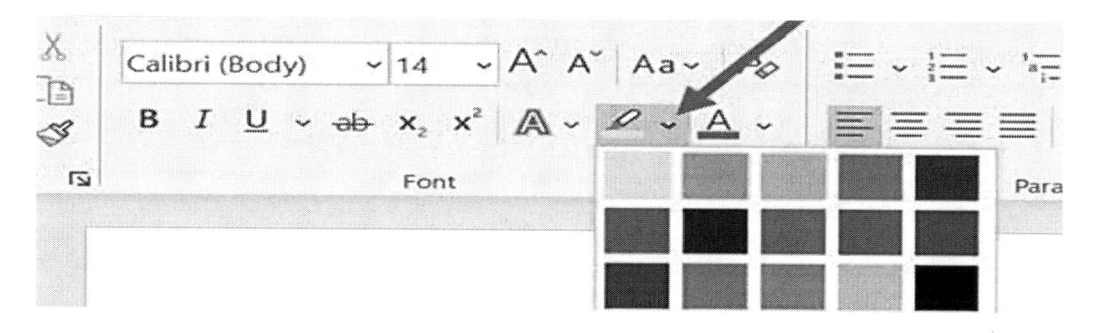

Note: More Colors are in the Font Color menu. To make your unique colors, click on it.

viii. **Caps Button**: This can be used to change the selected text to either upper case or lower case. This button is indicated in figure 8 below.

Figure 8: The Caps Button

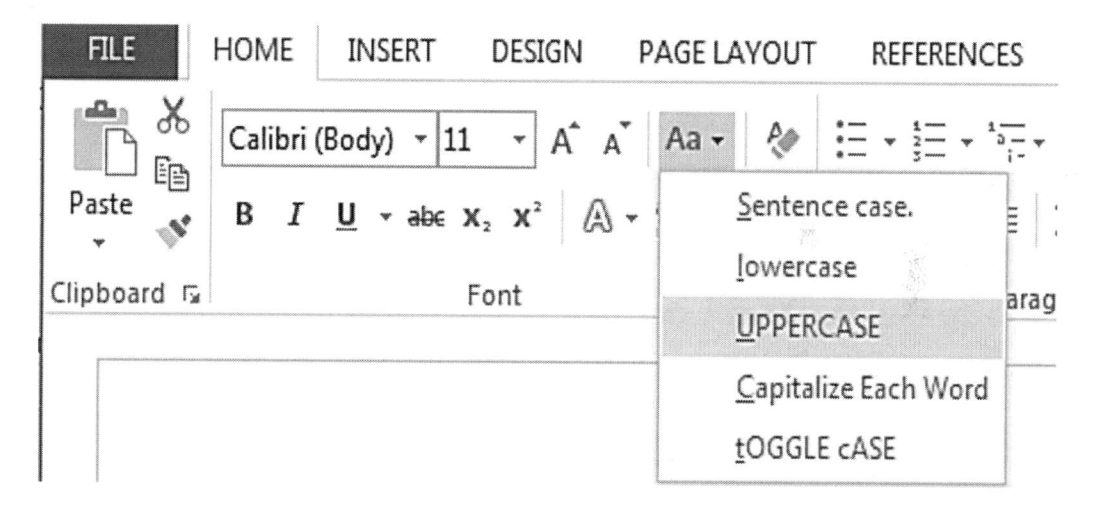

ix. **Shade the Background**: To change the color of the background of the text, use the Shading tool. Go to the **Home tab**. The **Shading command button** is on the Paragraph group. To use it, click the command button. The color shown on the button darkens the current word or block of text or sets the background color for new text that is typed.

To change colors, click the menu button to the right of the Shading command button and choose a new color. Choose a color from the list, or choose **More Colors** to make your color.

Note: If you want to remove the background color, you can choose "No Color."

Figure 9: The Shading Command Button

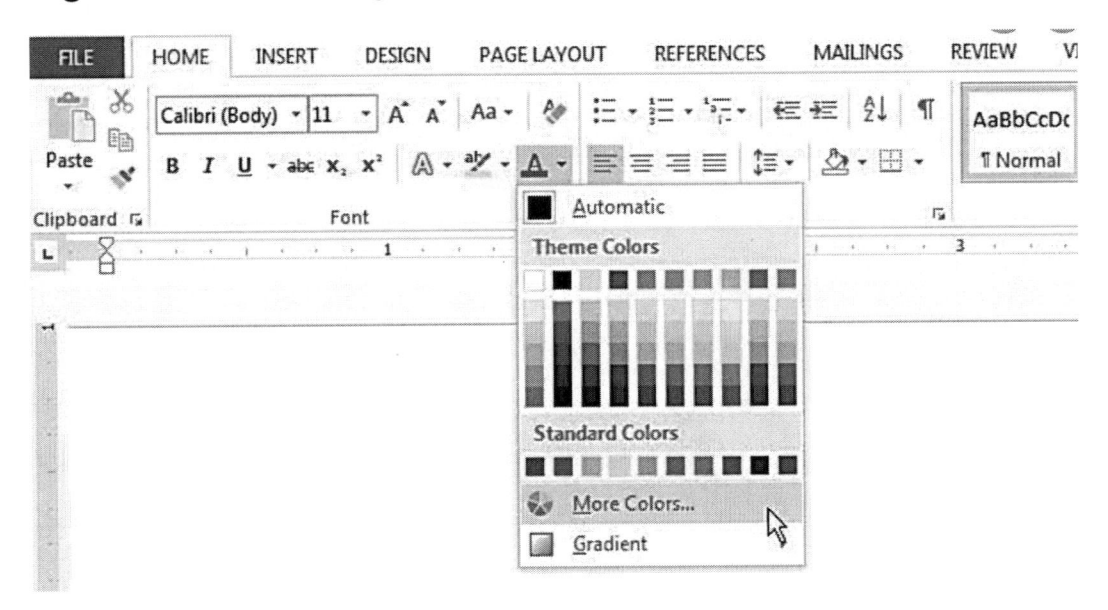

Paragraph Formatting

A paragraph is any chunk of text that ends when you hit the enter button in the text box. As long as you end the chunk of text by pressing the Enter key, it's a paragraph. In Microsoft word 365, there are a lot of options for how paragraphs are formatted. This is mostly because so many parts of a typical paragraph can be changed and customized to show text the way you want to.

The Paragraph symbol ¶ is used in a document to show that a paragraph has come to an end. It is usually hidden, but you can ask Word to make this character show up for you if you want it. Take the following steps:

- Click the **File** button.
- You can choose the Options command.
- The Word Options dialogue box shows up.
- Click on display
- Make sure Paragraph Marks are checked off by making a checkmark there.
- The click **OK.**

How to Format Paragraphs

Paragraph formatting lets you change how each paragraph looks. Among other things, you can change how the text is aligned from left to centre or how far apart each line is. You can indent paragraphs, number them, add borders and add shading to them

Alignment of paragraphs

One of the most important typographic rules for laying out paragraphs is how they will look next to the left and right margins. Alignment is what Word refers to this as. This is how the lines in a paragraph look compare to the left and right margins. The margin is the space between the edge of the paper and where the text is on the paper.

The alignment-formatting button is on the Home tab. They're part of a group called "Paragraph." To change the alignment of a paragraph, you can use the alignment buttons on the toolbar. There are four options as shown in figure 10

- **Left-aligned.** In this paragraph, all of the lines are close to each other on the left side of the text. The line doesn't get any extra space.
- **Centre-aligned.** All the lines in a paragraph are in the middle of the text margins on the left and right sides of the text. The line doesn't get any extra space.
- **Right-aligned.** This means that all the lines in a paragraph are aligned to the right side of the text.
- **Justified.** All of the lines in a paragraph are made bigger so they fit into both the left and right text margins at the same time. Space is added between words and characters as needed to fill out the line so that it looks good.

"Distributed text justification" is another way to align paragraphs that isn't in the official rules. This alignment is very similar to the Justified alignment, but it also makes the last line of the paragraph, no matter how short it is, stretch to the right side of the page.

Figure 10: Paragraph Alignment

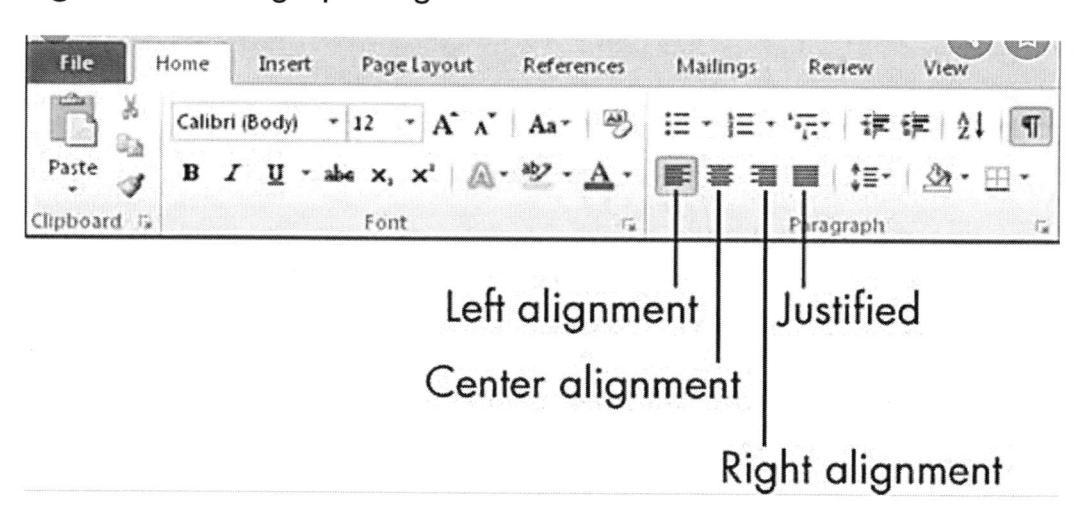

Spacing in Paragraph

Line space is how much space there is above or below a sentence. Instead of pressing enter to make space between paragraphs bigger, you can set a certain amount of space before or after paragraphs. To give an example, some paragraphs might be single-spaced 1.0, 1.5 and some double-spaced 2.0 as shown in figure 11 below

Right-click the Line Spacing button on your formatting toolbar and choose "Down Arrow" from the drop-down menu that shows up on the toolbar. Choose 2.0 if you want to double-space. Choose 1.0 to make the paragraph single-spaced again.

Figure 11: Spacing in Paragraph

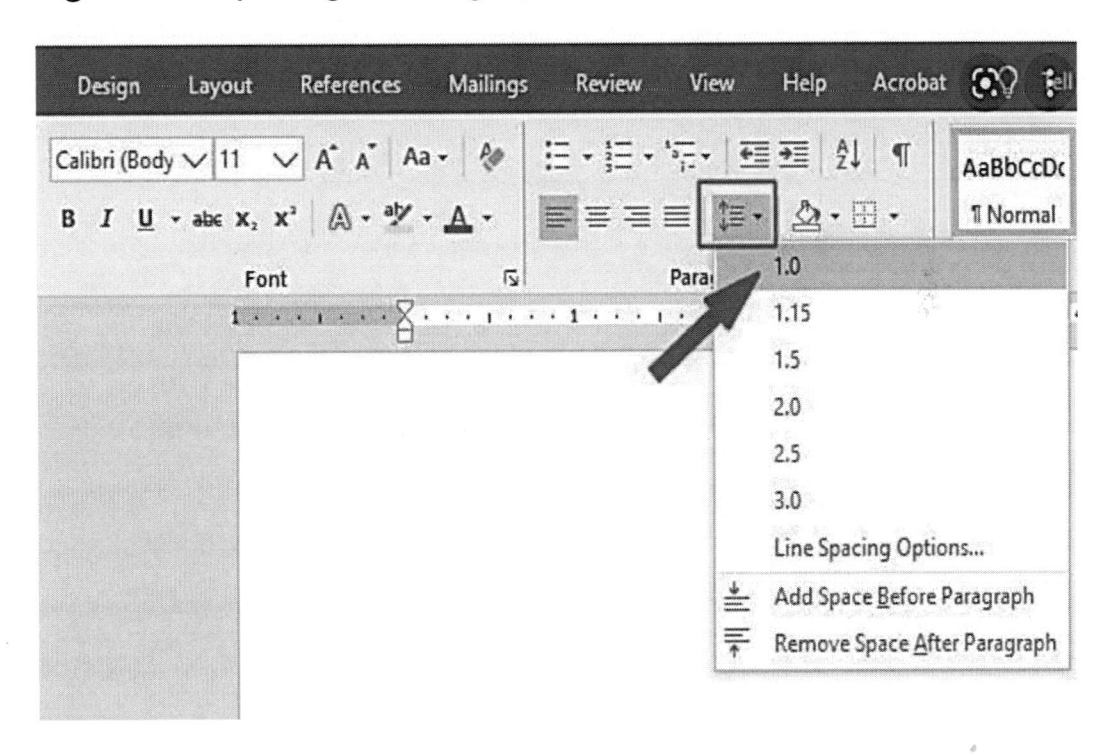

Paragraph indentation

There is a space called an indentation between the margin and the first character of a line of text. An indentation can be made on the first line of a paragraph as well as on all the lines in the paragraph. It can also be made on both sides.

Note: Adjusting a paragraph's indentation doesn't change how the paragraph is positioned on the screen. Paragraphs are indented based on the margins of the page.

Indent the First Line of a Paragraph

If you want to indent the first line of a paragraph, all you have to do is put your cursor at the beginning of the paragraph and click on the **tab key** on the keyboard. When you click on the enter key to start a new paragraph, its front line will be indented.

Alternatively, If you want first-line indentation, modify the Normal style:

Put the cursor anywhere in the paragraph and on the Home tab - click the Normal style, and then choose Modify. Next, select Format, and then choose Paragraph. Finally, on the Indents and Spacing tab, under Indentation, select the First line and select ok

How to Indent a Whole Paragraph

If you want to indent a whole paragraph, all you have to do is select the whole paragraph you want to indent. In the layout tab which is on the Ribbon bar, click on the indent left arrow upward within that paragraph section.

Tab Formatting

The Tab key can be seen on the right side of the keyboard. Table Key is its name. In Word, tab keys are used to make lists or make the text more readable by putting them in different places. Tabs are best used for a single line of text or the first line of a paragraph.

Seeing Tab Characters

When you press the Tab key on your keyboard, a tab character is added to your text. The only difference is that the width of the character that is inserted can be different. The width is set at a certain place across a page. That place is called the tab stop.

When you write, tab characters are usually hidden from view. The tab characters don't need to be seen to use them, but if you're having trouble setting tab stops and using tabs, looking at the tab characters can help.

Regardless of whether Word has the Show/Hide command set, you can tell Word to show tab characters at all times. Do the following

- Go to "**Files**"
- The Word Options window comes up.
- Tab characters can be selected. Make sure that the Tab Characters box is checked.
- Click **OK.**

Note: As long as you have the Tab Characters option checked, tabs will always show up in a text document. If you look at them in the text, you might be able to figure out some formatting problems.

Tab Stop

You can't see tab stops in your document, but they're real and they affect the text you type. To see where and how the tab stops are placed and to set new ones, you should check the ruler.

Take these steps: Click the **View** button. It's important that in the Show area, you make sure that there is a checkmark next to the Ruler item. Check the box to see if it's marked. The ruler is right above the document.

Figure 12: An image showing the ruler on Word

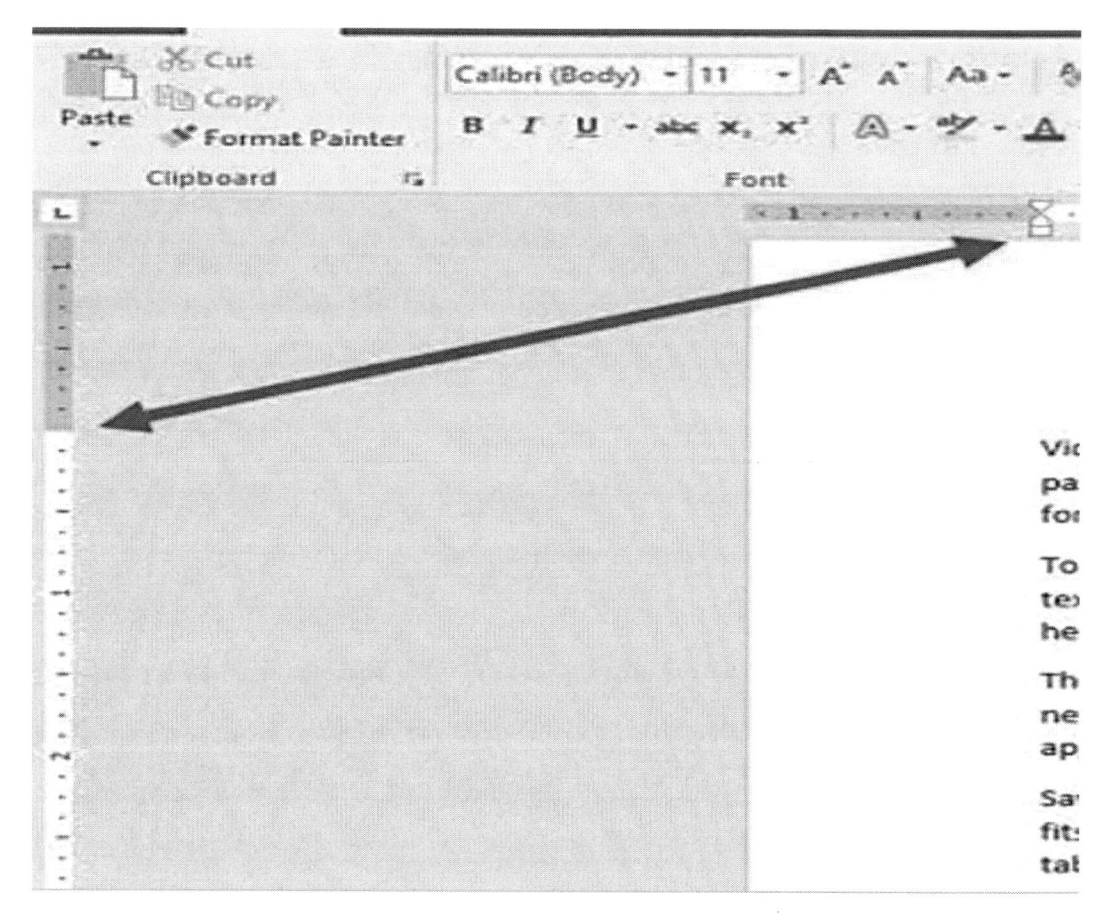

Setting Tab Stops

The best way to set a tab stop is to use the ruler. As long as the ruler is visible, there are two steps to the process:

i. Click the tab gizmo until the type of tab stop that you want comes up and then tap the ruler on the exact place you want the tab stop to be.

The Tab Stop icon shows up on the ruler to show where the tab stop is in the paragraph. You can move the tab even more by moving the mouse left or right. If there is already a tab character in the current paragraph, its format changes as you move the tab stop around.

Note: There is a tab stop at the end of each paragraph. The tab stop you set is for the current paragraph or any other paragraphs you choose.

ii. The Tabs dialogue box can be used to set tabs.

The Tabs dialogue box can be used to set tabs very precisely. It's also a way you can get to some types of tabs such as dot leader tabs, which are mostly hidden.

Keep in mind that the Tabs dialogue box isn't the same as a typical Word dialogue box: It doesn't work the same way. You have to set the tab position and type first, then click the Set button to do it. When you're done setting tabs, click the OK button. In general, the process goes like this:

- Click the **Home button.**

- Right next to the Paragraph group, click the button that opens up a dialogue box. The Paragraph dialogue box comes up.
- Right-click and choose "Tabs."
- In the Tab Stop Position box, type in the tab stop position that you want to set as shown in figure 12
- You can be very exact, like 3.11 inches.
- Choose a type of tab stop from the Alignment area, and then click on it.
- Then, click the Set button.
- The tab stop is added to the list of tab stops.

Note: If the ruler is visible, you can quickly open the Tabs dialogue box by clicking on the button. Double-click any tab stop on the screen.

Figure 12: The Tab Dialogue Box

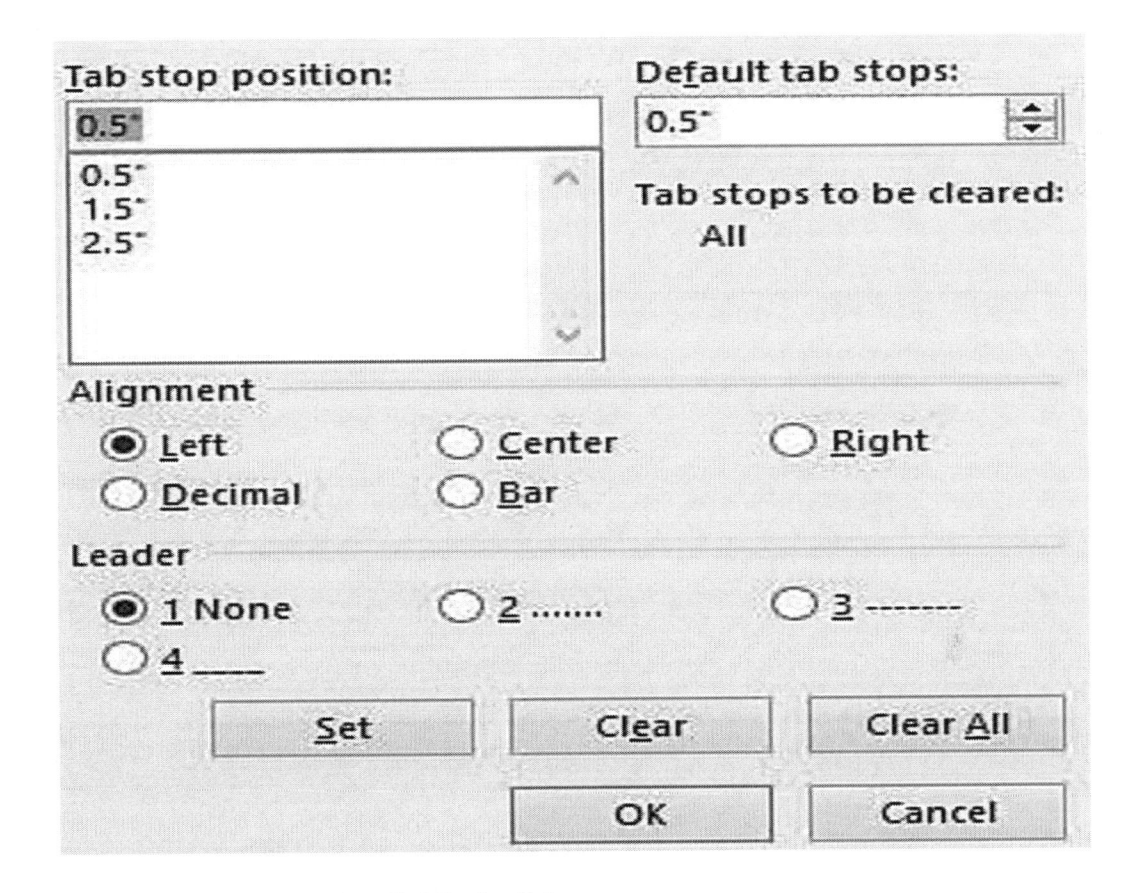

The Standard Left Tab Stop

If you want to keep things old, you should use the left tab stop. When you press the Tab key, the insertion pointer moves to the left tab stop, where you can type text. This type of tab stop is best for typing lists, putting information in single-line paragraphs, and indenting the first line of a multiline paragraph.

Creating a simple Two Column List

The left tab stop is often used to make a simple two-column list. Make this type of list by following these steps:

- On a new line, hit Tab.

- Type the first thing in the column. This should be no more than two or three words.
- Again, press Tab.
- Then, type the item in the second column. You can end that line by pressing Enter. you can thereafter start a new line.
- After you finish your list, you use the ruler to set the tab stops.
- Select all the lines of text you want to put in a 2-column tabbed list.
- Choose a left tab stop from the tab gizmo on the ruler, and then click on it.
- To set the first tab stop, click the ruler. A tab stop can be moved so that text doesn't line up.
- To stop the second tab, click.
- If you need to, you can move the tab stop to the left or right to help the text line up.

Note: You need only one tab between items in a column list. That's because the tab stop, not the tab character, makes your text line up.

The Centre Tab Stop

You can place text on a line with a tab at the centre. This is different from centring a paragraph, which means that only text that is placed at the centre tab stop is centred. To use this feature, you should put the text in your header or footer in the middle. That's when you'll need to use the centre tab stop.

The text on the left is at the start of the paragraph, which is left-justified but the text written after the tab is in the middle of the line. To do this:

- Start a new paragraph, one that has text that you want to put in the center of it.
- Set a tab at the 3-inch spot on the ruler.
- If you want to pluck a center tab stop, click the Tab gizmo on the ruler until a center tab shows up
- Start the line with some text The text you write should be short; it should only appear at the start of each line.
- Press the Tab key and type the text in the middle.
- As you type, the text is in the middle of the line.

Note: When you type, don't write too much. Remember that the centre tab is a single-line thing.

- To end a line of text, press Enter.

Making a Right-to-Left List

You can use both rights and left tab stops to make a two-column list look good. Make this list by following these steps:

- Begin on a blank line, the line that you want to change.
- Click the tab gizmo until the right tab stop comes up and you can see the tabs.
- An icon for the Right Tab Stop shows up in the margin.
- Right-click near the center of the ruler to set the tab stop.
- To get the tab gizmo to move, click on it until the left tab stop shows up. To get the Left Tab Stop icon, click and click.
- On the ruler, click to move one of the tab stops to the right side.
- Press the Tab button.
- When you move the insertion pointer to the right, it moves to the right tab stop.

- The text for the first, right-justified column should be typed in now.
- Press the Tab button. Some text should be written in the second, left-justified column of the table.
- To end a line of text, press Enter.

Note: If you need to make more changes after you're done, select all lines and move the tab stops on the ruler as needed.

The Decimal Tab

The decimal tab can be used to make two columns of numbers line up next to each other. The decimal tab doesn't align text to the right as the right tab does. Instead, it aligns numbers by their decimal, which is the period in the number. The decimal tab is shown in figure 13. To make the decimal tab stop show up on the ruler, click on the tab gizmo until the tab stop shows up.

To use the decimal tab

- Start a blank line of text. On the ruler, click the Tab gizmo until the decimal tab stop appearing.
- To set the decimal tab stop, click on the ruler, and move it to where you want it. Later, you can change the position.
- Type the first column text and press the Tab button.
- Then, type the number. Until you press the Period key, the number is aligned to the right until you do so. After then the rest of the number is left-aligned.
- To end a line of text, press Enter.

Note: After the list is done, you can make changes: Make sure all the lines in the list are checked off. Then, move the decimal tab stop to the left or right to change the direction.

Figure 13: The Decimal Bar

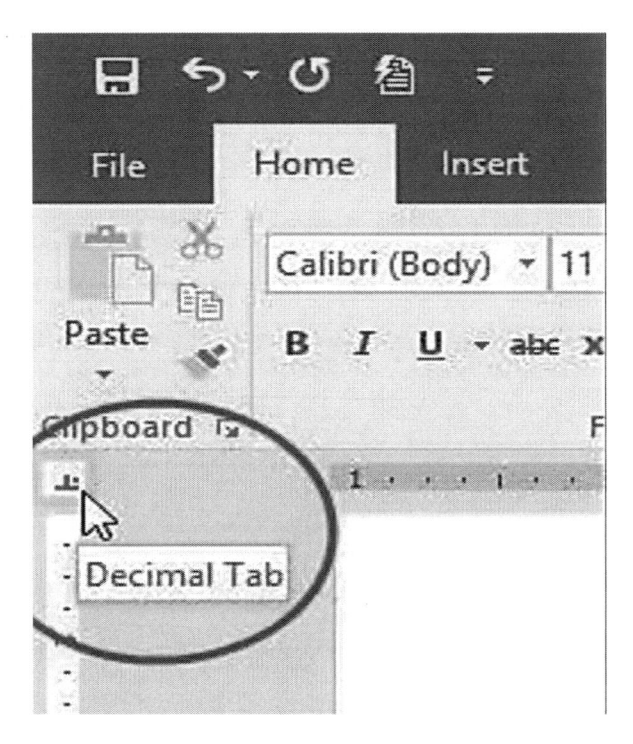

The Bar Tab

The bar tab isn't a real tab stop in Word. It doesn't change the tab character. Instead, the bar tab is just a piece of text art. The bar tabs are used to make lines of text look like they have vertical bars in them. The bar tab icon is shown in figure 14 below

To set a bar tab stop, do the following:

- Turn on the tab gizmo until the bar tab stop comes up and you can click on it. The bar tab icon is shown in figure 13

- Click the ruler to set the stop on the bar tab. At each place in the text, a vertical bar shows up. The bar shows up whether or not the current line has any tab characters.

Note: To get the most out of the bar tab stop, mix in a few other tab stops.

Figure 14: The Bar Tab Icon

The Fearless Leader Tab

The leader tab shows a group of dots or other symbols where the tab is on the page. You can press this tab key to move the pointer to the next tab stop.

Dot, dash, and underline are the three styles of leader tabs

To set this

- Create a tab-style list and Select all of the text as a block.
- When you open the Tabs dialogue box, double-click a tab on the ruler.
- Select the tab stop from the list of Tab Stop Positions that you want to use.
- In the Leader area, choose the style of leader.
- Then, click the Set button.

- Then click ok.

CHAPTER 11

HOW TO FORMAT A PAGE ON MICROSOFT WORD 365

In this chapter, we will discuss how to choose a page number, switch orientation, set margins, color background and watermark. It's important that your document has a cover page and that you know how to add a header or footer. This will be discussed in this chapter

Page Setup

Word lets you set the page format, which includes the page size, orientation, margins, as well as other page formats and attributes. This will be discussed.

I. How to Change the Margin Of a Page

- Click on the **Layout Tab** and the **P**age setup shows up
- Click on Margin and you can see all the Margin (Normal, Narrow, wide, moderate and then select the margin that suits you and start typing) as shown in figure 1
- Choose any type and then you can start typing wherever the cursor is.

Note: If you are not satisfied with the Margin you can choose to customize your margin. To do this; still, on that page, click on the customise Margin as shown in figure 2 and then the dialogue box shows up. The dialogue box gives you the full authentication to change the top height, left height or width, bottom to whatever you want and then click OK. Note: Leave a space between the text and the edge of the page, which stops the text from spilling out of a document and onto the screen.

Figure 1: The Margin Option

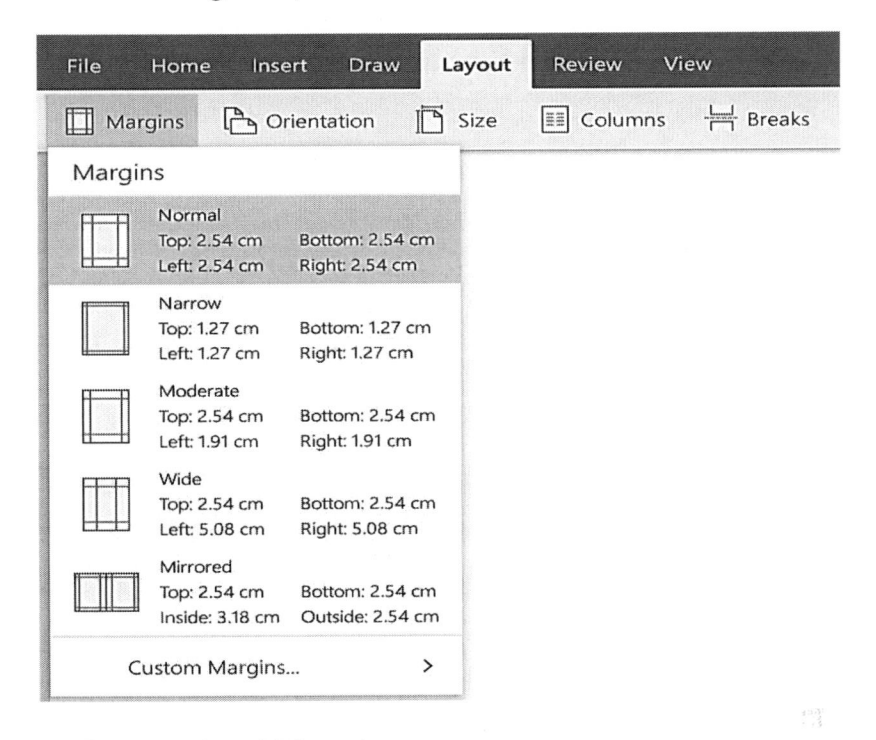

Figure 2: Customized Margin

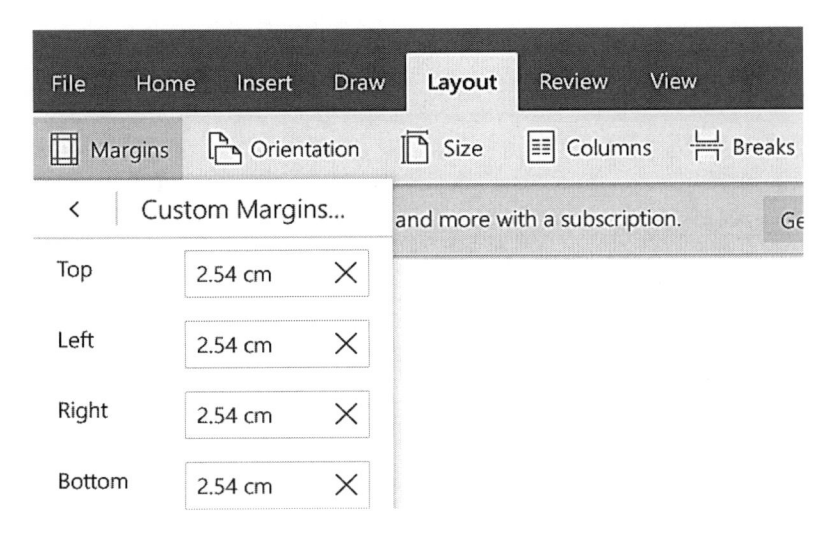

ii. How to Change the Orientation of a Page

The orientation can be in portrait or landscape. To do this.

- Go to the **Layout tab**
- Click on the Page setup
- And then on orientation. Click on Portrait or Landscape depending on what you want and click OK.

iii. The Page Size

There are different page Sizes such as the A4, A3, A5 or legal-size paper. In the United States, the normal page Size is 81/2 by 11 inches. In Europe, the size A4 is used. Neither size is a bad choice. That's because the size of the page is part of the page format. To change the page Size

- Click on the **Layout tab**
- In the Page Setup group, click the Size button size of the page.
- Choose a page size from the drop-down list as shown in figure 3 and click **OK**

If you want more page sizes, click on the more page sizes and you can select any document size.

To customize your page Size, when you click on the more options there's a dialogue box that shows up, you can input the width and height of the page size you want and click on Ok, then the page Size will automatically change.

Figure 3: The Page Size Options

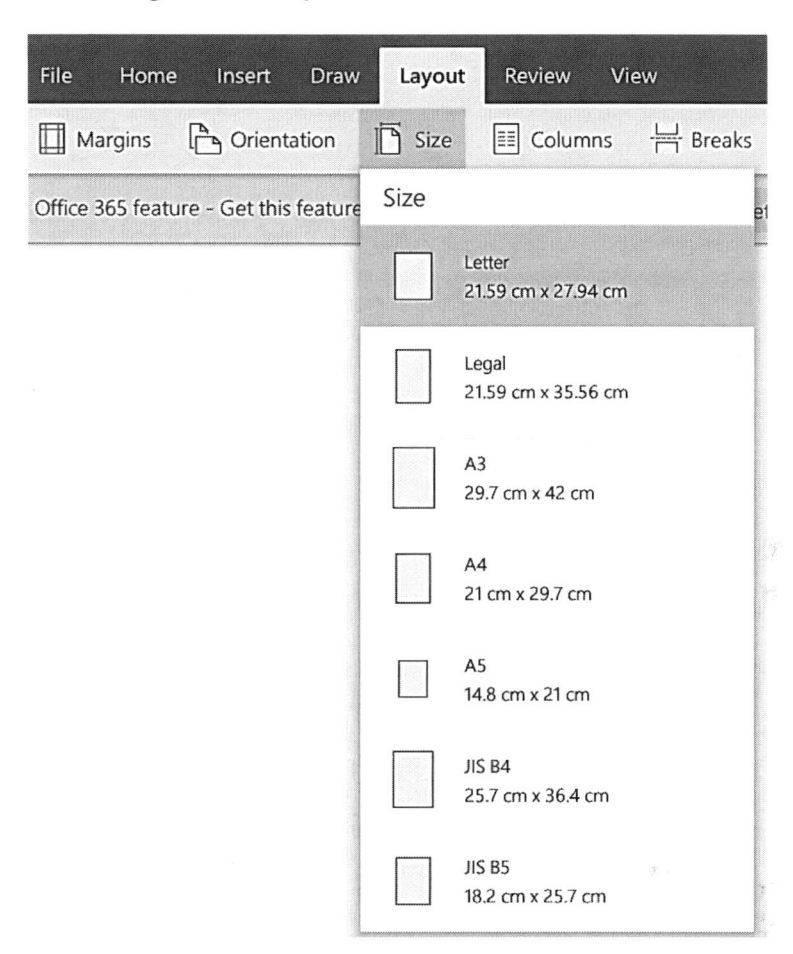

iv. Columns

To create a column on a page, put your cursor on the place where you want to create the column in the word document

- Click on the Layout tab and then on the page setup group, click on the column
- On the drop-down list, click on the column you want (one, two, three, left or right column) Click on the column you want and click OK.

v. Page Break

To create a page break

- Click on the l**ayout tab** and click on **breaks**
- There is an option as page, then click on it and the changes takes place

Alternatively, you can use the **Ctrl + Enter**

Note: You can also break a column. After creating a column Place your cursor on the column you want to break. Click on the layout tab, and click on the breaks. Finally, click on columns, and the column breaks to another page.

vi. Line Numbers

If you want to give line numbers to your page, follow these steps:

- On the Layout tab, click on line numbers
- On the drop-down list, click on the continuous options and the line number shows from each page as shown in figure 4

Note: if you want each page to start a new number, click on line numbers and click on " restart each page" and each page starts from number 1, the next page starts from number 1 also. If you don't want any line numbers, click on none as shown in figure 5

Figure 4: Line Number

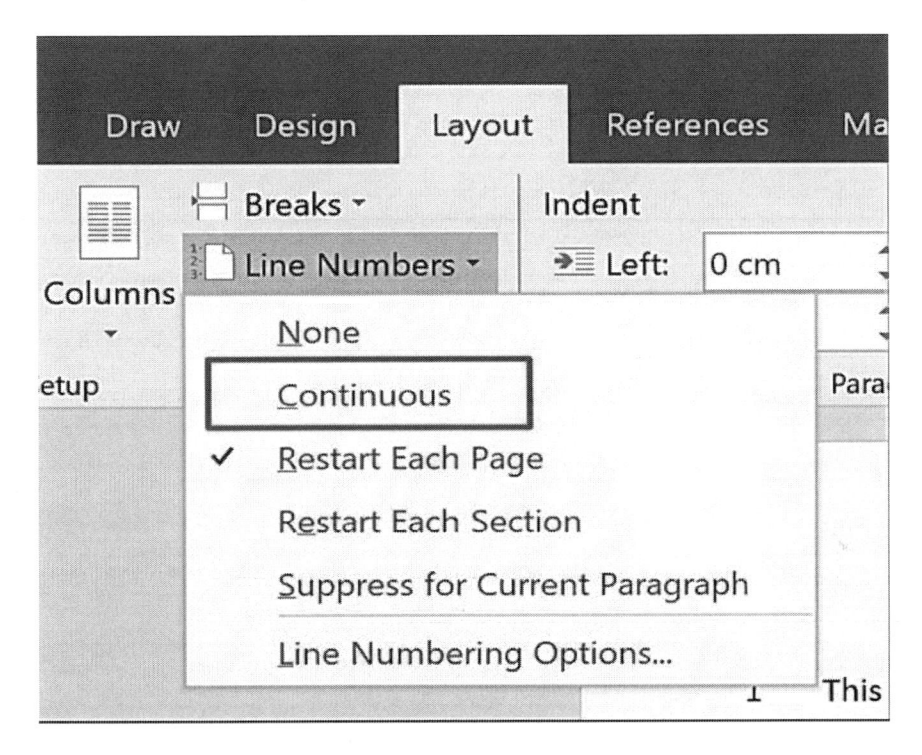

Figure 5: Line Button (None Option)

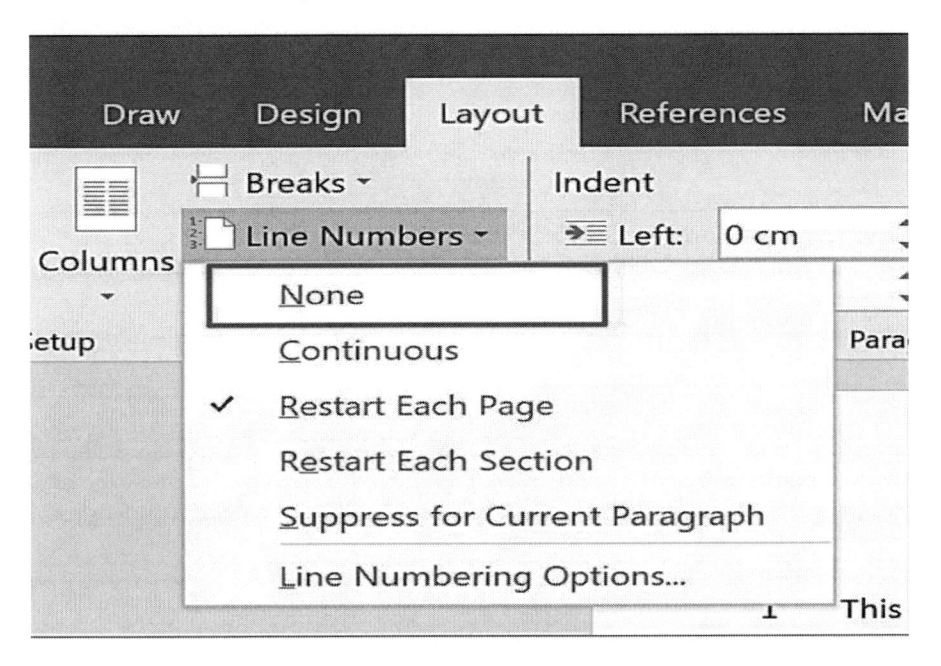

vi. Hyphenation

This adds hyphens between syllables in longer words at the end of a line. To do this:

- Click on the **Layout tab**
- On the Page Setup group click on hyphenation as shown in figure 6
- From the drop-down list click on **Automatic**
- And hyphens are added to the long text at the end of each line

Figure 6: The Hyphenation Option

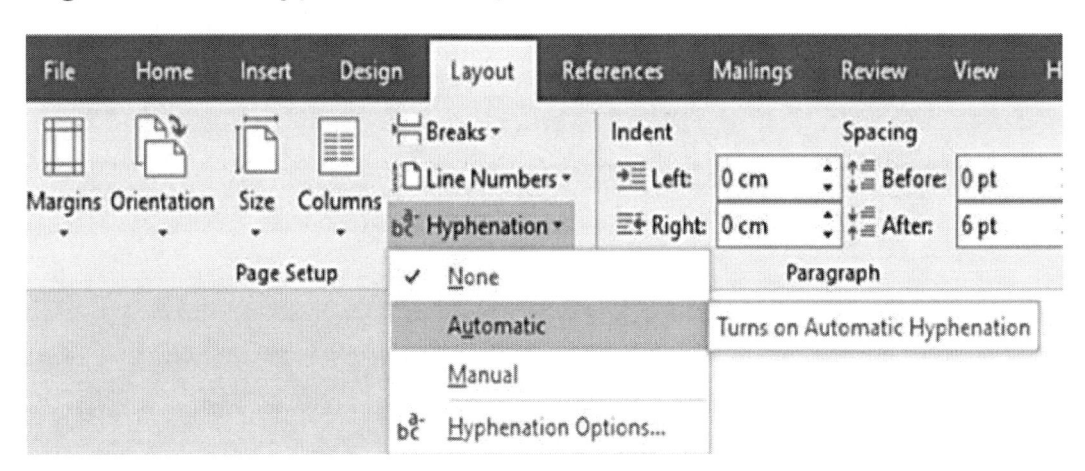

Page Numbering

How to Add Page Numbers in Microsoft Word

It is important to add page numbers before adding other elements to the header or footer of your page otherwise other elements will replace page numbers.

To add a page number;

- Select the **Insert Button** on the Ribbon
- Then select the Page number button on the header and footer group
- On the drop-down menu, select the location to insert the page number (You can choose the top of the page which is the header, bottom of the page which is the footer, page margin, or the current position which is the place where the cursor is on the text).
- Once you make choice then you can select your style options on the submenu, the options depend on the location you chose.
- Once you make your choice, the page number appears immediately

How to Format Page Numbers

- Click on the Insert button
- Click on the page number button on the header and footer group. Followed by " **format page number**" in the drop-down menu
- Now select the option you want from the page number format dialogue box.

Note: Number format lets you choose numerals, letters, and a Roman numeral. They include chapter number options only if you have already established a chapter number in the scheme.

- When "**continue from previous section**" is selected your sections will be numbered continuously. When you've selected your choices, click the Ok button and the number will be applied immediately.

How to Remove a Page Number from the First Page

If you want to remove a page number let's say from the title page which is the first page. To do this

- Select the Insert tab from the Ribbon
- Then select header if your page number is on the header or footer if your page number is in the footer.
- Next select edit header or edit footer from the down menu and select "different first page" in the option group on the header and footer tab

Note: The header or footer tab only appears when you're working on the header or footer

- The page number on the first page should disappear. If it doesn't, then select the delete button to delete it manually

How to Start Numbering From Second Page

After the previous section of removing page number from the first page, you want to start the Numbering for the second page. Do this:

- Select the page number button in the header and footer group
- Then select a format page number from the drop-down menu
- Then enter 0 in the page format dialogue box and then select the **OK** button

- Then the second page will start with number 1

Then close the header and footer button. Always remember to save your document to save your changes.

Page Background

i. How to Insert a Page Color

- Click on the Design Tab and on the right-hand side, you will see the page background
- Click on the page color and select any color you want to change the background as shown in figure 4

Note: To get more color, click on more colors to see more color and click **OK**

There is another option called Fill Effects. Here, you can add multiple colors on one page, select color 1, select color 2, and then you can choose how you want the 2 colors to look (horizontal, vertical, diagonal up, diagonal down, etc) and then click OK. It will show on your page background.

You can also click on Texture to get other textures to use as a page background. There are other options like patterns too.

To insert a picture on your page background, click on the fill effect dialogue box, click on insert pictures and select a picture, click on Insert and the picture selected is shown on the page background. If you don't want any color, just click on "No Color "

Figure 7: Page Color

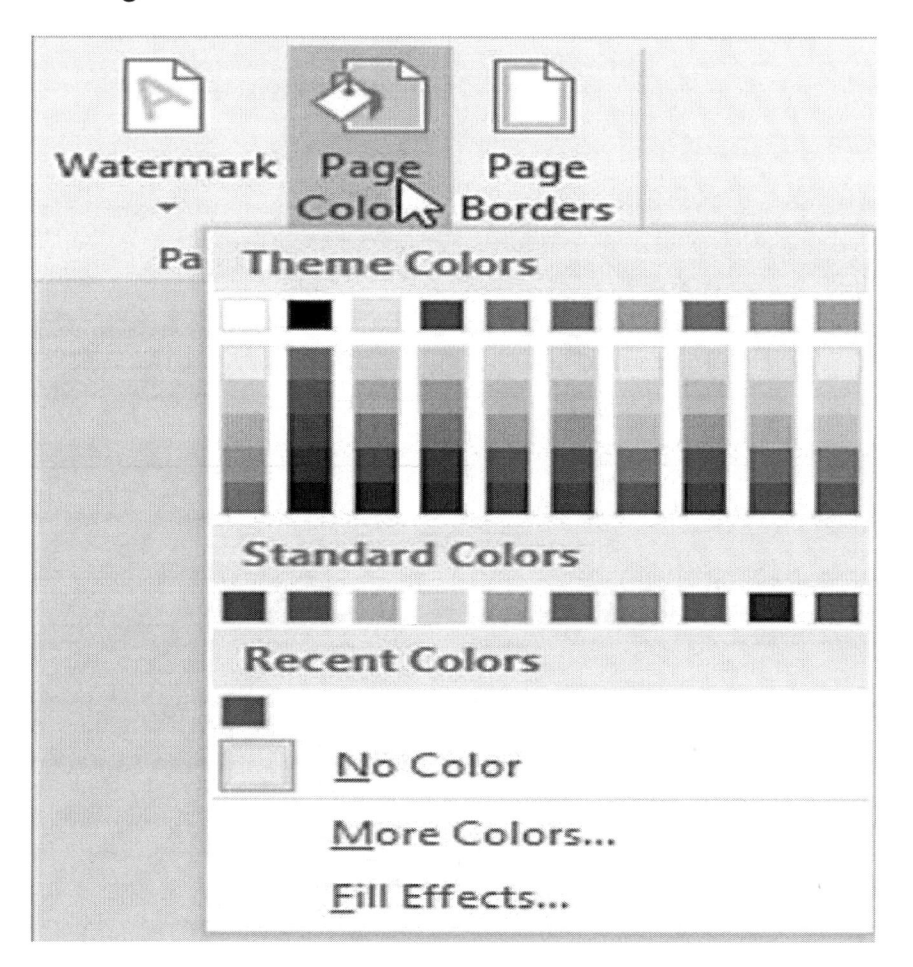

ii. How to Insert a Page Border

- On the Design tab, click on page border and the dialogue box shows up, showing different options of borders (box, shadow, 3D, or none) as shown in figure 7
- Click on the one you want and click ok.

If you want to choose how the line will look on the border (continuous line, dotted line, double line, etc). You can choose it from the dialogue box as shown in figure 8

Figure 7: The Page Border

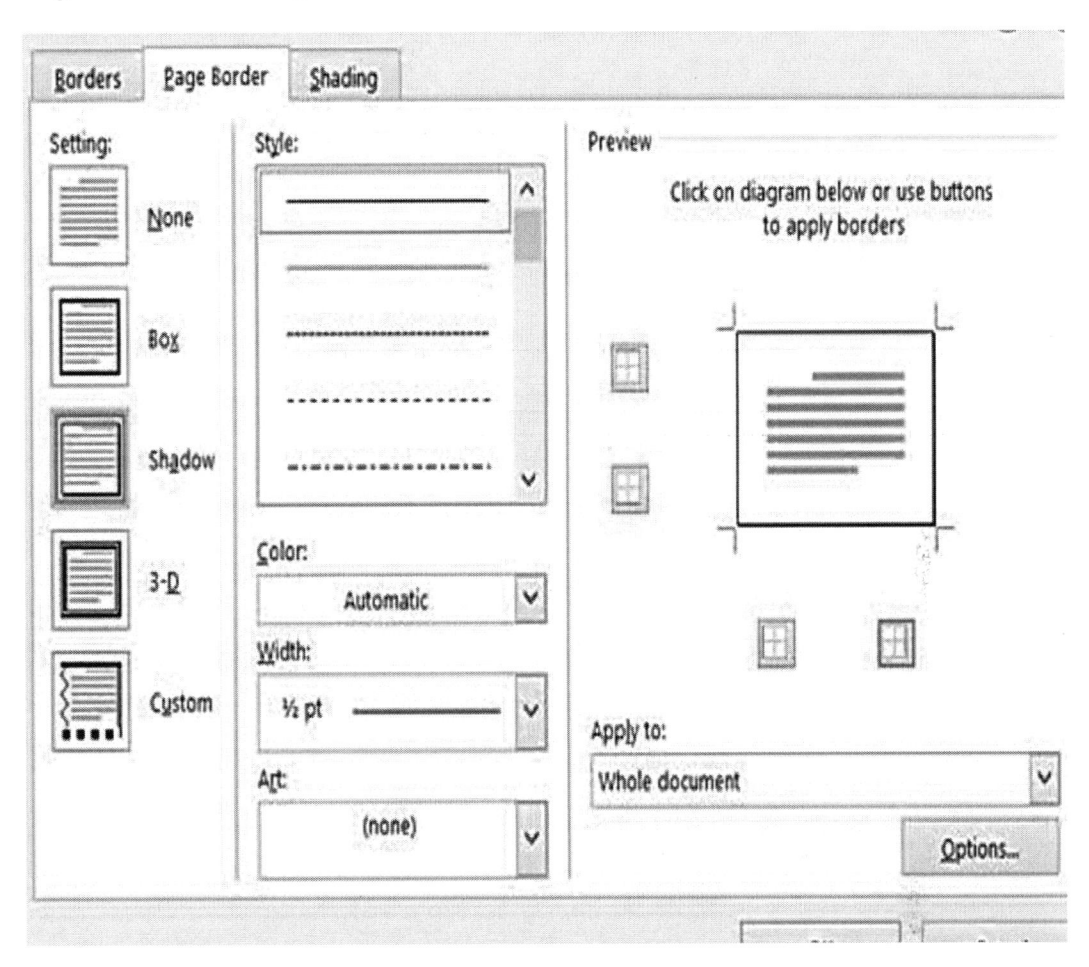

To increase the thickness of the border: On the dialogue box on the page border, you can see the option of the weight of the border, click on the drop-down button and choose a number. Also on the color of the border, click on the drop-down button select a color and then click on OK.

Figure 8: The Page border

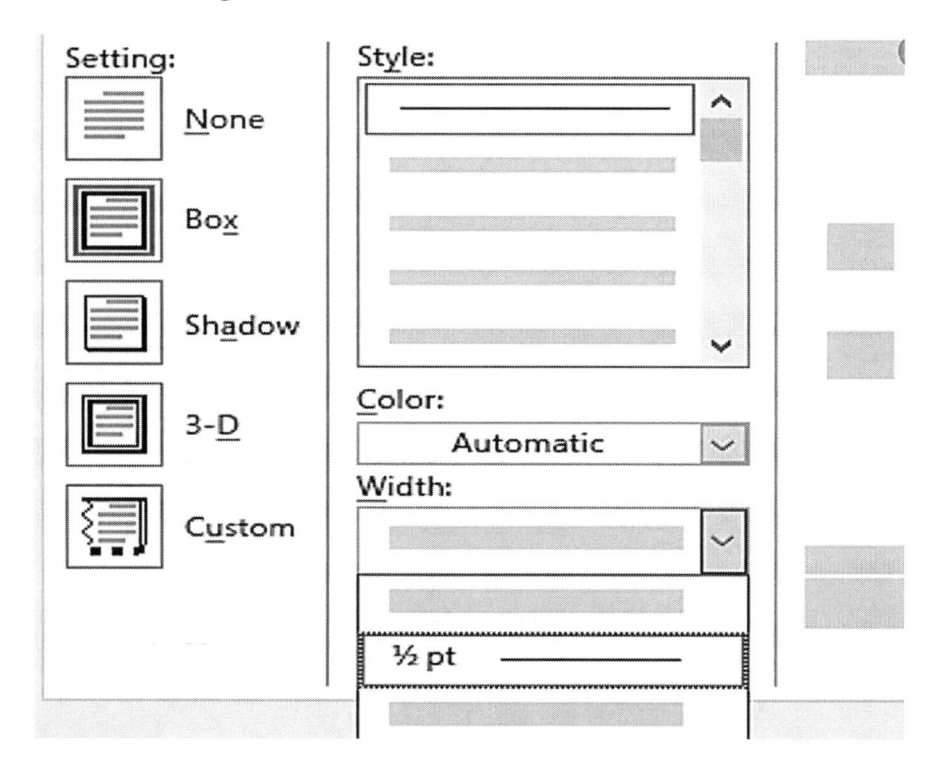

iii. Water Marks

A watermark is an image or text that appears behind the main text of the document. It is always lighter than the text, so you can read the document easily.

a. How to Add Watermark

- Click on the Design tab and on the right side, you will see an option on the page design known as Watermark.
- Click on the drop-down menu and you will see some options (Confidential, diagonal, confidential vertical, etc)
- Click on anyone and it shows on your document page

b. To Edit a watermark

- On the watermark options, click on the Custom Watermark, a dialogue box shows up with different options (no watermark, picture watermark, text watermark)
- If you click on the text watermark, click the text you want, the font, the color, layout, size, and then click on apply. An example of a customized watermark is shown in figure 9 below
- Then the text you typed is applied based on what you filled on the dialogue box.
- To add a picture watermark, select a picture from any folder on your pc click on Insert, and then click on apply. The picture shows on your document.

c. How to remove a Watermark

- Click on Design
- Go to watermark and click on Remove Watermark

Figure 9: A Document with A Watermark

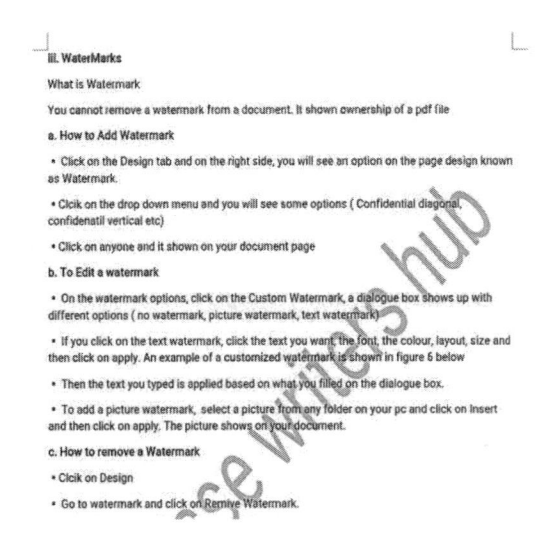

CHAPTER 12

SECTION FORMATTING

Sections Breaks

Sections are the part of Word that controls pages, headers, footers, orientation, margins, and columns on Microsoft Word. Section breaks allow you to space up your document into independent chunks. It shows which parts of a document have different page orientations, columns, or Headers and footers.

Uses of Section Breaks

- If your document needs different headers and footers on different pages, you would use Section breaks to do this.
- Using Section breaks, you can make a table of contents, index, and Appendices with different types of numerals.
- For a document with two pages, you'll need a Section break between the two pages.
- If you need to mix pages that are portrait-oriented with landscape-oriented pages, you can use section breaks
- Section breaks can be added before and after Word's newspaper column feature, so you can use it in the middle of a page.
- You can start page numbers again at any point in a document by putting a section break in the middle of a document.

How to create A Section Breaks

- Click o**n Layout**
- And click on Breaks and then **Section Breaks** comes up as circled in figure 1
- Several options show up (Next page, continuous, even pages, old pages). Click the one that best suits you and section break is applied on the point where you put your cursor.

Figure 1: The Section Break Option

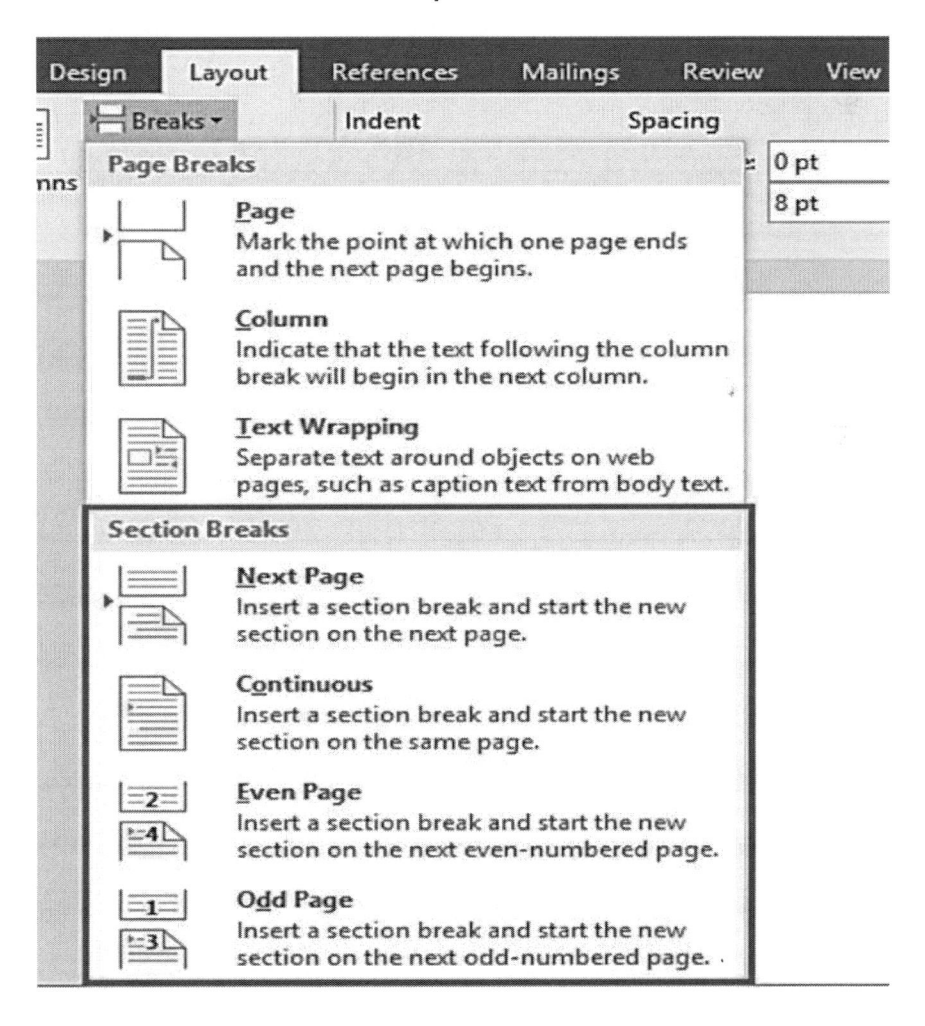

Note: You choose Next when you want to create a section break on a new page, click on Continuous if you want to create a section continuous that is, start a new section on the same page. If you click on Even, the section breaks on the next even paged number and the same applies to the odd Click on Show/ Hide button on the Home Tab to know where the section breaks are applied,

How to Remove Section Break

Before you start, click on the Home tab and click on the Show/Hide to reveal all the formatting on the word document including the section break. To delete it, put your cursor before the section break and click the delete button.

Alternatively, you can use the Replace option on the home tab, click on it to open. Then click on special and select section break from the list and then click on Replace all and click Ok.

Headers and Footers

Headers are information that is placed at the top of each page of a document. You can include any information you want on the header provided that it is small enough to fit into the available space. It may include the date, page number, author's name, etc. The footer is a piece of information that is pointed at the bottom of each page of a document.

How to Add Headers to Word Document 365

- Click on the Insert button. Once the Insert tab is visible.
- On the right side of the ribbon, click on the header
- On the drop-down menu, click on the type of header you want to use

- The header document template will appear on your document
- And where it says " type here" . Start typing
- Once you're done typing, click on close header and footer

How To Add Footer to Word Document 365

- Click on the Insert button. Once the Insert tab is visible.
- On the right side of the ribbon, click on the footer
- On the drop-down menu, click on the type of footer you want to use
- The footer box will open and you can start typing whatever you like on the footer
- Once you have your information entered, click on close header and footer as shown in figure 2 below

Note: If you don't like any of the headers options on the drop-down menu, click on the Edit header at the bottom of the drop-down menu. And the header box will be opened and you can start typing in any format you want. This applies to the footer also.

Also note that when the cursor is on the header or footer area of your document, a new tab called the " headers and footers tools design tab" is available. You can experiment with all the different options that are available in this Ribbon so you can have your header and footer look exactly how you want them to look. On the Home tab, the font features available can be used to customize the font, size, style, and text color of your headers and footers.

Figure 2: Close header and footer button

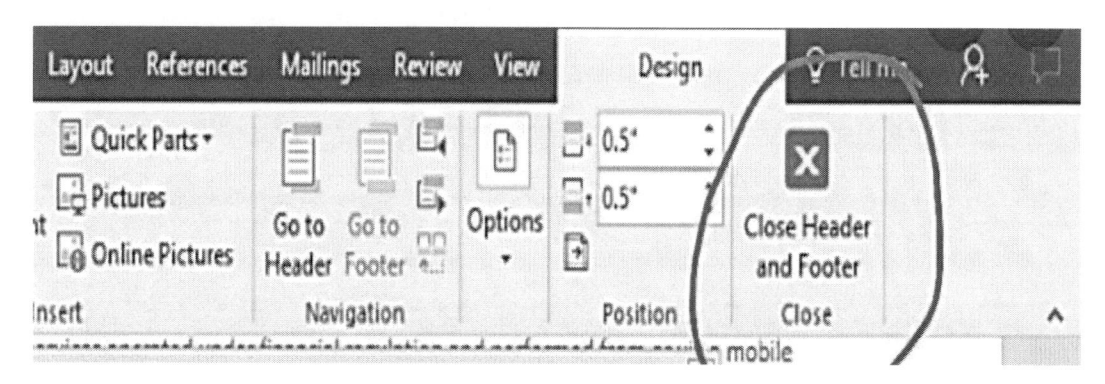

In addition, you can toggle between the header and footer area in the main area of your document by double-clicking. For example, if you have finished working in the header area, you can double click anywhere in the main area on your document and the header area will close and the cursor will return to the main document. You can also go back to the header and footer area to do the same thing. The image of the footer and header button is circled and shown in figure 3.

Figure 3: The Header and Footer

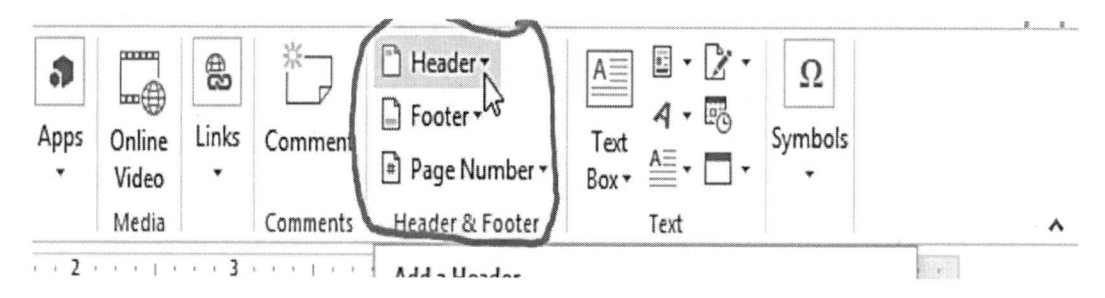

How To Delete Headers and Footers

- Click on the Insert button and click on the header or footer. The dialogue box will show, scroll down and you will see remove headers click on it as shown in figure 4 and the header will disappear. Same with the footer, click on Remove footer and the footer will disappear.

Figure 4: The Remove Header Button

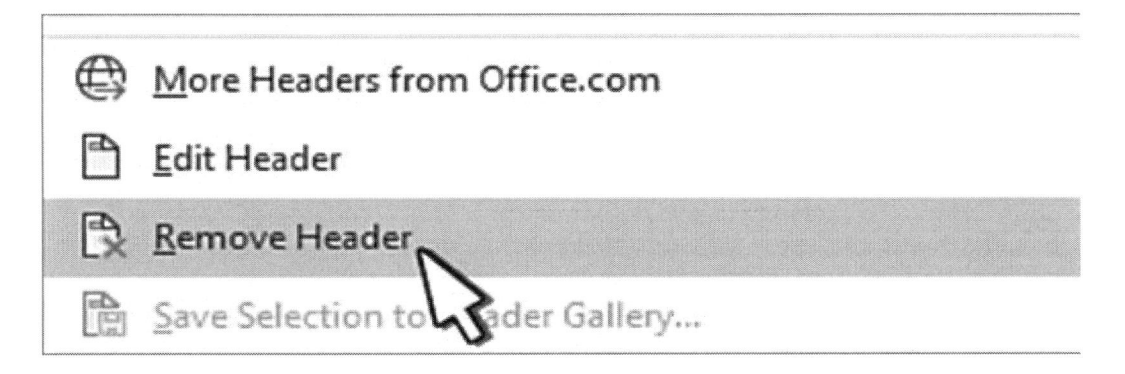

More Headers from Office.com
Edit Header
Remove Header
Save Selection to Header Gallery...

To Insert Any Word on the Header and Footer

On the top of the page, that is the header area, double click on it, and the header displays. In this area, you can Insert anything you want. For example, you can insert a table. Just click on Insert and click on the table with the number of rows and columns you want. Then you can type any text you want. Specifically, you can insert the following:

I. To insert Date and Time: After you double click on the upper area of the document and click on the Design tab. Click on the Date and Time and the dialogue box comes up which will you different formats for date and time. After choosing the one you want, click OK and the date shows on the header area of your document. Remember to always save your document.

To change the position, on the right-hand side of that same tab, click on the Insert Alignment dialogue box. Then it shows options (left, right and center). Click on the position you want and click OK.

ii. To insert Pictures: After double-clicking on the header area, on the Design tab, there's an icon given as Pictures. Select a picture from any folder on your pc and click on Insert. Minimize the picture to the size you want. The pictures are on the header of each page. You can use the alignment tab to change the position

iii. To Add Document Info: Similarly after Double-clicking the header area. On the Design tab, click on document info. Then click on add, the name or author of that file is displayed on the header area. Also if you click on the file name, the name of the file is displayed on the header section of each page. You can add document name, address and so on.

iv. Options: Sometimes, you have a title page but on the first page you don't want to show the header and footers. Then click on a different first page. On the first page, you won't see the header and footer area but on other pages, you will see the header and footer. It also has another option given as different headers and footers for odd and even pages.

Note: If you want to increase the gap or space used by the header. Click on the header from the top and keep increasing the number as shown in figure 5 and the space increases. Same with the footer, click on the footer from the bottom and the footer is increased.

Figure 5: To increase the space between headers/footers

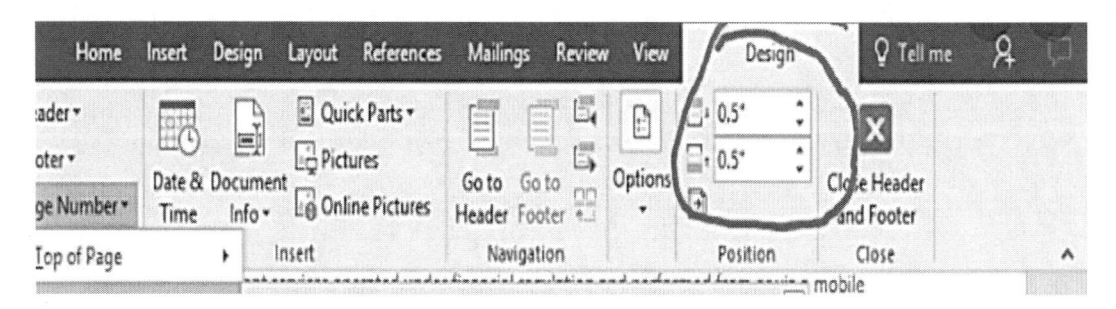

How to Add Border to Headers or Footers in Word

- Click on the **Insert Tab** and Click on **Headers**
- Scroll down to **Edit Header.**
- Then click on the Design tab and go to Page Border
- A dialogue box is displayed that has different options of borders, styles, color, width, and other options which you can use to edit the border to your preferred choice.
- Click Ok after choosing and close the header and footer tab.

How To Create Cover Page in Microsoft Word

To create a Built-in Cover Page

- Click on the Insert tab on the Ribbon
- Then select the cover page from the pages group as shown in figure 6
- Here, you can choose a built-in design from the drop-down menu. For more options, click on more cover pages options
- To insert your cover page, right-click your preferred built-in design and choose a location from the shortcut menu (Insert at Beginning of section, insert at end of the section, insert at Beginning of document etc) as shown in figure 7 below
- When the cover page appears, place your cursor in the sample text and type in your information

Note: To delete a section of sample text, right-click on the text and click on the option that says Remove content control from the shortcut menu.

- When you finish putting all your information, save and it is now part of your document.

Figure 6: The Cover Page Option

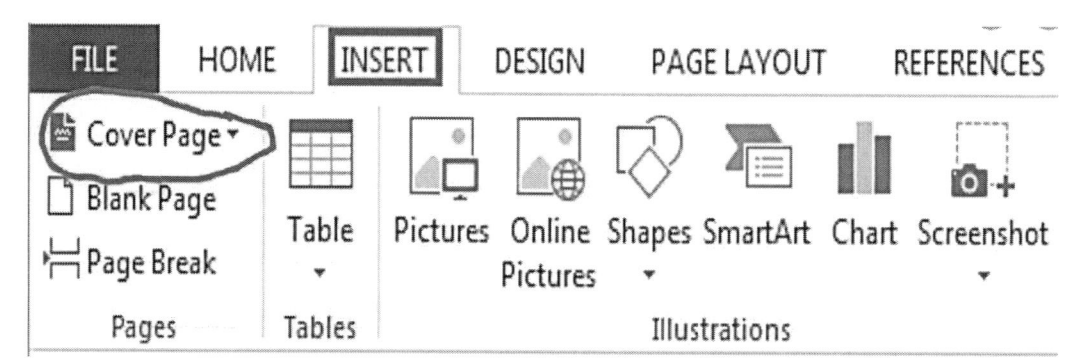

Figure 7: The different options to place your cover page on Word

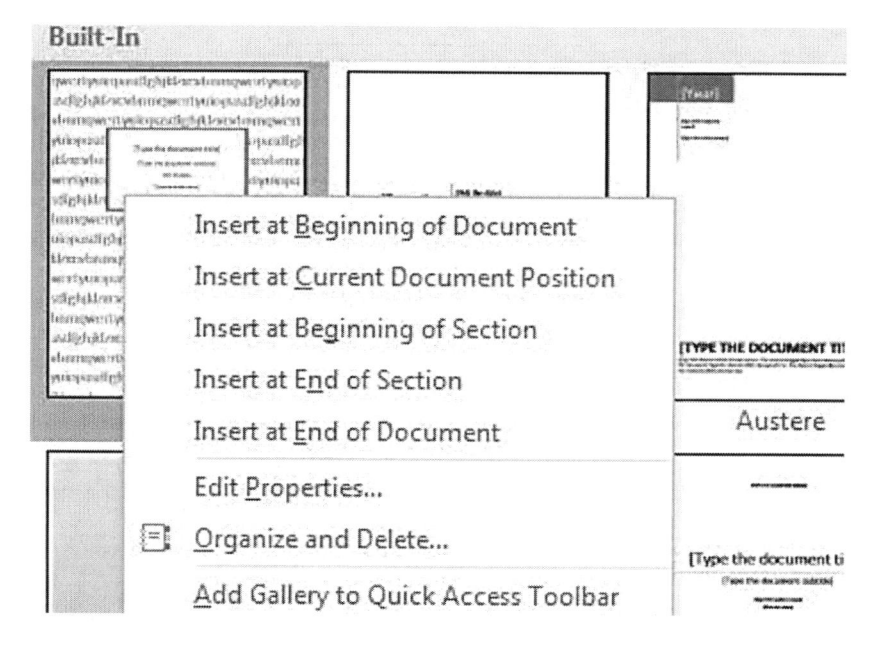

To Create Custom Cover Page

- To begin, **open** a blank document.
- Select the Insert tab in the Ribbon and cover page on the pages group

142

- Next, select Save Selection to Cover Page Gallery as shown in figure 8.
- The create new building block will appear. Now type your unique name in the name text box, then add any additional information into the description text box if necessary

Note: It is better to leave the default settings for the other option in the style box.

- When you are done, click the OK button and it should be added to the cover page Gallery. Save and close the document used to create the custom cover page
- Now open the document to which you want to use the cover page. Select the Insert tab and select your custom cover page from the bottom of the cover page Gallery in the drop-down menu. The cover page should now be added to your document.

Figure 8: Custom Cover Page

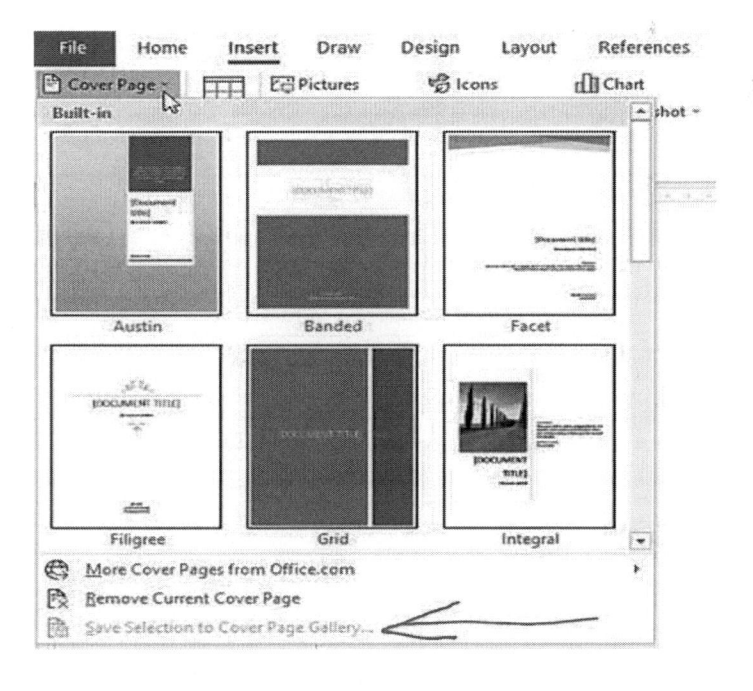

To Delete a Custom Cover Page

If you want to delete a custom cover page from the cover page gallery, right-click the cover page drop-down menu and then select organize. Next, select the delete button and click yes to delete. Finally, you can close your document.

CHAPTER 13

STYLE FORMATTING ON MICROSOFT WORD 365

Word has great features called styles which you can use to control the font, color, and formatting of your document. You can use this feature to get a more professional look and try out different looks on your document. Simply, styles are a collection of all the formatting tools or a mixture of formatting tools in one place (font, size, bold, color). It allows you to quickly format specified content.

Uses of Styles

i. To use a style in Microsoft for Headings: Highlight all the different headings on your document. There is a section called styles on the home tab as shown in figure 1, just click on the style you want and that style will be applied to the selected headings.

Figure 1: The Style Group

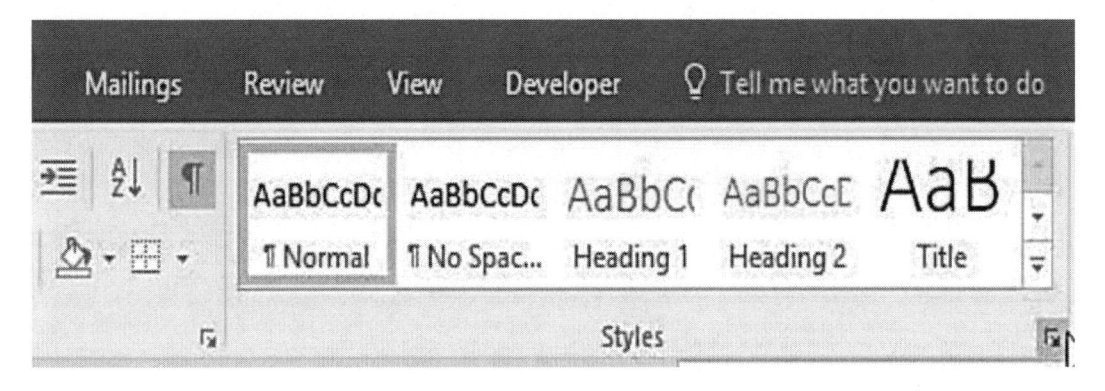

Note: One great benefit of styles is that as you make changes to a style, it applies to all selected headings.

ii. To Insert Table of content on Microsoft Word using Styles

- The best way to do this is to first type out all your headings and then you can add each heading as a section for your table of content
- Click on the Reference tab. On the references tab, there is an option to insert a table of content as illustrated in figure 2.
- You can easily insert an automatic table content as shown in figure 3.
- Immediately a table of content is inserted in your document with all the page numbers matching the page that the headings appear on.

Figure 2: The Table of Content on the Reference Tab

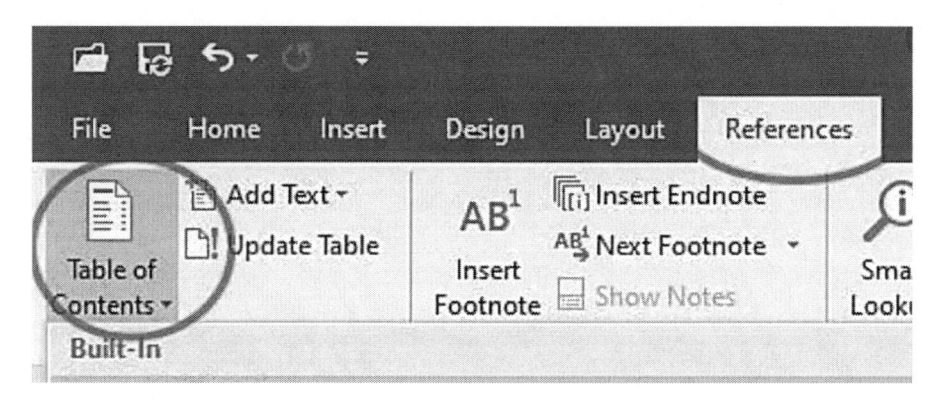

Note: The table of content is leveraged on the fact that you put down all the headings within the document first

Figure 3: Automatic Table of Content

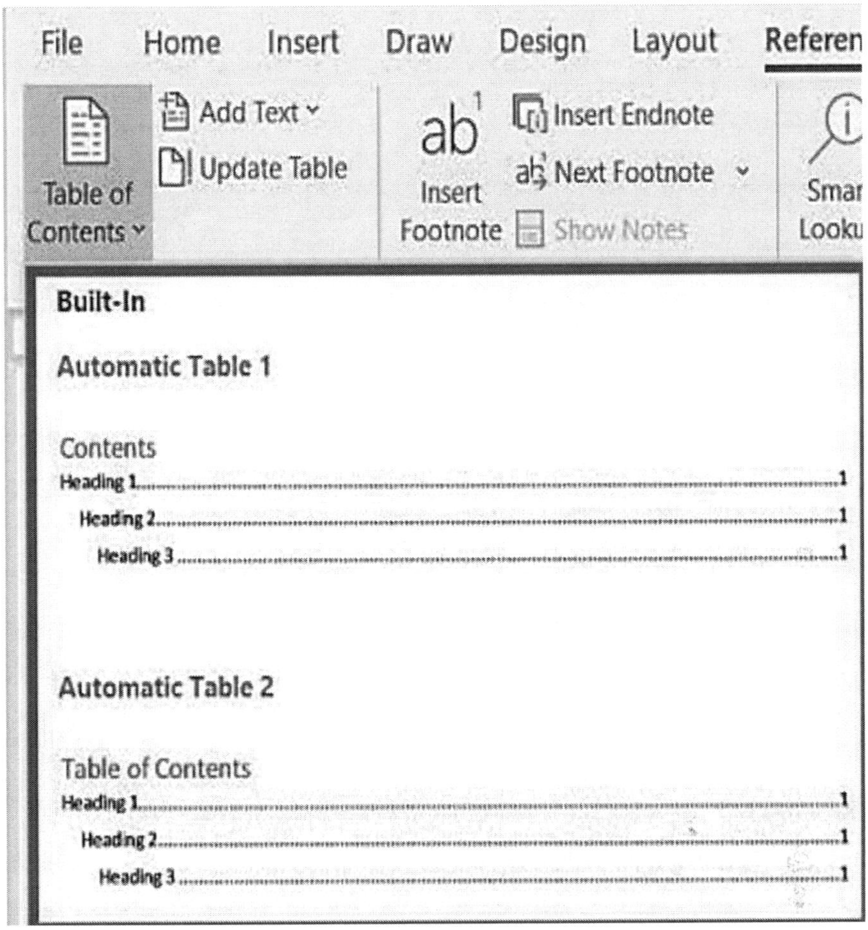

Creating a Customized Table of Content

Instead of clicking on the automatic table of content, scroll down and click on the custom table of content as shown in figure 4, a dialogue box like figure 5 shows which shows different options (headings 1, headings 2, headings 3), you can take advantage of those options and you can define more styles on your document, the table of content will take advantage of that.

Figure 4: Custom table content

Figure 5: Dialogue box of the custom table of content

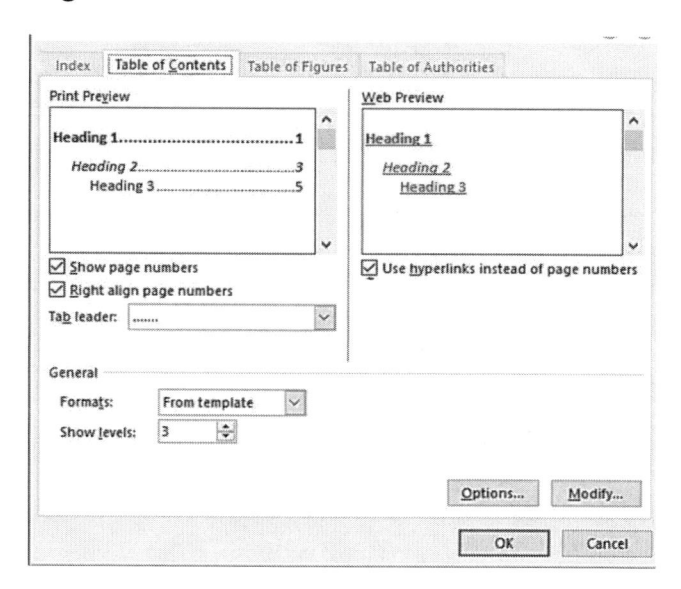

iii. To Navigate throughout your document using Style

- Click on view and click on the Navigation pane as shown in figure 6.
- This will display a quick view of all the headings on your document. If you want to go to the last heading on your document just click on that heading and it will throw you to that spot in that document

Figure 6: The Navigation Pane

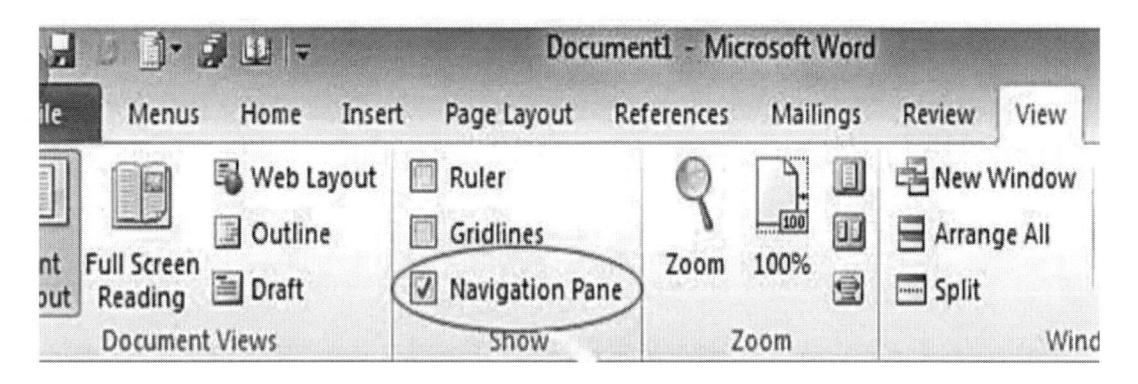

How to See All Styles In Microsoft Word

On the Home tab, look at the style option and click on one style, for example, it will highlight all text around the style.

Microsoft word doesn't load all the styles, all you have to do is to click on the small icon on the bottom right corner of the style pane(This is circled in figure 7) and all the style shows up. You can further click on the options button and you see the option select style to show. Click on all styles and click on OK. Then all styles that are missing will show up

Figure 7: The Style Pane arrow

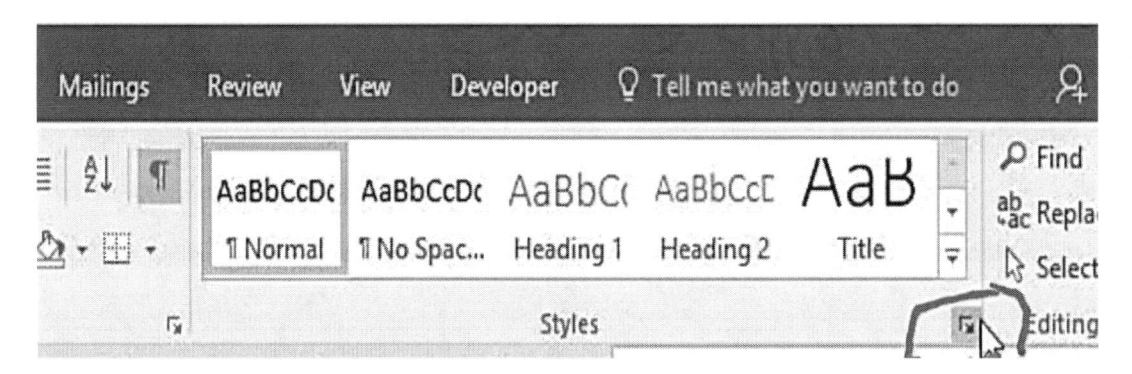

Why Uses Styles in Words

i. You can be sure that all the headings, paragraphs, subheadings, etc have the same correct consistent formatting

ii. It is faster to apply style than doing it individually

iii. Helps to navigate through your document faster.

Types of Styles in Microsoft Word 365

I. Paragraph Styles: it apply formatting to an entire paragraph (indentation, justification, line spacing). It can also include font settings that apply to the entire paragraph

ii. Character Styles: apply formatting only to selected text. It includes font name, font size, italics, bold, color, and another formatting you can use for individual words

iii. Linked Style: This means that they can be used as either a paragraph style or character style. Note: The Linked style must be enabled.

iv. List Style: This style determines the looks of the list such as bullet style, number scheme, indentation, etc.

v. Table Style: it determines the looks of the table such as text formatting of the header rows, guidelines, and colors for rows and columns.

How to Apply Styles on Microsoft Word 365

- Start by placing your cursor next to a line of text, then go to the Styles group and choose any of the styles. To get the fullest, click the drop-down arrow as shown in figure 7 and choose any option from the drop-down list. (The drop-down list is shown in figure 8 and on figure 9 more clearly) You can do it to each line (title, heading, subheadings) to change how it looks

Figure 8: The Styles Options

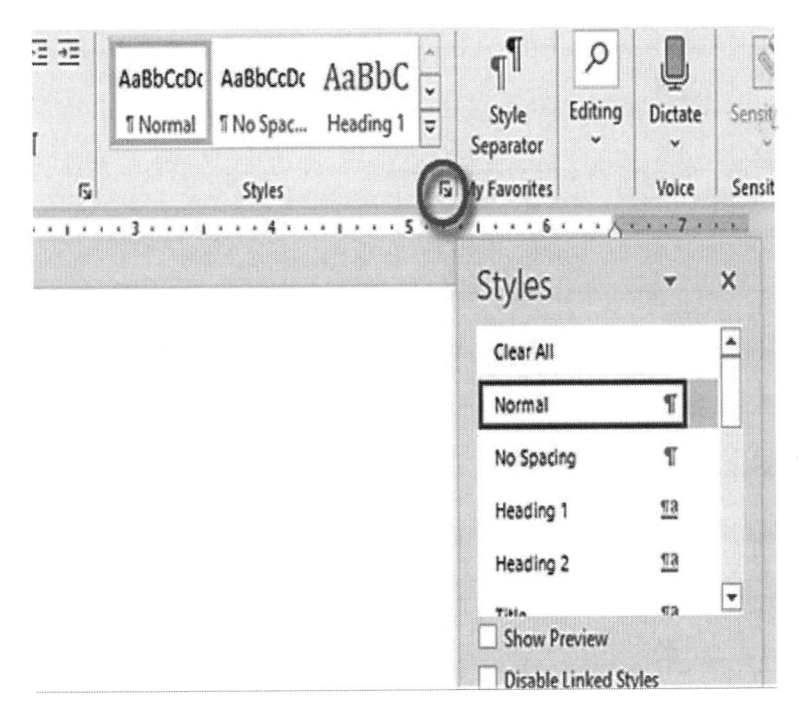

Figure 9: The Style Options

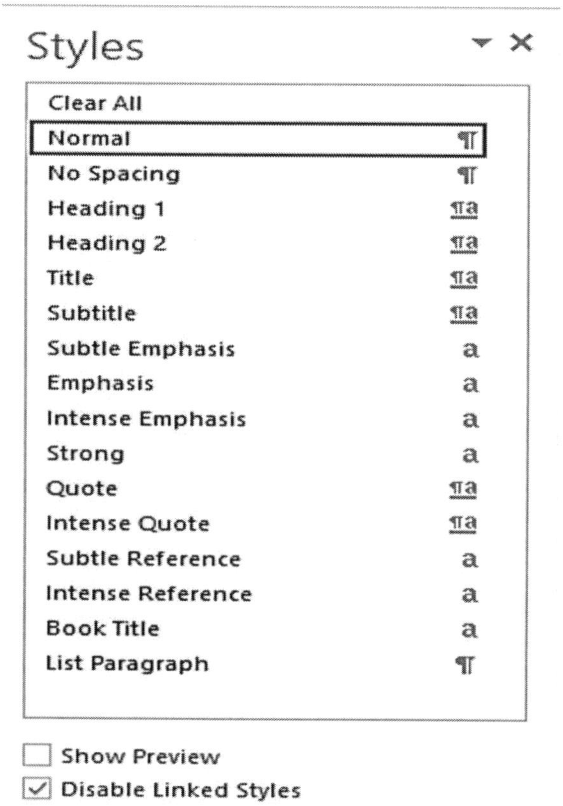

```
Styles                          ▼  ✕
┌─────────────────────────────────────┐
│ Clear All                           │
│ Normal                            ¶ │
│ No Spacing                        ¶ │
│ Heading 1                        ¶a │
│ Heading 2                        ¶a │
│ Title                            ¶a │
│ Subtitle                         ¶a │
│ Subtle Emphasis                   a │
│ Emphasis                          a │
│ Intense Emphasis                  a │
│ Strong                            a │
│ Quote                            ¶a │
│ Intense Quote                    ¶a │
│ Subtle Reference                  a │
│ Intense Reference                 a │
│ Book Title                        a │
│ List Paragraph                    ¶ │
└─────────────────────────────────────┘
 ☐ Show Preview
 ☑ Disable Linked Styles
```

Modifying a Style

Click on the style group, right-click and choose Modify. A drop-down box that has different options to change your document appears (font, size, paragraph options, spacing, and others). Fill in the words to Modify it. Then click Ok and the style is updated on the highlighted text

Note: When you modify a style, know that you're changing every essence of that style in the document. Meaning, you can use styles to change several things at the same time without selecting each document especially if the document has a lot of text.

Creating a New Style

- On the **Home** tab, click on the drop-down arrow beside the style groups/gallery and there's an option that says create style on the style task pane as shown in figure 10.
- Click the new style icon at the bottom left corner of the style task pane to bring up the create a new style from the formatting menu.
- On the dialogue box that pops up as shown in figure 11 enter a name for your style, you can then choose any formatting you like (style type, paragraph options, size, font, color, bold, underline, etc).
- There is also an option "base on the option", it allows you to choose an existing style on which you wish to base your new style which you can use as a template for the new style.
- Then click OK if you're satisfied with the style and close the list, then your style has been applied.

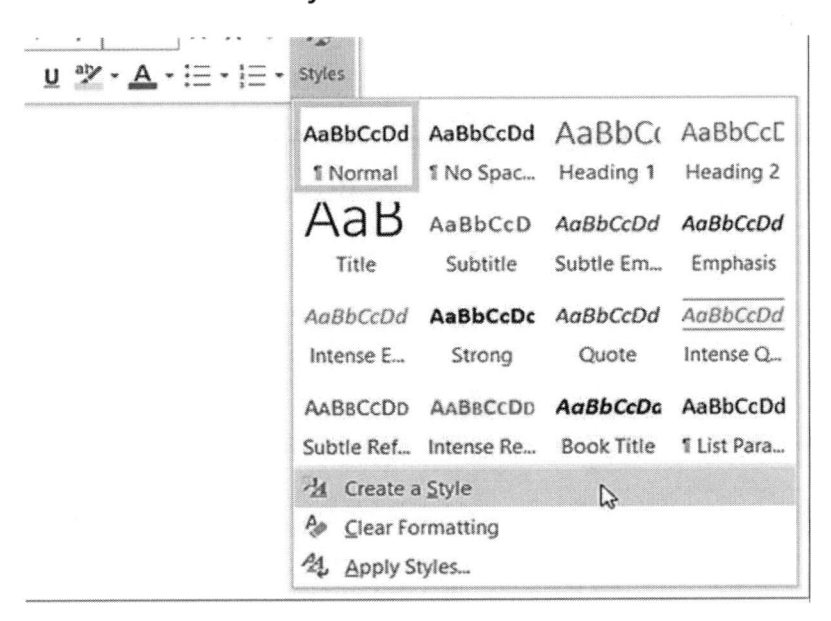

Figure 10: Create New Style Icon

Figure 11: Create New Style dialogue box

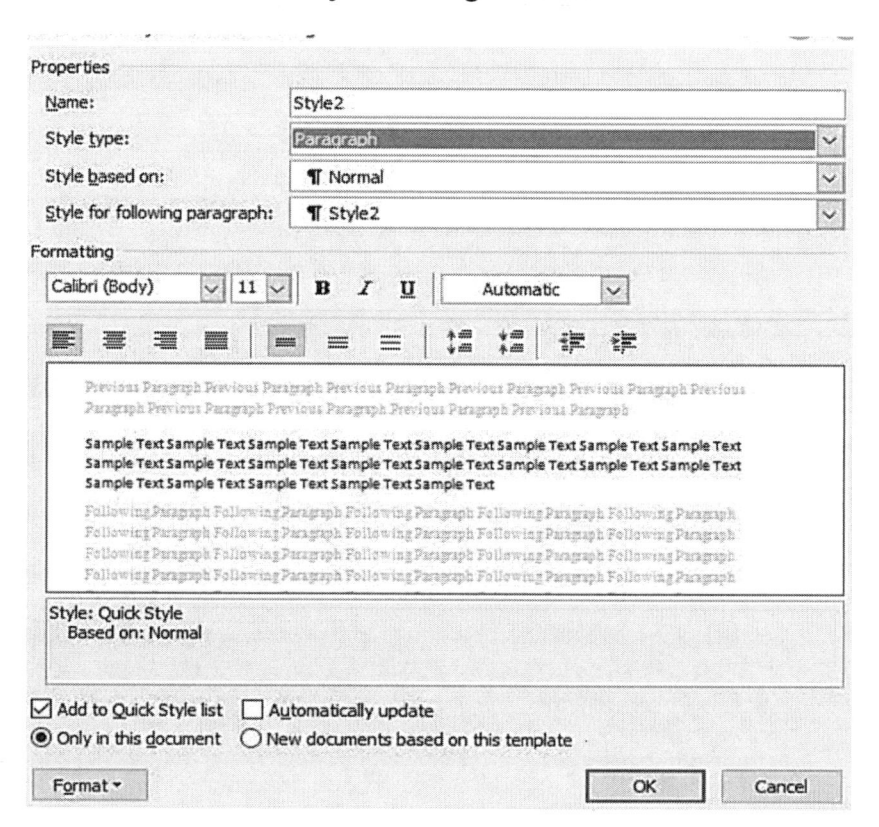

How to Delete Styles

Click on the arrow on the home tab on the style groups. Click on the particular style and the drop-down arrow click delete. It asks if you're sure you want to delete it click yes. Once done, the style will no longer appear on the style menu.

Alternatively, on the style pane on the home tab, click on the managed file at the bottom of the style pane. Select the name of the style to delete and then delete. Click the yes button on the Confirmation box that appears.

However, to permanently remove the style from the template you need to take an extra step. Click on the import and export button at the bottom of the dialogue box and on the left side, you will see a template of document name list in the styles available in the drop-down. Choose the name of the template within which the style you want to delete has been saved from the styles available on the drop-down. Then in the template document name list, select the customized style to delete. On the Confirmation box that appears, click yes to the question and close.

Restricting Styles Changes on Microsoft Word 365

To turn on style restrictions:

- Click on the **File** Tab and then select protect a document in the back icon as shown in figure 12
- On the drop-down menu, select **Restrict Editing (**Figure 12)
- Next, on the restrict editing pane, select formatting restrictions and then select the settings
- On the formatting restrictions dialogue box, check/mark "limit formatting to a selection of styles" as shown in figure 13
- Now check or uncheck the individual styles you want to allow in the document, or select one of the preset option buttons or click "All" to check every style currently allowed in the document. Click on "Recommended Minimum" this option checks comment style options currently allowed in the document but uncheck fewer comments styles such as a table. "None" unchecked all style options (figure 13)
- Then check or uncheck the three optional formatting choices (i. allow other formats to override formatting restrictions this first option implies that you should allow other formats surpass the option selected in the formatting restrictions

style or box ii. Block theme or scheme switching prevents other users from changing the document to a different theme in the design tab or a separate scheme such as the color scheme iii. And the last option is to block Quick Style set switching which when clicked on helps prevent other users from using the style options on the home tab) When you're Done select Ok. This is circled red in figure 13
- A dialogue box will show asking "The Document may contain formatting or styles that aren't allowed. Do you want to remove them"? Select No if you want to keep all of your existing styles while preventing other users from using them
- Next select yes on the start enforcement button and enter a password on the start enforcing protection dialogue box and then select OK as shown in figure 14

Figure 12: Restrict Editing Button

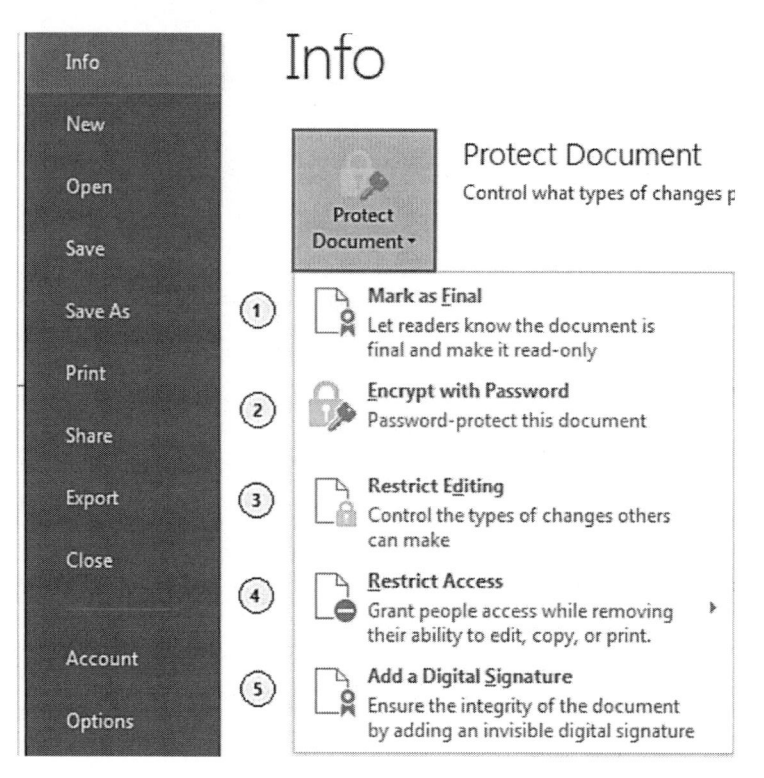

Figure 13: Formatting Restrictions Icon

Figure 14: Start enforcement button

Turning Off These Style Restrictions

Return to the restrict editing task pane, and select the stop protection button (figure 15). Enter your password in the unprotected document dialogue box and click OK. When this is done, it turns off the style restrictions from the password-protected copy of the file that you have shared with other users.

Figure 15: Stop protection button

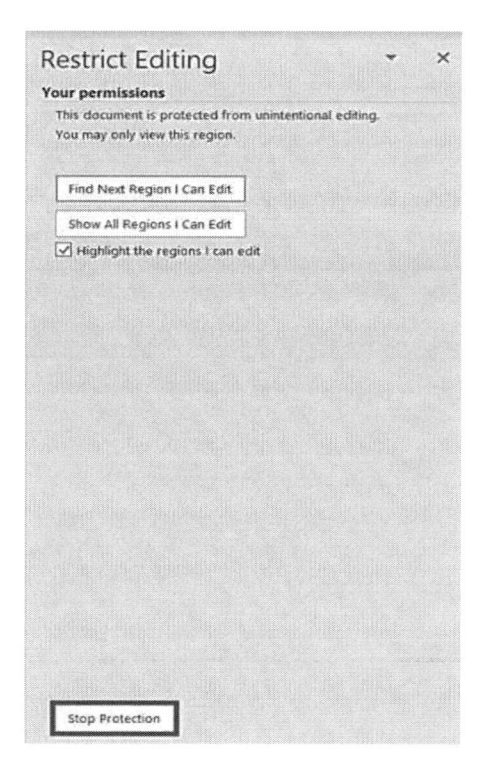

Note: You will have to share your password with them if you would like them to turn off the protection also.

Template Formatting

A template is a document that when opened contains the basic text and formatting needed for a purpose such as a Resume, CV, invoice, report, or legal document. All you have to do is to edit and fill in the template as needed and save it as a new document. It serves as a master or pattern from which other things can be made,

Creating a Template

i. Saving the template

- To save any file as a template: Click on the File Tab. From the options that show up, click on Save As (figure 16)
- Double-click on any folder to save your template either on the computer or PC. The Save As dialogue box shows a list of folders where you can save it

Figure 16: The 'Save As' Button

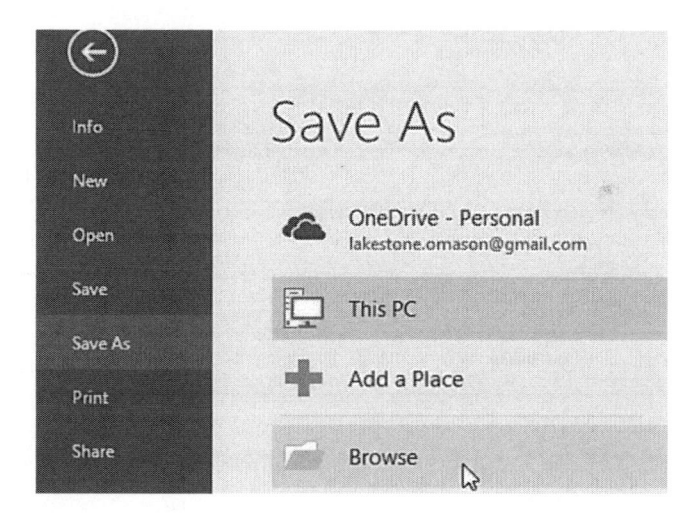

- Type a name for your template in the File name box. There is another box known as "Save As type list" scroll down and click on Word Template. It automatically goes to the Custom Office Templates folder.
- Finally click on **Save.**

ii. Modify The Template

To modify a template in Word;

- Click on the **File tab** and click **Open.** Thereafter, click on a template you want to edit.
- Open the template, edit all the text on the template
- When you are done with the editing, click on the save icon.

Note: Any changes you make on the template will be updated on your template

Making a New Template from Scratch

To create a new template from scratch. Open a blank document and type in any text you want to appear on the template.

Then you can create your style as discussed in the upper section of this chapter and any text formatting you want on the template

When you're satisfied with the styles and everything about it, click on the save as button and save as a template.

Theme Formatting

A theme in Word is a collection of a style set, color set, font set, effect, paragraph spacing, etc that you can apply to your document.

To Apply a Theme in Word

Go to the **Design tab** on the ribbon, then click the themes drop-down button in the document formatting button group to open a drop-down menu of theme choices as shown in figure 17. To preview a theme in your document, hold your mouse over themes in the drop-down menu and to apply a theme to your document, click the theme to apply in the drop-down menu. You can click on the color buttons to change the theme color, the same applies to the font, effect, and paragraph spacing.

Figure 17: The Theme Group

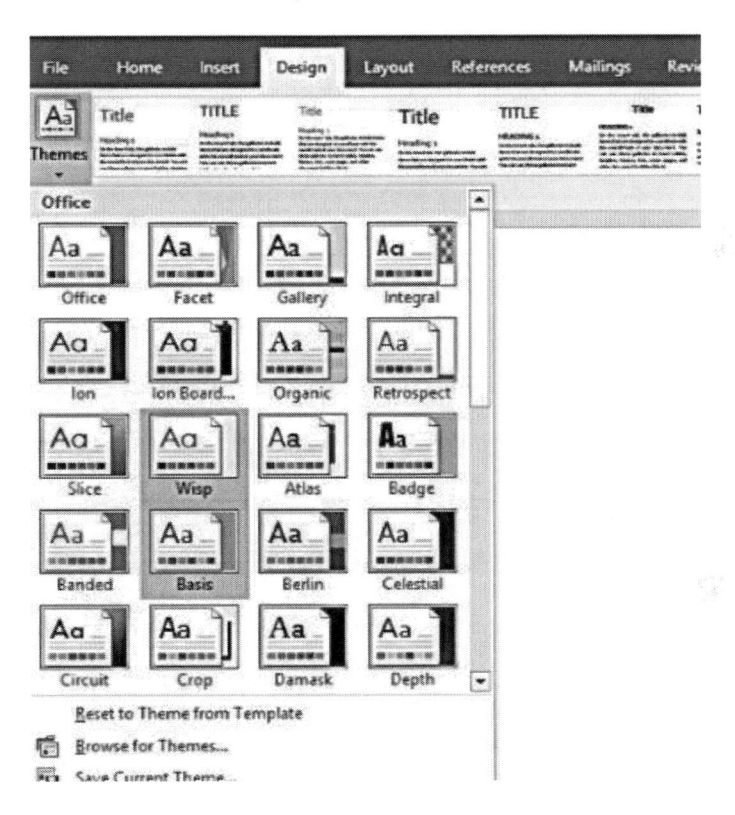

How To Remove an Applied Theme From Your Document

Click the **Design tab** on the Ribbon. Then click the theme drop-down button in the document formatting button group. Then click the Reset to Theme from Template command from the drop-down button as shown in figure 18 below

To Revert your Document to the Default Theme for its related document template. You have to customize the individual elements of the theme by changing the font set color set, style set, and paragraph spacing after making changes on a theme, you can now save it as a new theme you can later apply to other documents in word.

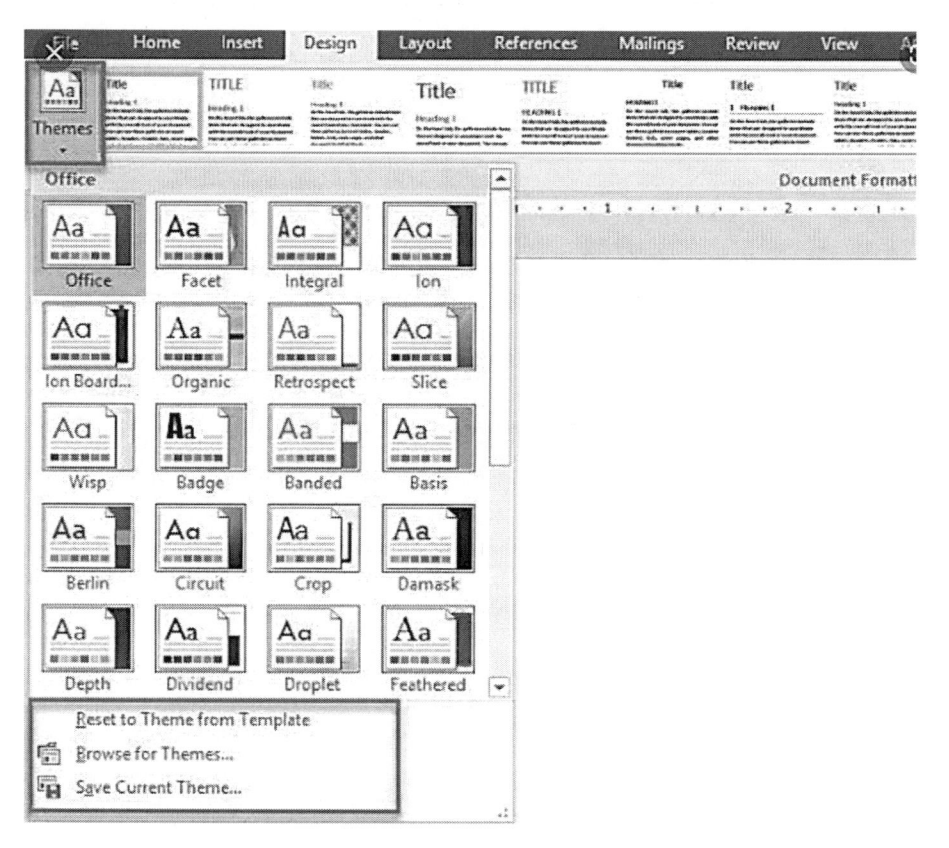

Figure 18: The Revert Theme from Template Button

Note: Always remember after applying a theme to your document, you can change the color scheme and font which will be applied to your document. To save this as a custom theme, let's say you want to use it in other documents perhaps. On the drop-down menu. Click on save current theme (figure 18) and a dialogue box shows where you name this document and click on save.

How to Create a Custom Theme

When you open your document, go to the Design tab and on the document formatting group, there is the font group shown in figure 19, which shows all the font types. If you change the font and click on anyone, it will change all the font in your document. Next to the font is the color scheme shown in figure 20 where you can choose from a list of colors that looks good together. As you scroll through the colors, the color changes depending on what you're highlighting. It will change the color of the fonts of the headings, subheadings color in your document. When you are done with the font and color editing of your choice, click on save

Figure 19: The font Group on the theme

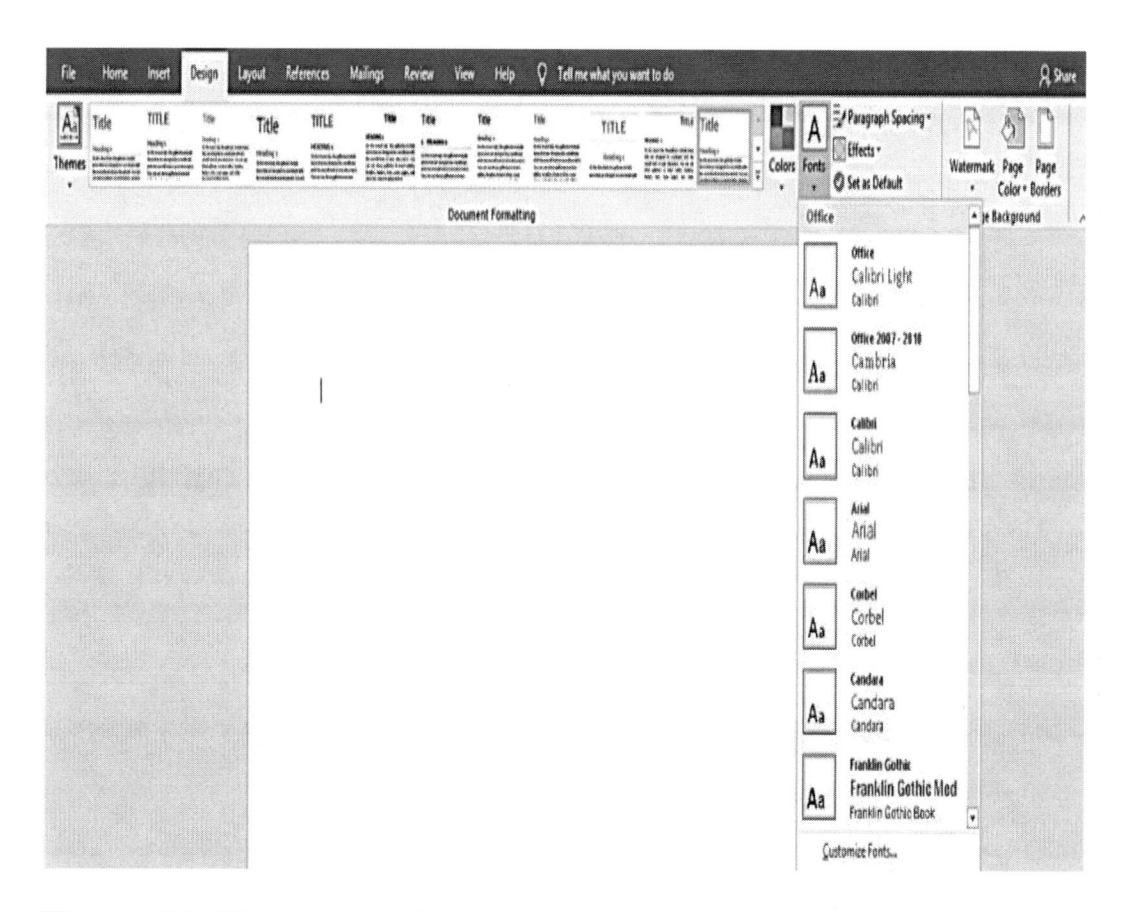

Figure 20: The color scheme group

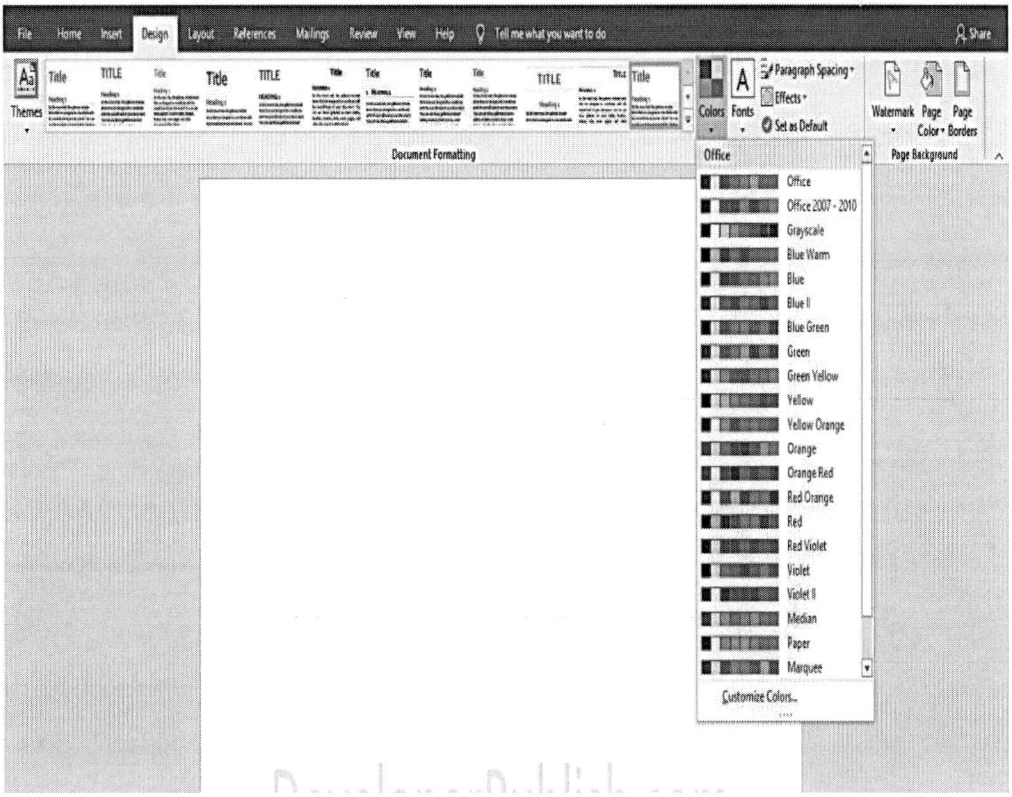
File
Home
Insert
Design
Layout
References
Mailings
Review
View
Help
Tell me what you want to do
Share
Themes
Colors
Fonts
Paragraph Spacing
Effects
Set as Default
Watermark
Page Color
Page Borders
Document Formatting
Page Background
Office
Office
Office 2007 - 2010
Grayscale
Blue Warm
Blue
Blue II
Blue Green
Green
Green Yellow
Yellow
Yellow Orange
Orange
Orange Red
Red Orange
Red
Red Violet
Violet
Violet II
Median
Paper
Marquee
Customize Colors...

CHAPTER 14

BORDERS, TABLES, ROWS, AND COLUMN ON MICROSOFT WORD 365

In this chapter, we are going to learn how to create, insert or remove borders, rows, and columns. We will further discuss how to create a table of content, bullet and numbering list, endnote, and footnotes, and finally the graphics in Microsoft Word 2019.

Borders

A border is like a line coupled into a text, paragraph, or page of a document. This line can be in a different format, either thin or thick, single, double or triple, dashed, or with various art and color

How to Add a Page Border in Microsoft Word 365

Open a blank document or any document on your pc. Then click on your **Design** tab on the Ribbon. Then click on the **page border**. And scroll down to **borders and shading** And the dialogue box showing borders and shading shows up as shown in figure 1. On the settings section, click on any type.. box, 3D, shadow, etc. Click on apply to which will prompt you to choose where to apply it on the document and click Ok You can also edit the border in terms of color, style, art, width, etc.

Figure 1: The Border and Shading Dialogue Box

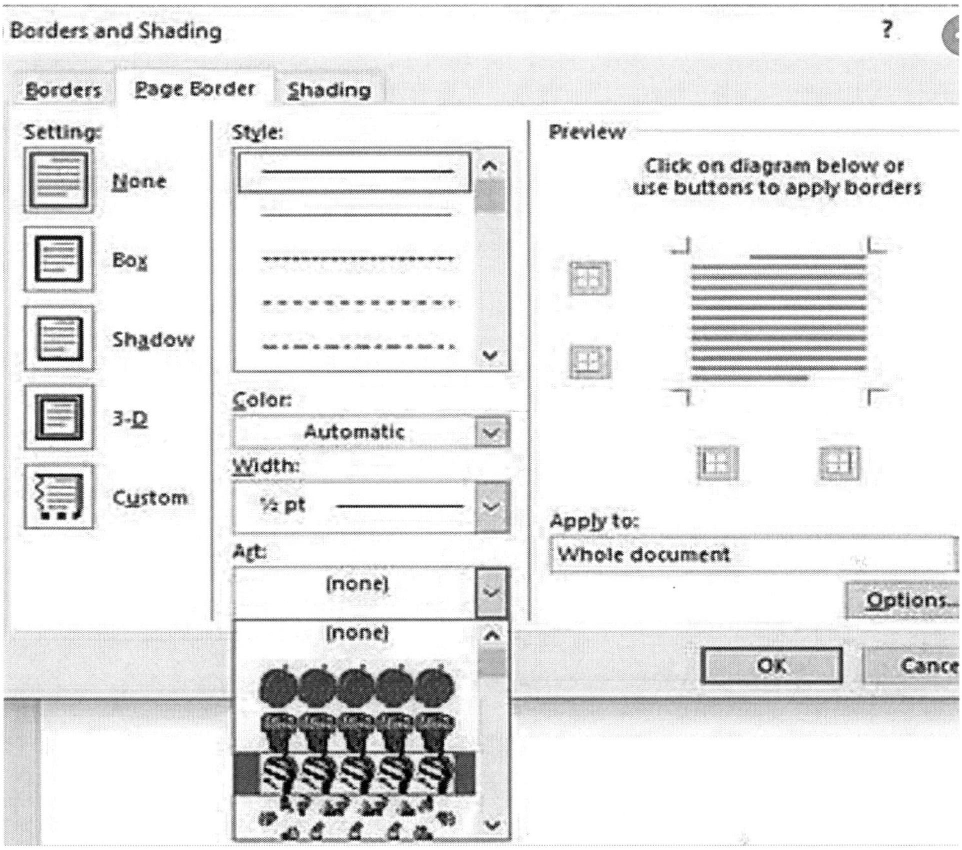

How to Add Border to a Part of Text

Select the text you want to apply the border to. Click on the **page border** on the design tab and the dialogue box, click on any type and click Ok. The border will be added to that selected text in the document. Note you can also edit your border with the elements shown in figure 1

How to Add Border to a Paragraph

Select the paragraph. Click on the border on the design tab and click OK to apply a border to a paragraph.

To Remove a Border

Click on the None option on the dialogue box that pops up when you click on the page border button on the Design tab.

The table on Microsoft Word 365

How to Insert a Table

Start by opening a document on your PC. Put your cursor in the document where you want to insert the table. Click on the Insert tab, and click on the table in the table group. Now move your pointer across and down to select the number of cells organized as rows and columns needed in your table. The selected cells will turn orange then click Insert table. This is illustrated in figure 2.

Figure 2: The Table Group

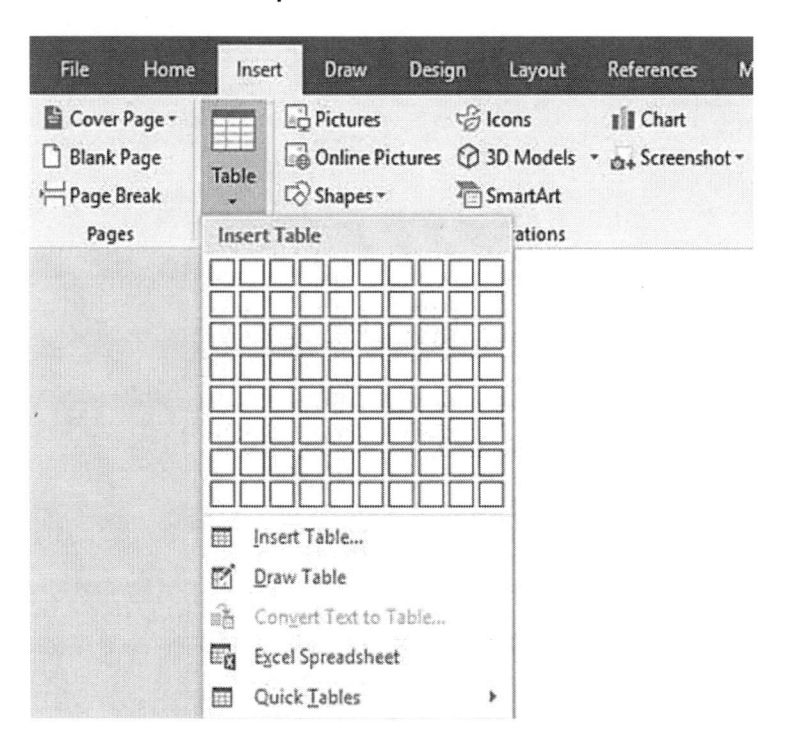

Quick Table

Quick tables are tables you can modify for your use. To begin, Put your cursor where you want to Insert the table. Click on the Insert tab on the Ribbon. Select table in the table group followed by quick table from the drop-down menu as shown in figure 3. Choose the table you want from the gallery. Then enter your content by typing over or deleting the table example text.

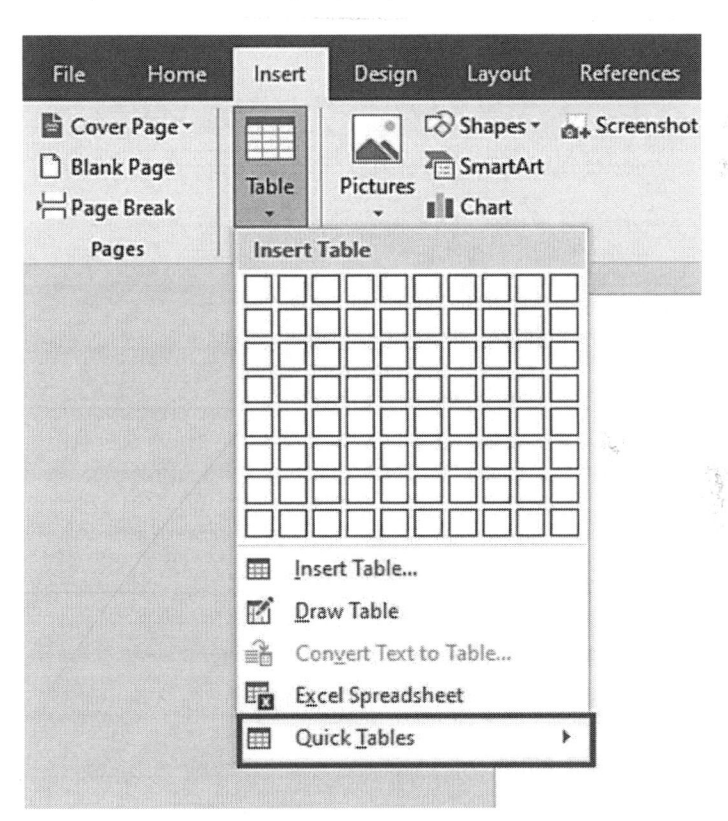

Figure 3: The Quick Table

How Do I Enter Text into a Table

To do this, place your cursor into a cell and type as you normally would enter a text into a table.

Table Styles

Click on the Design tab and then on Table Style, click on the drop-down button circled in figure 4 below, and different table styles show up then you can select any one of them as shown in figure 5

Figure 4: Table Style drop-down arrow

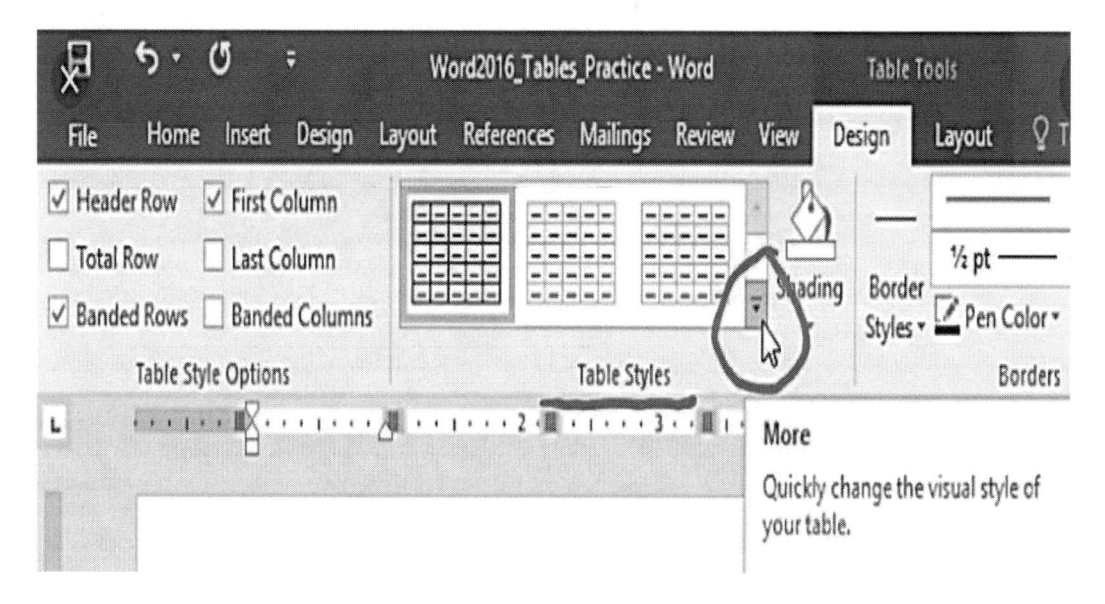

Figure 5: Table Styles

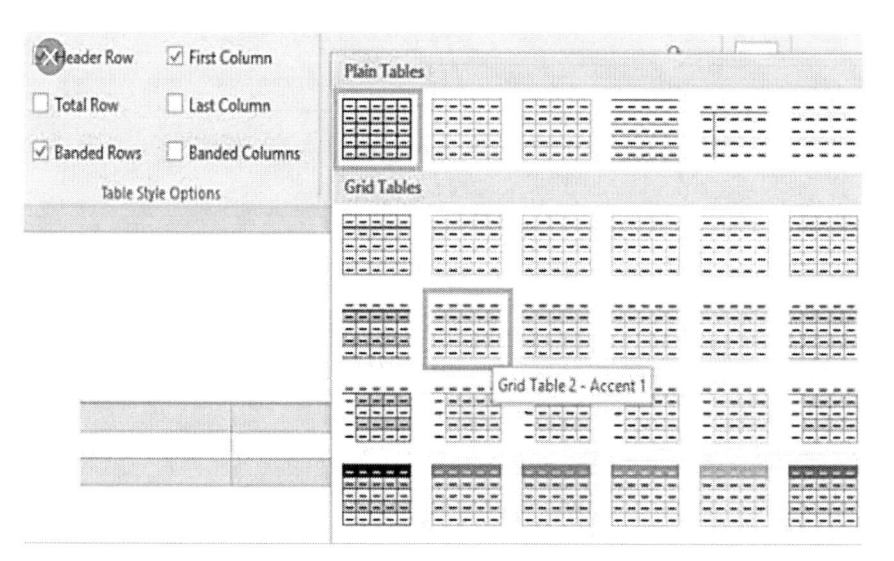

170

Note: You can use the shading menu to add a custom menu to individual rows and columns.

- **Header Row:** Only the header row is colored, the first row is highlighted
- **Banded Rows:** Alternate rows are highlighted
- **Total Row**: All rows are highlighted
- **First Column:** The first column is highlighted
- **Last Columns:** last columns are highlighted
- **Banded Column:** Alternate Column are highlighted

To create your table styles

Click on create new table style on the table style group and do lots of formatting on the dialogue box. Click okay when you're done.

Insert Rows and Column

After creating a table, place your cursor beneath any row, to add another row beneath it. Click on the **+** sign. To Insert a column, click on the layout tab and an option shows Insert left, insert above, insert right and insert bottom. Just place your cursor on the position where you want to add and click the Insert column, choose any position where you want the column to be added and it is updated in your document

Cut, Copy, Paste, and Delete Rows and columns

Click on the row and column on the Layout tab, you will see delete. Click on it to delete the column or just right-click with your mouse. It displays different options to cut, copy, paste or delete rows and column

Alternatively, to delete a table, select the table selector which is a + plus. It will select the entire table. Note that you may have to use the pointer over the table to reveal all the table selectors. Then right-click the table and select the delete table from the shortcut menu,

Resize Rows, Column, and Tables

Place your cursor on any column, click on the layout tab and click on cell size group there is a height option, click to expand it and the height of the column increases, same with weight, etc.

To Get an equal height of each column, click on distribute rows and all rows will have equal height. Same with the column, click on distribute column to get an equal column.

To resize an entire table, click the resizing handle in the bottom right of the table. You may be required to move your pointer over the table to reveal the handle. Then drag the table to the size you want upon the + sign on the bottom side of the table

Split and Merge Cells

Select all the cells, click on the layout tab and click on merge cells while on split cell place your cursor on the cell, click on split cell, a dialogue box shows up to type in how many rows and columns you want, type in the number and click OK. That cell will be split into the number of rows and columns you typed in.

To split an entire table, keep your cursor anywhere you want to split the table. Click on the split table and it will be split.

How to Convert Text to Table

First, select your text. Click on the Insert tab and click on the drop-down arrow on the table groups. Scroll down to convert text to table. On the dialogue box, choose an option for separating your text. This is how word knows what to put in each column. Then click OK.

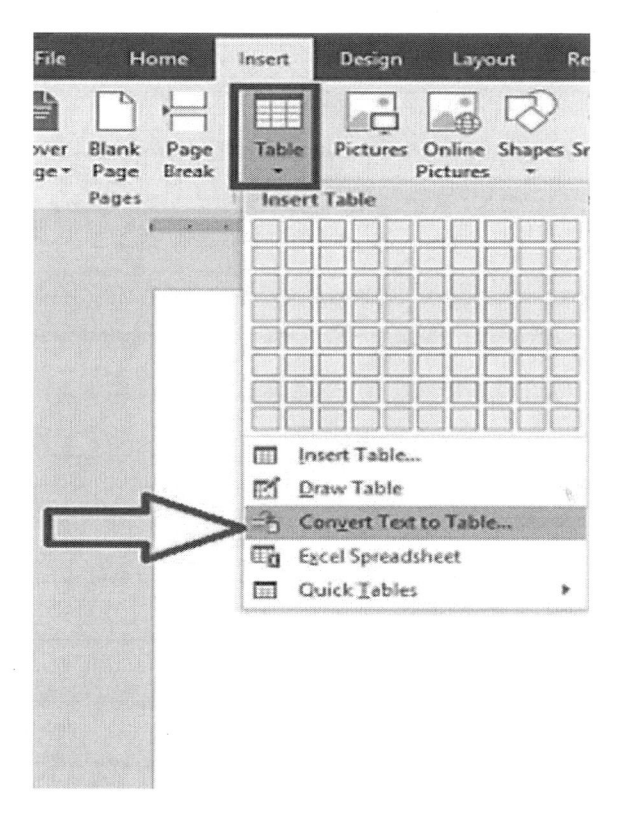

Figure 6: Convert Text to Table

Placing a Column Break

In Word, you can break a column as you can break a page too. This column can break works only on multicolumn pages. It helps the column's text to stop at some point down the page and then continue at the top of the next column.

To do this: Click to place the insertion pointer in your document which will be the start of the next column and click the **Layout** tab. Thereafter, click on the **break** button located on the **page setup group**. A menu appears to click on the column. The text immediately moves to the top of the next column.

Note: Column breaks don't end column instead, they split a column, ending text at a certain point on a page and starting the rest of the text at the top of the next column.

How to Create Bulleted List in Microsoft Word

Bullets lists are helpful when creating a list that stands out from the text. To create a bulleted list. Place your cursor on where you want to insert the bullet list.

Go to the **home** tab, and on the **paragraph group,** click on the bullet, on the drop-down arrow, click on any bullet that suits you the best. Then type your first list item, after that, press enter and the second line start with the same bullet style. Double-click the enter key to end your bullet list.

Figure 7: Bullet Styles

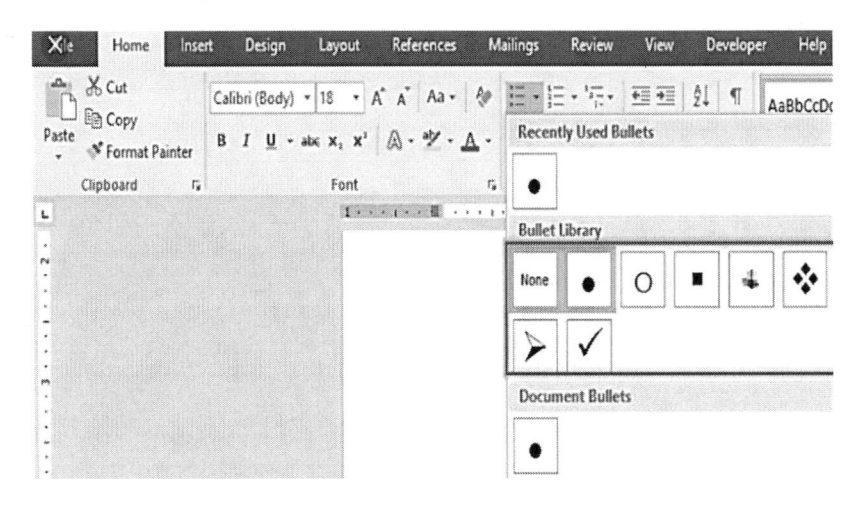

How to Create a List from an Existing Text

The first thing to do is to select the text you want to turn to a list by highlighting the text. Then go to the home tab and select bullet on the paragraph group. Bullets are automatically updated on your selected text.

To Remove the Bullet and Numbering

Just open the document and go to the home tab, click on the bullet icon and choose none.

How to create an index in Word

An index is something you can insert into any word document particularly in a long document. An index is a list of items or topics discussed in the document listed in alphabetical order. Always found at the end of the document, showing you the page number where those topics are located.

To create an index, the first thing to do is to **mark the entries.** Select the text you'd like to use as an index entry, or you can just click where you want to insert the entry.

Then go to the **References tab,** and on the Index group, click **Mark Entry.**

Then mark all your entries. Note, you can edit the text in the Mark Index Entry dialogue box., you can also add a second-level in the Subentry box.

Next, if you want to format the page numbers that will appear in the index, select the Bold check box or Italic check box below the Page number format. Then click **Mark to** mark the index entry or click on Mark all to make it easy.

Then to **Create the index**, after you mark the entries, you're now ready to insert the index into your document. All you have to do is click on where you wish to add the index and on the **References tab**, in the Index group, click **Insert Index**. On the Index dialogue box that shows up, you can choose the format for text entries, page numbers, tabs, and leader characters. Then click OK.

How to Insert Endnote and Footnote on Microsoft 365

Footnotes are at the bottom of a page while **endnotes** are found at the end of a document. To begin, place your cursor where the superscript number for the footnote should appear. Select the **Reference tab** and select the dialogue box launcher in the footnote group. Now select footnote or endnote and choose the note designated location at the drop-down menu (figure 8). Be sure to explore other options on the dialogue box including the number formatting. Next select insert to create your footnote. Afterward, create your superscript number your cursor will automatically move to the new location designated in the footnote and endnote dialogue box (figure 9) Now, write your note and Double click on the number before the note to return to the location of the corresponding superscript number in the body content. Place your cursor on where the superscript number for the next note should appear and then select Insert footnote or endnote in the footnote and endnote group to Insert the next note.

Figure 8: The Footnotes and Endnotes button

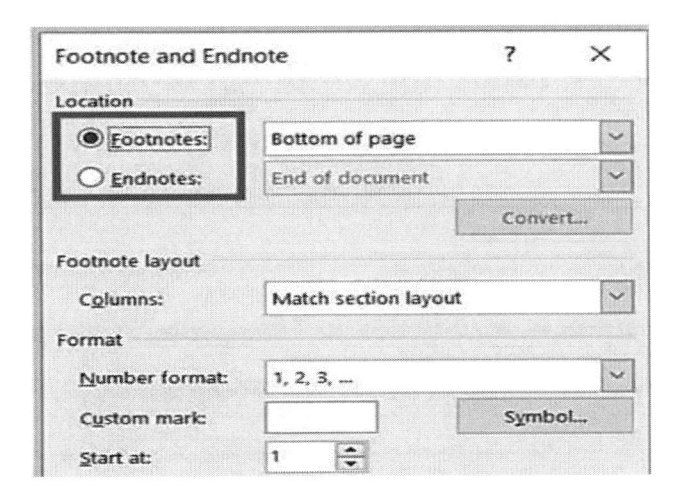

Note: You can use footnote and endnote in the same document. Also, note that if you move the text connected to footnote or endnote, the sequencing of the superscript numbers or letters and the notes themselves will be automatically updated. In addition, if you add or delete footnote or endnotes between existing notes the sequencing of the superscript numbers or letters and the Notes themselves will be automatically updated.

Figure 9: Endnotes and footnotes location

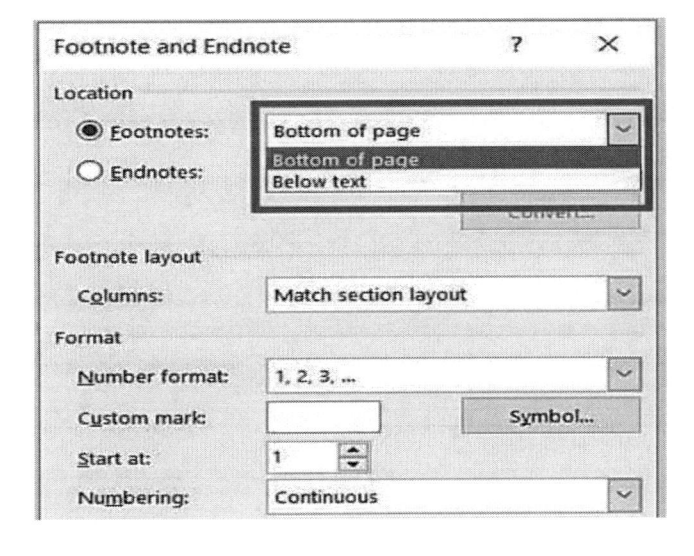

Graphical Works in Microsoft Word 365

Most of the graphical tools are found on the Insert tab of Microsoft word 365. Here, you can insert anything into your document including pictures, shapes, text, etc.

To Insert pictures: Put your cursor to the point where you want to insert the image and click on the Insert tab on the ribbon. One of the commands is the picture tool format tab. When you click on it, it will take you to locations where you can insert different images into your document. When you have selected the image, click on Insert, and the image is automatically updated into your document. Use one of the command buttons to choose which type of image to add.

Figure 10: Insert Pictures

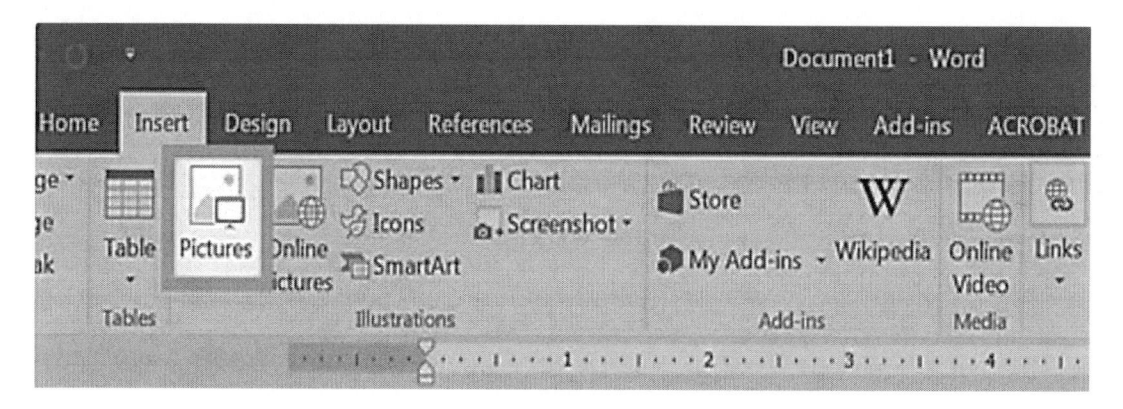

Note: You can also insert online pictures, by clicking on online pictures from the Insert tab. Then copy the image from the web and paste it into your document

- **To Delete an image,** click on the image, select it and click on the delete button.

- **To Copy and Paste an Image;** Select the image you want to copy from another document. Alternatively, press Ctrl + C to copy the image. Then go to the new location where you want to paste that image and click Ctrl + V to paste. Alternatively, right-click the mouse, and options are displayed, choose the paste option to paste the image

How to Insert Shape into Your Document

You can Insert shapes into your document. Word has a section that contains some common shapes such as circles, squares, arrows, geometric figures, etc. To do this; Click on the Insert tab and click on the shape button as illustrated in figure 11. This menu has lots of shapes that you can choose from. Click on your preferred shape and it is updated into your document.

Note: you can adjust the shape in terms of size or colors. All you have to do is use the drawing tool format tab. This can be seen on the Ribbon. Just select the shapes to effect those changes. You can use the **Shape Fill button t**o set the fill color and you can use the Shape Outline button to set the shape's outline color. You can also adjust the outline thickness (Shape outline button menu) weight and effect (3D, shadow, or any fancy formatting)on the selected shape.

Figure 11: The shape button

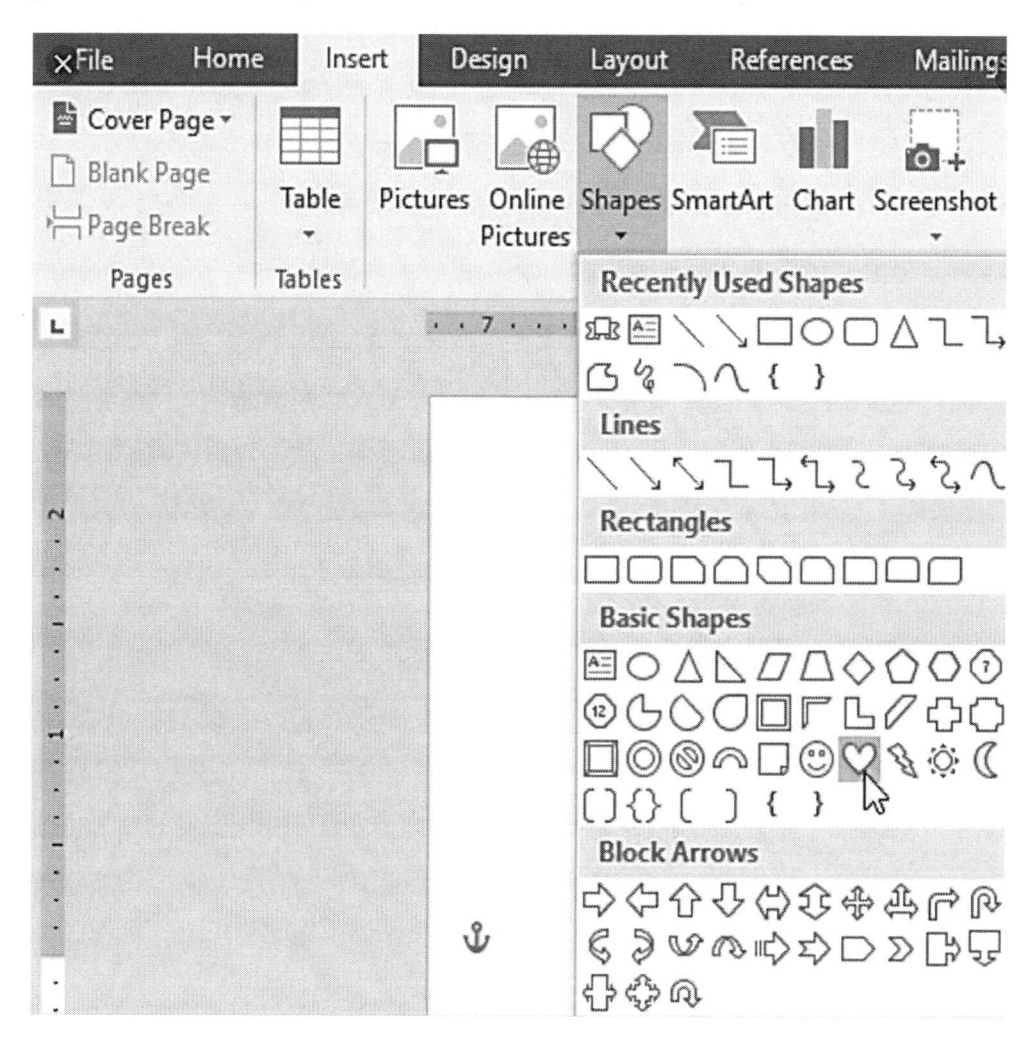

How to Create Picture Layout on Microsoft Word 365

First of all, select the picture and a new box appears on the selected picture. On the **picture style group,** there is an option for a **picture layou**t. Click on it and then a list of different Layout will be displayed. Click on the one that suits you and resize to the box.

Figure 12: The Picture Layout

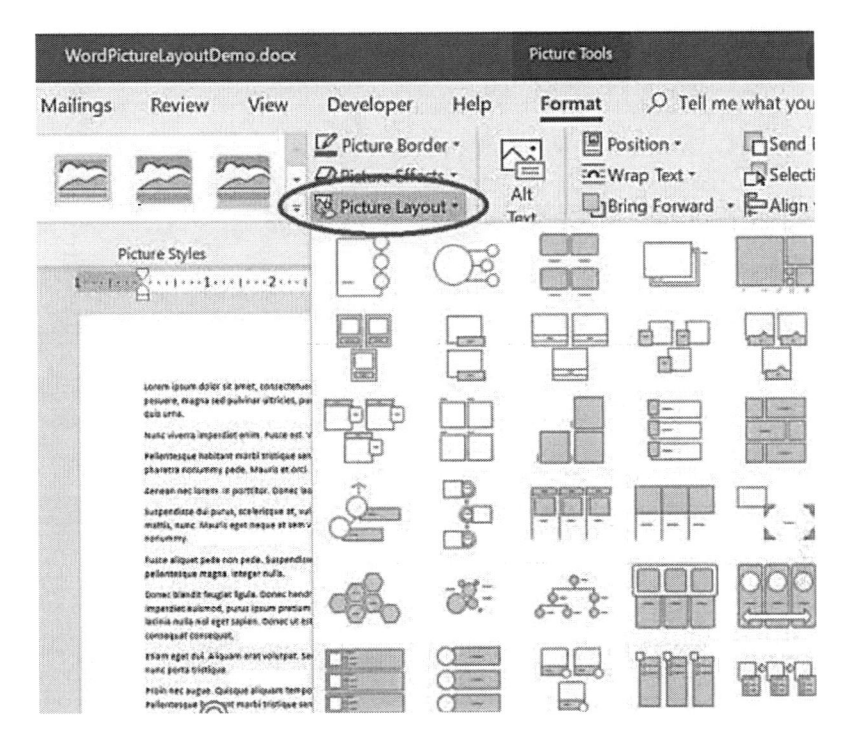

How to Wrap Text Around an Image

It is important to provide a proper layout option to keep all text and images in your document well organized. This layout has 3 general groups. The **Inline** (where the image is inserted into the text and the image acts as a character), **wrapped** (text stays around the image), and **floating (** where the image is seen at the front or behind the text).

To insert an image Layout, first of all, select an image and then click on the Layout Options button, and a list of various layouts settings is displayed. Some of the options are Inline, square, tight, through, behind the text, top, and bottom, front if text, behind the text, wrap text, etc. To get more options, click on more options. Select your preferred and click OK.

Figure 13: Wrap Text

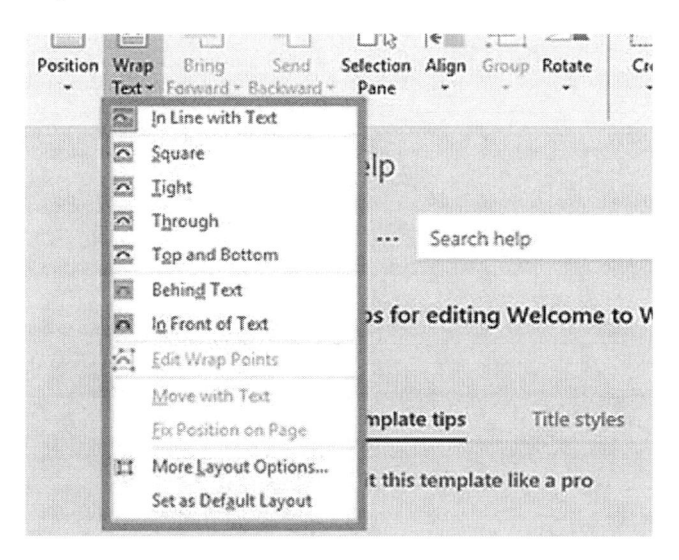

How to Resize an Image

Click to select the image and some dots around the image appears like 8 corner handles (as shown is circled in figure 14). This is what is used to resize the image either bigger or smaller. The top long handle circled on the image and has the rotate icon is used to rotate the image.

Figure 14: The resize Button

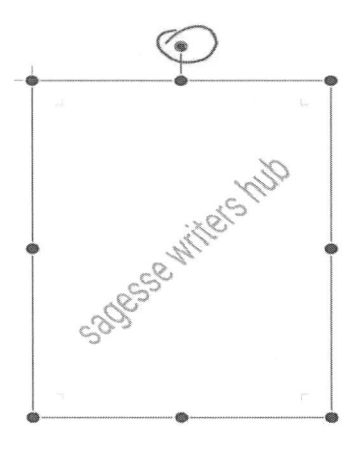

How to Crop an Image

To crop an image, click to select the image and on the picture formatting tool in the size group, there is the crop button. Click on the button and press the enter to cut out any part of the image.

Figure 15: The Crop Button

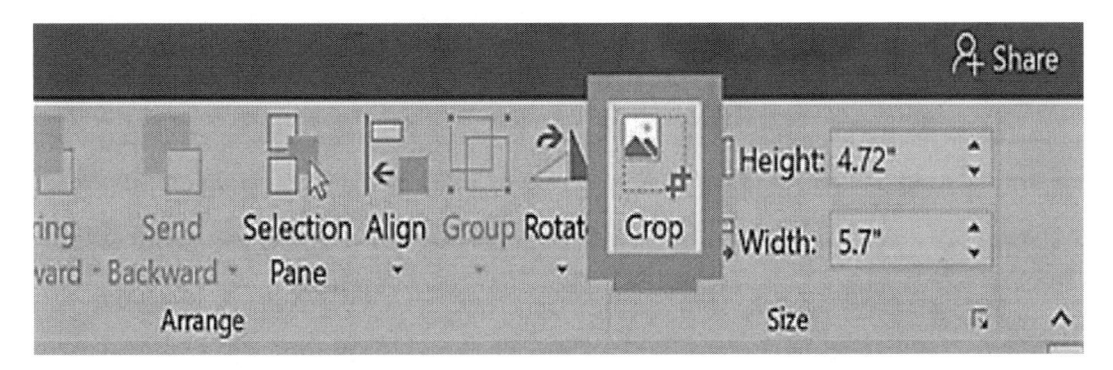

As a way of conclusion, all images can be edited to suit your choice. You can choose to rotate or change the position of the image. This can be achieved with the picture formatting tool.

CHAPTER 15

MAIL MERGE

Mail merge is a great time saver if you need to create multiple documents that are the same but unique in their ways like In terms of name tags and address. With Mail merge, you can send an email, print a document, and edit any document using mail merge.

Email using Mail Merge: To send an email to multiple people, first of all, you need source data which can be a list of names and addresses and can be in excel or outlook contacts which is one database and the other database is the Generic letter.

To Use Mail Merge to send an email to different people with the letter containing different names and addresses, follow these steps:

Click on Mailing and click on **Start Mail** Merge as shown in figure 1 below. Then select **Step by Step Mail Merge Wizard** (figure 1) and the Mail Merge dialogue box comes up.

Figure 1: The Start Merge Mail button

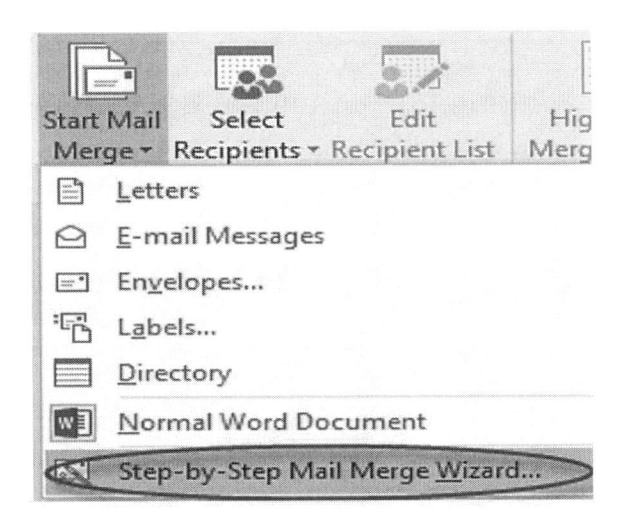

There are 6 steps to complete this mail merge.

Step 1: After clicking on start mail merge, It will ask you what you want to do (letters, emails messages, letters, labels, directory). Select your preferred and click on next. For the session, we click on step by step mail merge wizard.

Figure 2: The Start mail merge box

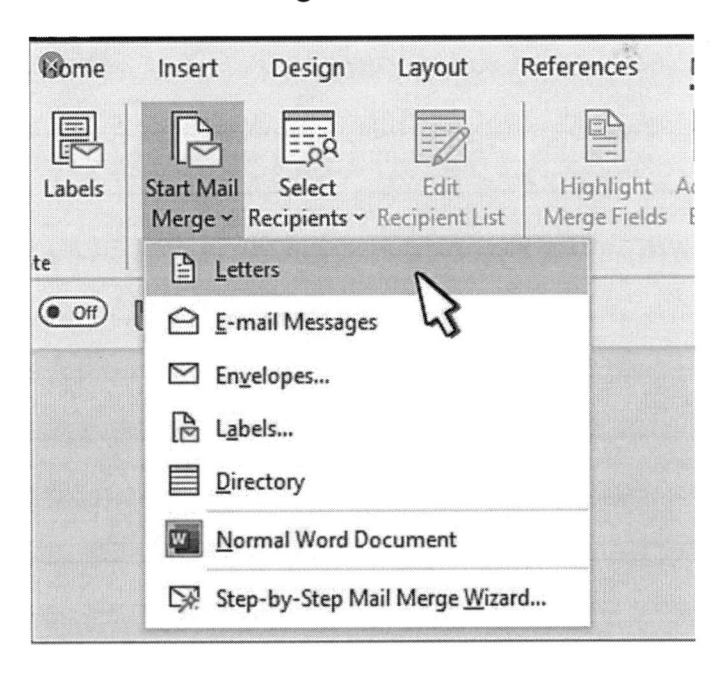

185

Step 2: It will ask the location of your document (Do you want to use a current document or an existing document). Select the recent document and then click on next and select recipients.

When you click on **select recipients,** there are some options displayed (use an existing list, select from outlook contacts, type a new list). If you have created a database as discussed earlier, then click on browse and select the folder where your database is. Click on open and your worksheet is displayed. Then mark the 'first rows of data contain column headers' and click OK.

Step 3: When your database is displayed, select the recipient you want to send the mail to. Select and click on OK and the data is now inside your Microsoft word. Then put your cursor where you want to Insert the data. Click on the Insert merge field. Select what you want to Insert from this field (first name, last name, email, contact, address, etc). Write your letter which you must have done (it is stated as one of the requirements above)

Step 4: Preview your letter where it shows how the email will be sent to the person.

Step 5: Click o**n Complete the Merg**e

Step 6: Click on **Finish and Merge** (edit the individual document, print document or send email messages). Click on send email messages and it brings a dialogue box where you can manage the options such as to, Subject line, mail format, and click on OK.

Figure 3: Finish and Merge Button

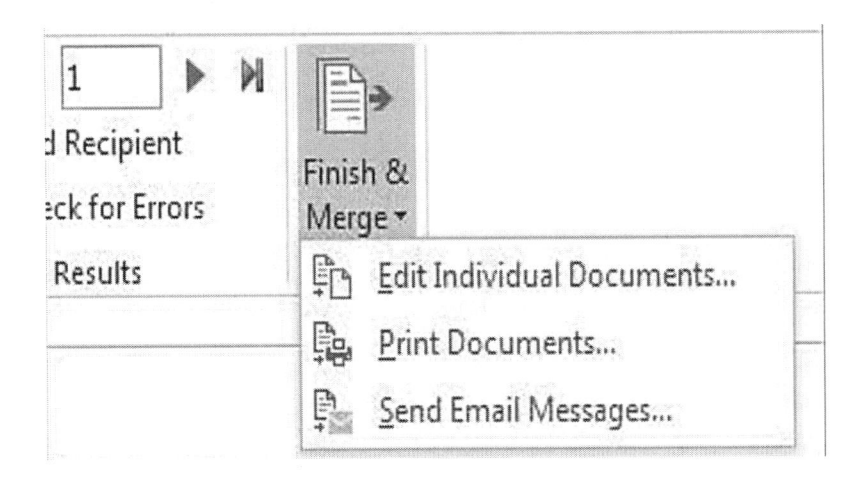

This will be updated on your document and al, the emails will be sent to the recipient.

Working with Labels And Envelopes in Microsoft Word 365

Working with Envelops: On the Mailing Ribbon, click on Envelops. The envelope and label dialogue box pops up. The first thing to type in is the delivery address (on the drop-down, you can pick it up from your outlook address book). Next is the Return address where you can put an address to return the letter to if it doesn't get delivered to the recipient. On the preview windows, two items will appear there when you want to print out the envelope.

Note: If you don't want to put in a return address, just click on the omit button and on the preview section it will disappear off the preview.

There is a check box to add electronic postage. If you click on it, a message shows up that says "you need to install electronic postage software before you can use this feature, would you like to visit the Microsoft Office website or to find out more about electronic postage addresses" you can choose or choose not to.

Another option is the Feed, which shows you how to feed your envelope into your printer so you don't get it wrong. There is an options button, you can choose your envelope size here. You can change the delivery address, return address, spacing from the top and left on this option button. And of course, you'll get the preview as you modify the settings which will reflect on your work. There is a printing options box that shows the different feed methods you can have when putting your envelope into the printer (face up, face down, clockwise rotation)

Finally, you can choose to print or add to the document. If you click add to document, It will say ' do you want to save the new address or go back to the default return', choose your response and then your document is updated. You can make some Adjustments to your document. Your envelope is ready.

Figure 4: The envelope option button

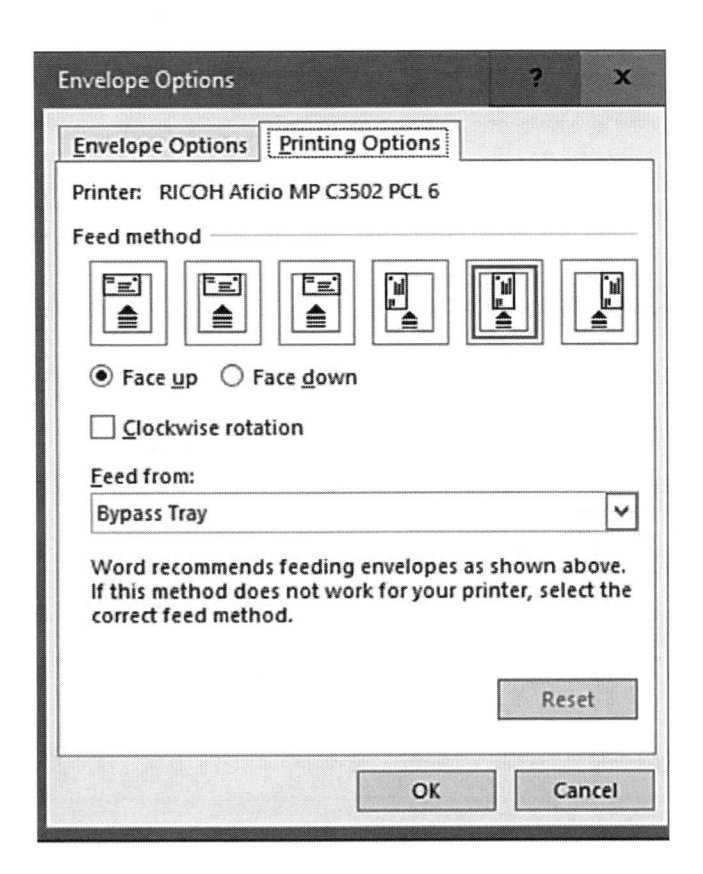

Working with Labels: Labels are sheets that are sticky and you can peel off and stick to anything. To do this go to the label option on the Mailing tab. The same dialogue box comes up. Fill in the fields according to what you want (address, an option of what to print either a full page of the same label or a single label, etc). After filling all the required fields, click on the print or add to document option. You can go ahead to print or add to the document.

Figure 5: The label option

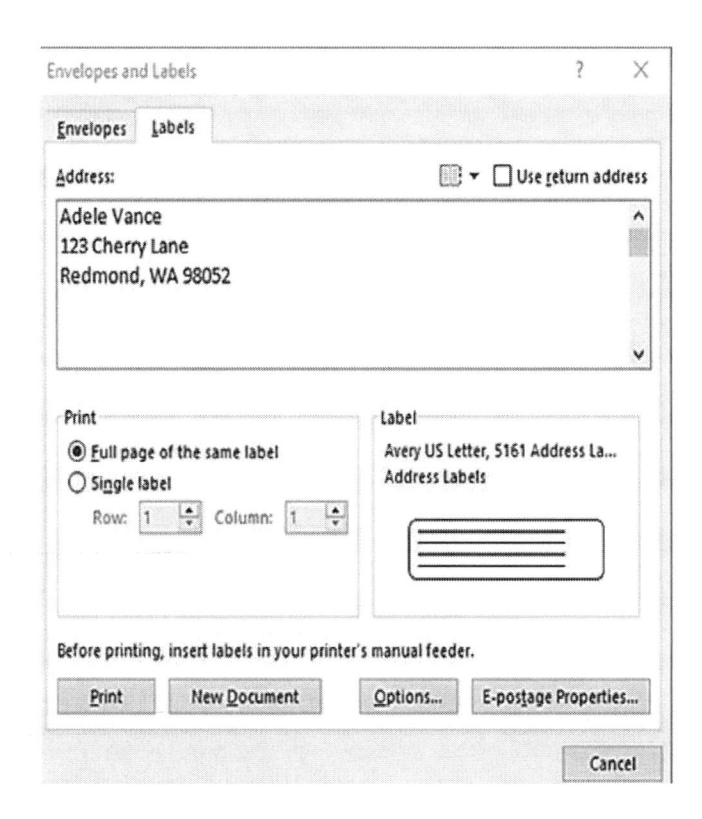

Multiple Document

Ways to Combine Multiple Word Documents into One Document on Microsoft Word 365.

First, open a blank document where you will want to Combine these multiple documents. Go to the **View Tab** on the ribbon, click on the outline, and then on Show Document and select insert, it will take you to your file storage where you select the first document you want to add say file 1, and click open. Then go back to Insert and select the next document let's say file 2 and click open. Repeat for other documents you want to add. Then go back to the View tab and click on Print Layout. It is then arranged on one document.

Alternatively, go to the **Insert tab,** on the top left-hand corner, click on **Objec**t. On the drop-down arrow, select text from the file. Select your files copy all the files you want to merge and click insert. It is automatically combined into a one-word document.

Figure 6: The Object button

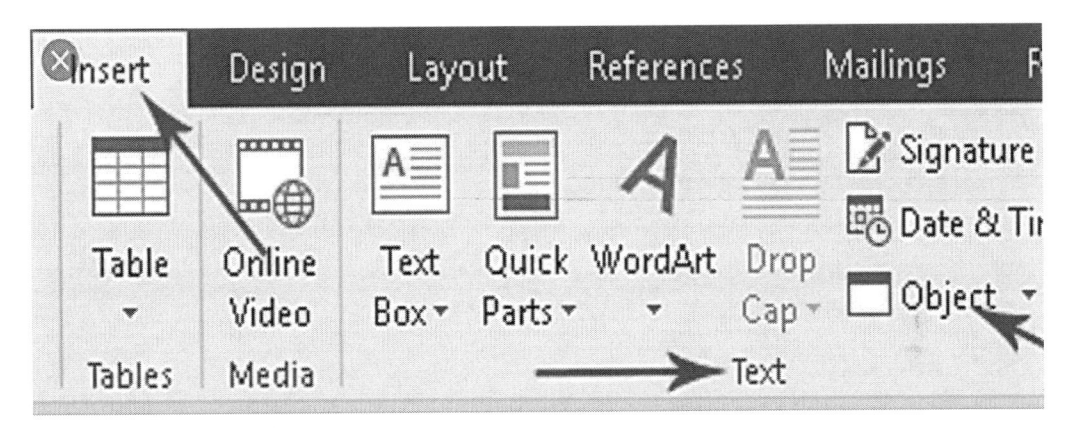

How to Customize Your Ribbon on Microsoft Word 365

You can create your tabs and add options to your tab. To create your tab which may have your required command, click on the File tab and select options. Then select Customize Ribbon. On the right-hand side, you'll see the main tabs, scroll down and click on New Tab. There is a new tab alongside a new group. First, click on the new tab and select Rename to give your tab a name. Then you can click on the New group to add some commands, just select the command you want and click on Add. When you have selected the command on your new group, click Ok. Then your tab is automatically updated on the Ribbon.

Figure 7: How to customize Ribbon

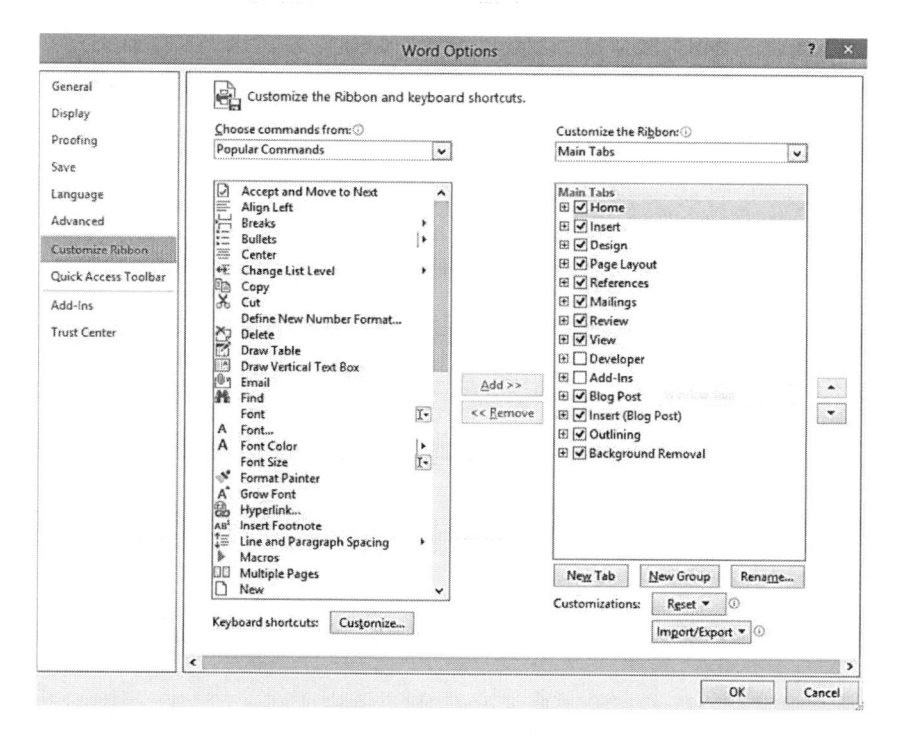

How to Add Commands to Quick Access Toolbar on Microsoft Word 365

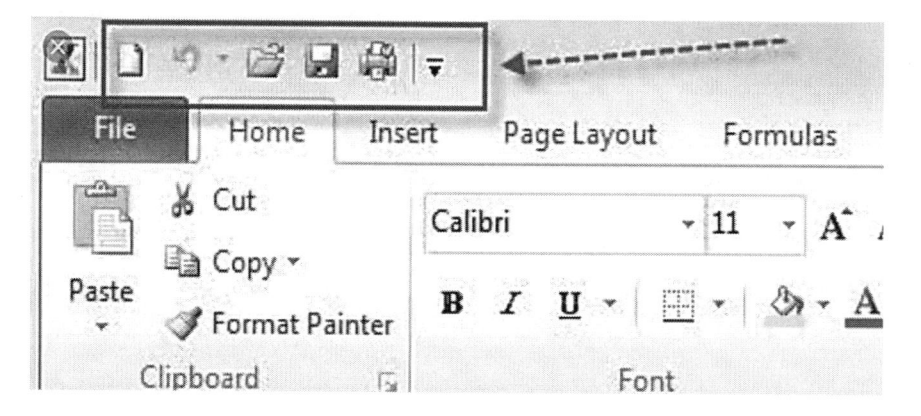

There are some commands in word that are hidden at the back which are not too visible. You can bring them forward or just attach them as a shortcut toolbar. Let's assume you want to convert a text

192

to speech. There is an option known as to speak. You can bring that speak the command to the Quick Access toolbar and the text will be read by Microsoft Word.

To do this; Click on the File tab and select Options. Select Quick Access Toolbar and you'll see an option called Popular command, when you click on it, select All Command. It is from the All command, you'll select the speak command and select add and it is moved to the Customize Quick Access Toolbar (save, undo, redo). Then click on OK. It will be added to the Quick Access toolbar.

Figure 8: Customize Quick Access toolbar

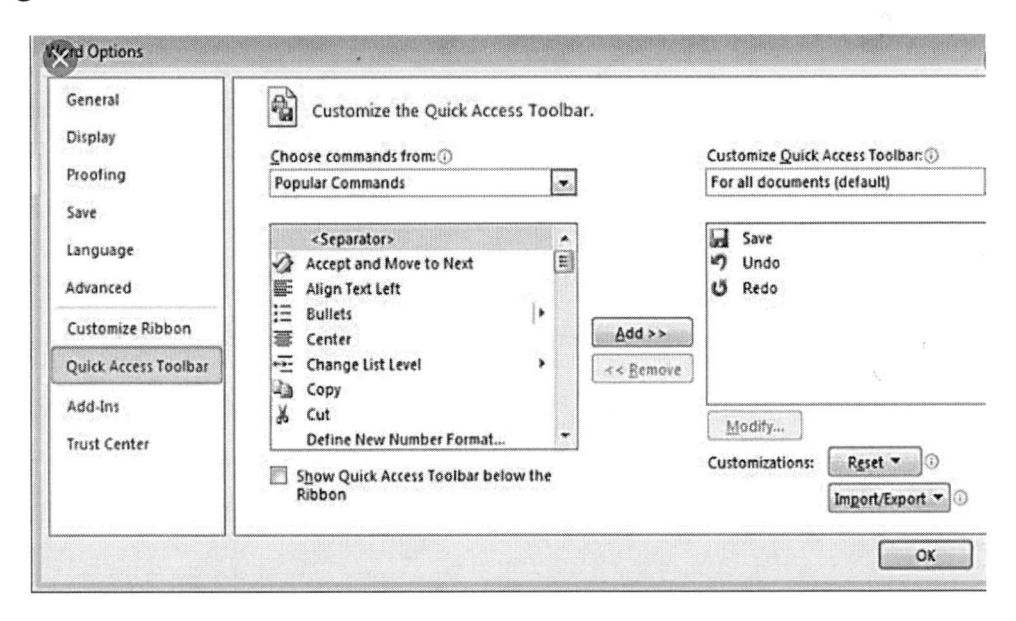

To enable it, select the text and click on the Speech command and it will be read by Microsoft Word.

CHAPTER 16

TOP TIPS AND TRICKS IN MICROSOFT WORD 365

Dark Mode

Do you know you can turn on dark mode on Microsoft Word 365 especially at night to give your eye a break? To turn on dark mode, go to the top left corner and click on the **File** Menu. Within the file menu, scroll down to the bottom left corner and click on Account. This opens up the account screen and right in the middle, there is a section called **Office Theme.** By default, it's always on the colorful screen which tends to be bright. Click on the drop-down arrow to see other colors (dark grey, white, black) You can select dark grey or black to make your screen dark

Note: When you change the office theme, not only will it affect word, it affects all other Office apps (excel and PowerPoint).

When you go back to the word, all the ribbons tabs are dark but the document still looks bright. To change this; Go to the **Design tab,** on the right-hand side, click on the page color. Click on the theme color, and choose the dark color. Your document color changes to black and word change your font color automatically to white.

Note: It doesn't affect your document when you want to print. It comes out in its standard color (white).

Figure 1: The Dark Mode Theme on Word, 365

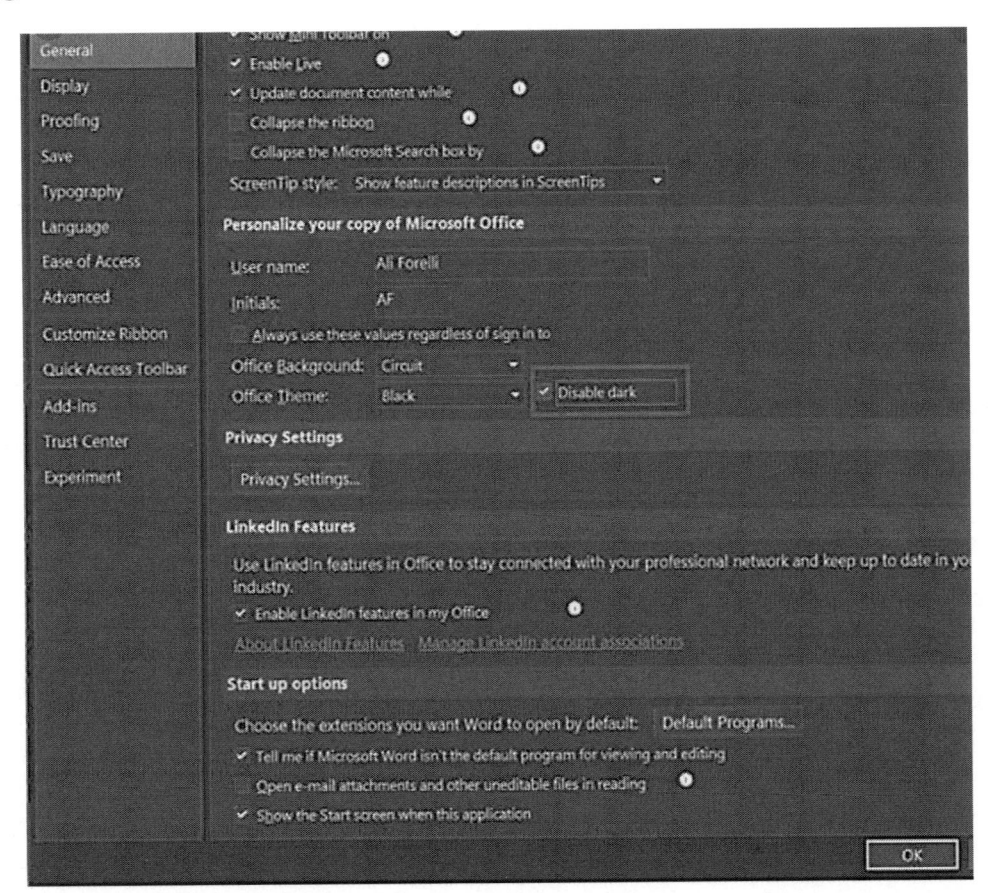

Turn Your Word Document Into an Interactive Web Page

You can turn your document into an interactive web page that looks great on any device. To do this; click on the File tab. Then click on the option called Transform. On clicking it, it opens a pane on the right-hand side where you can transform your document into an interactive web page. There are lots of styles, you can choose from, select any one and click on transform. Then you can see a preview of your word document as an Interactive web page.

Figure 2: The Transform Icon

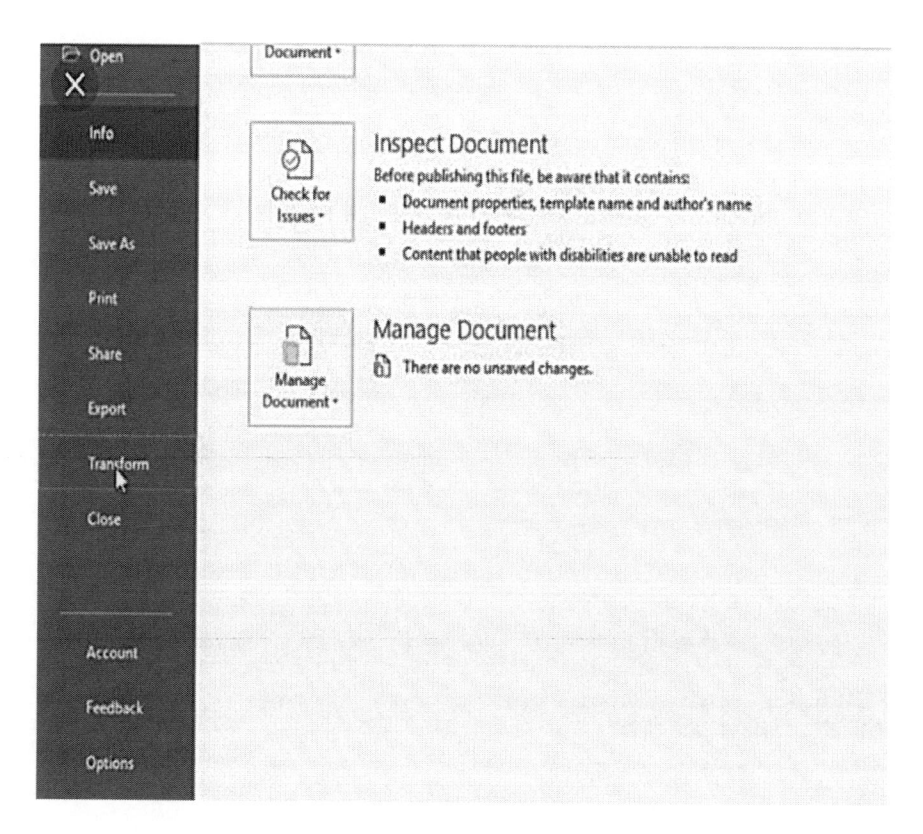

Note: To make any changes, click on Edit above and you can Modify the look of your webpage, you can also review the navigation and share (share this sway)

Convert Photo or Document PDF to an Editable Word Document

You can convert from PDF with ease and edit your files without restrictions. To do this; Go to the File Menu and click on Open. Navigate to where you have your PDF file on your computer and then open it. You get a prompt telling you that it wants to convert your PDF file to a word document. Click on OK. Then you can go through and edit it.

Using Equation/Formulas in Microsoft Word

Formulas and Equations are not limited to Microsoft Excel alone. You can use formulas in Microsoft word.

All you have to do is, click on the **Layout tab**. Within the Layout ribbon, over on the far right-hand side, there is an option for Equation. Click on it and it opens a formula dialogue box. You have to select the formulas you want to use, fill in the figures into each box and click on Ok and you'll get the value.

Note: On the paste functions button, there are lots of different calculations you can run also.

Figure 3: The Equation Button

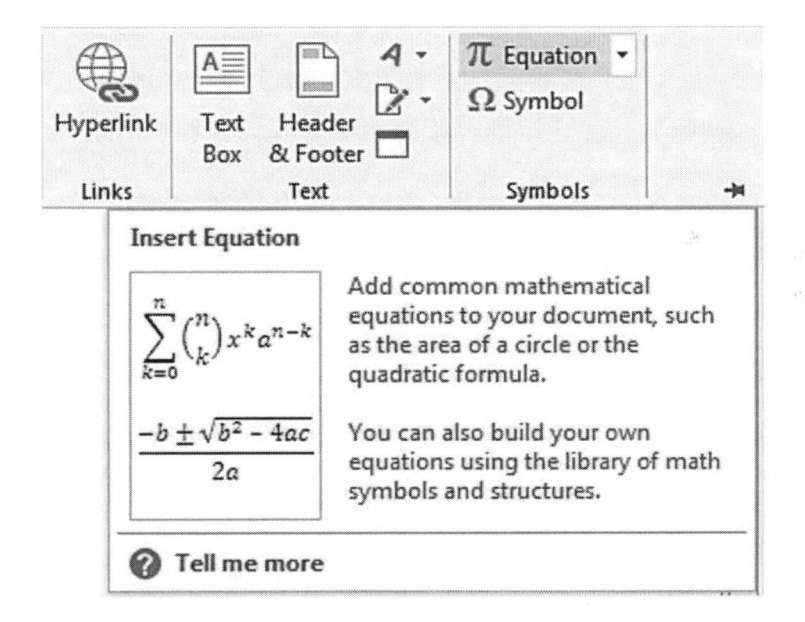

Sort List in Word

To sort the list on Microsoft word. First, select all the lists and click on the **Home tab,** and right in the middle there is an option as **sor**t.

197

Click on it and the sort text box opens. There are different options like the sort by option (by paragraph, headings, field) and the text option (Ascending or Descending order), Number option, or the date option. Then click on OK and it is automatically updated.

Figure 4: The Sort Icon

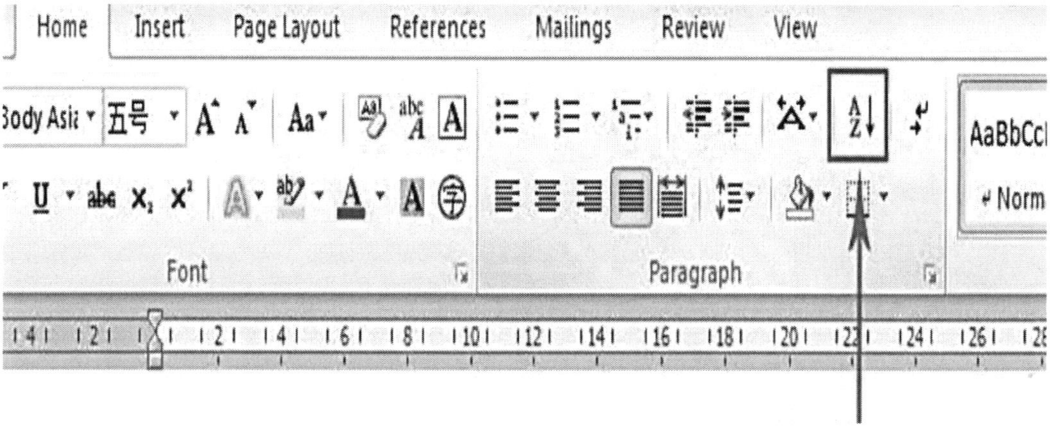

Collaborate With Others

In Microsoft word, you can easily collaborate with others on a document at the same time. In the past, to work with others on a document, you have to email someone else an attachment, they make an edit and send it back then you have to all the edits together and work on them. Fortunately, it is now a lot easier. To do this: On the top right-hand corner, there is an option for Share. Click on it and it opens the share dialogue box, you can share it with others.

By default, it says Anyone with the link can edit. When you click on it, you can define specific persons to share it with. You can go to the Settings and edit as you want. Then type in an email address and copy the link to share with anyone.

If you want to call out someone or ask a question or you want them to work on a Sentence. All you have to do is highlight the sentence. And on the top right-hand corner, there is a button on Comment. Click on it and click on New Comment. It opens the Comment box at the right-hand side of the document and you can type in your comments. You can put @ to select a specific person to direct the question or sentence to. Then they will get a notification about that specific section of the document. Then when you click on the specific person's name, you can share your document with the person.

Pin Document

You pin your document so you can easily and quickly get back to them in the future. To do this: Click on the File tab and this brings us to the word backstage. Within the home view, you can see all your recent documents. If you select the document and hover around it, there is a pinned icon (figure 5). Click on it and click on Pinned.

Figure 5: The Pinned icon

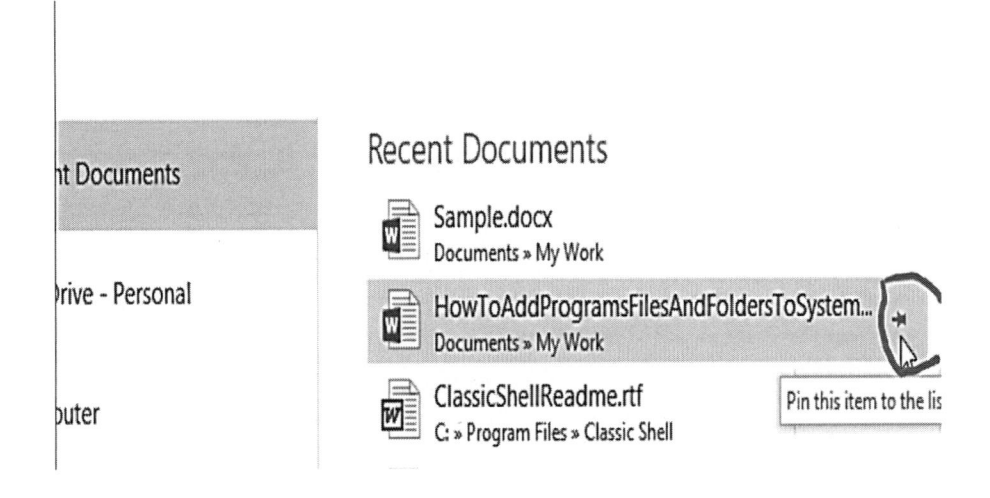

Whenever you want to get back to where your document is, just click on Pinned as shown in figure 6 and the document appears

Figure 6: The Pinned Document

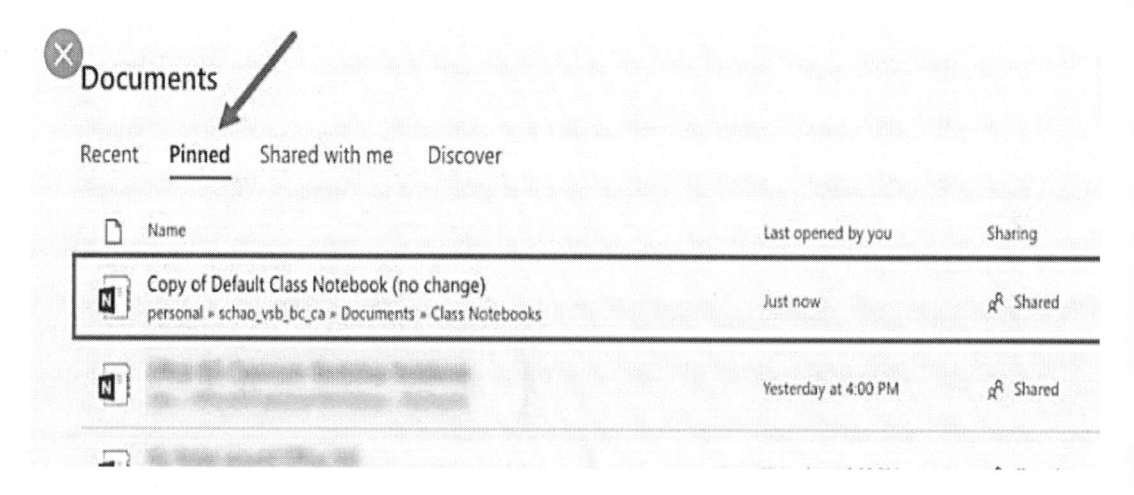

How to Rewrite a Text

On Microsoft Word, you can rewrite a text or a phrase. To do this: Highlight the word and right-click on it. There is an option as Rewrite Suggestions. When you click on it, different ways to write the highlighted or selected text will be displayed. Select your preferred choice and it is updated on your document.

Figure 7: Rewrite Suggestions icon

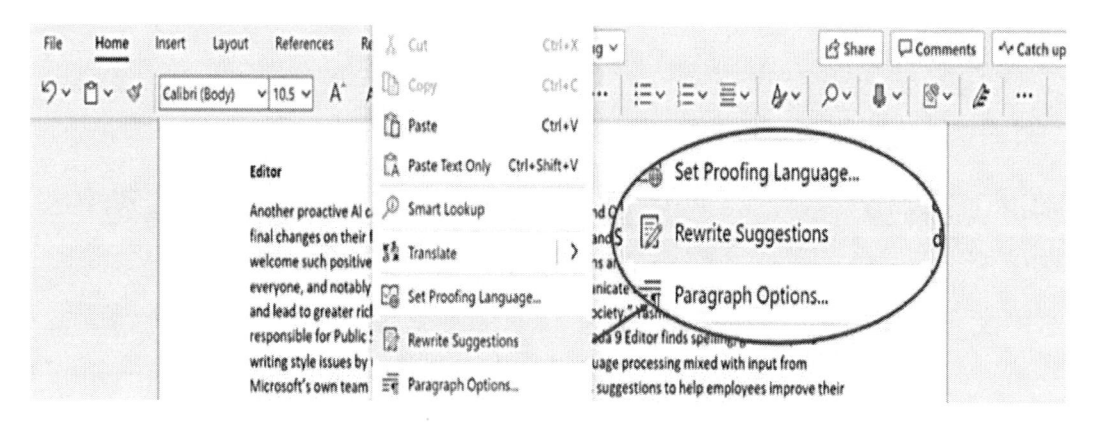

200

Resume Assistant Powered by Linkedin

This is a feature created by LinkedIn on Microsoft word that helps you write your Cv or Resume. To use this feature: click on Review. On the right-hand side, there is an option called Resume Assistant. Click on it and it opens a pane for resume Assistant. Then you can fill in the required field. There are also some bullet points to help you with the skills, you can learn from them to put yours together. When you're done, click Ok and your resume is ready.

Translator

Microsoft Word comes with a built-in translator. To use the built-in translator, go over to the Review tab and under language, there is an option to Translate. Within the submenu, you can translate selection or translate an entire document. When you click on Translate Selection, it opens the translator in the right-hand pane. Then select some text select the language you want and click on Insert.

Figure 8: The Translator button

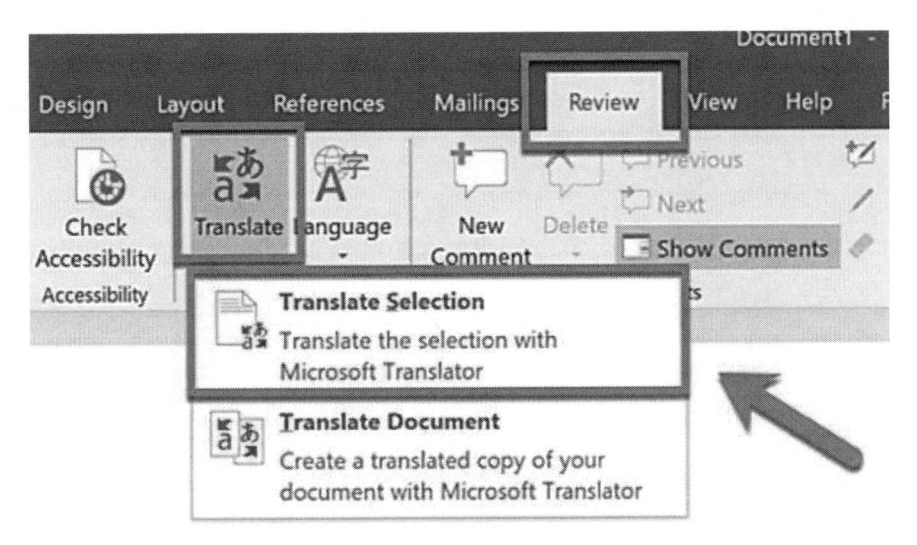

Citation

Microsoft word makes it easy to work with citation. To Insert a citation on any quote, click on the Reference tab and click on Insert citation (figure 9). First, you have to add a new source. Click on Add New Source. This opens up the create source dialogue box and you can add information related to what the source is (book, journal article, report, conference proceedings, etc) (figure 10). Then you can fill in the Author, title, year, city, publisher. Once you've finished typing in all the information, click on Ok and it will be updated in your document.

Figure 9: The Insert Citation button

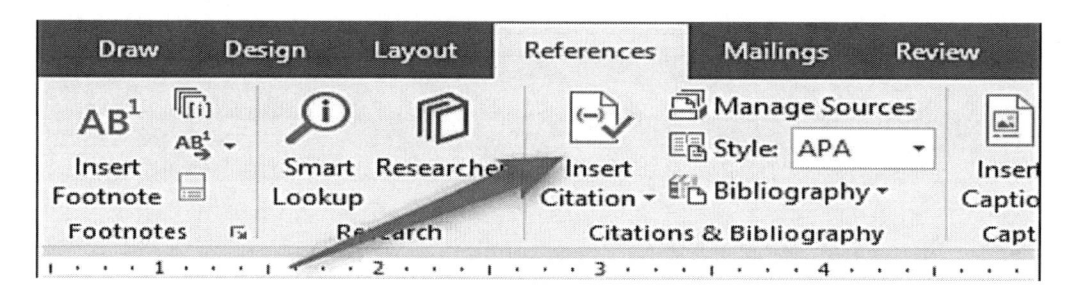

Figure 10: The Create Source Dialogue Box

Also, to Insert a work cited section. Go to the citation option, there is an option for Bibliography. First, select your style, and next click on bibliography. (figure 11) Within here you can Insert a few different build-in formats and the works cited on your doc will be updated on your document

Figure 11: The bibliography section

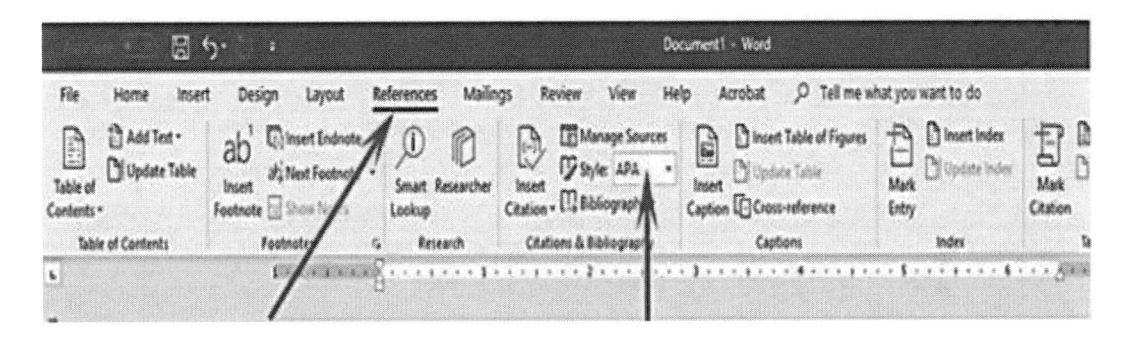

Format Painter

First, select the formats you want to copy, then go to Home Ribbon and click on the format painter. This then copies the formatting and there is a big brush close to your cursor. Then highlight the text you want to apply in the same format and it is automatically updated on your document.

Figure 12: The Format Painter icon

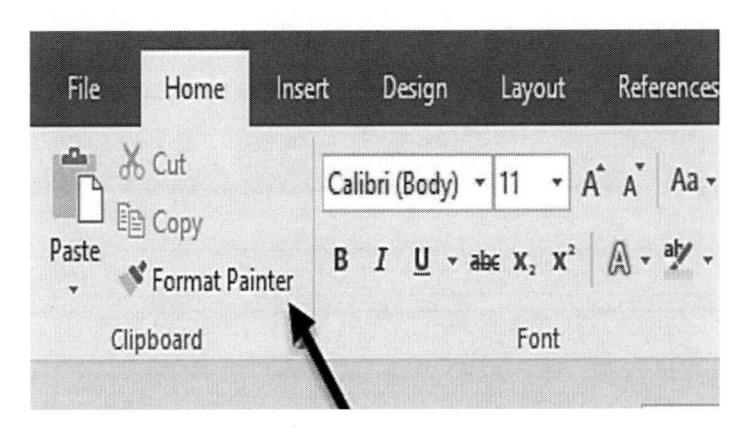

Read Aloud Voice

This is a feature that reads out your selected text. First of all, select the text and click on the Review Tab. And select the Read Aloud option, it automatically reads out the selected text on your Word document There is also a backward, pause, and a forward option you can select from. You can also further change the voice to either a male or female.

Dictation

On Microsoft Word, you can dictate your Words and Microsoft word listens to your Words and types them in. Click on the Home Tab and then click on the Dictate button. As you dictate your words, Microsoft word types it in. There are also Settings options where you can turn on auto Punctuation. There are language options also on the Dictation button.

Figure 13: The Dictation Button

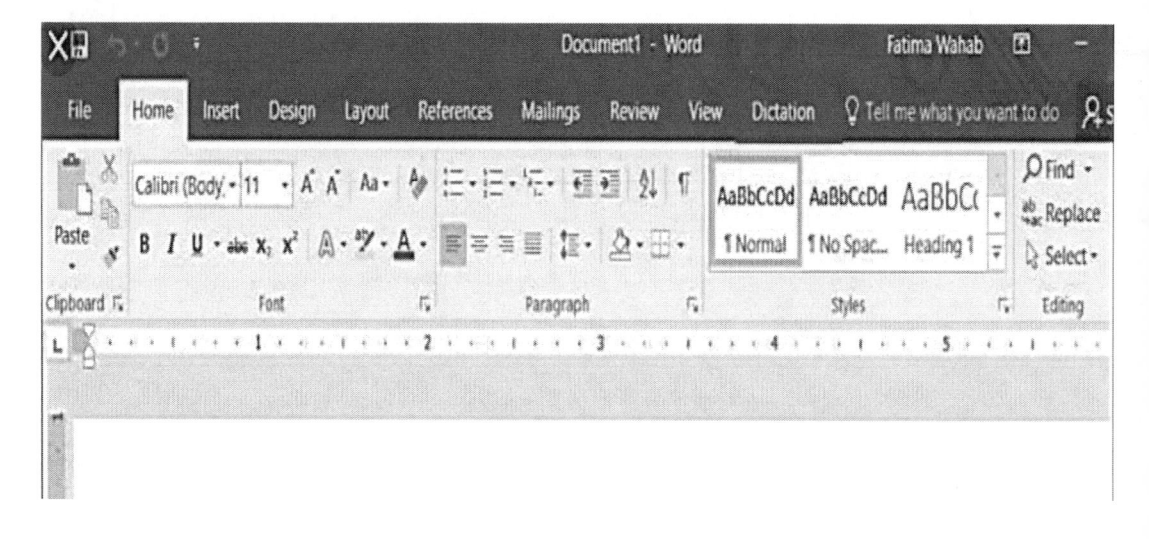

Convert Word to PowerPoint

Open your document and click on the File menu, then click on export. There is an option for export to power presentation (preview). Click on it and it fetched lots of themes for your presentation. Click on any design you want and click on Export. A few seconds later it is open, click on open presentation. Your Powerpoint is ready.

Figure 14: Export option to PowerPoint

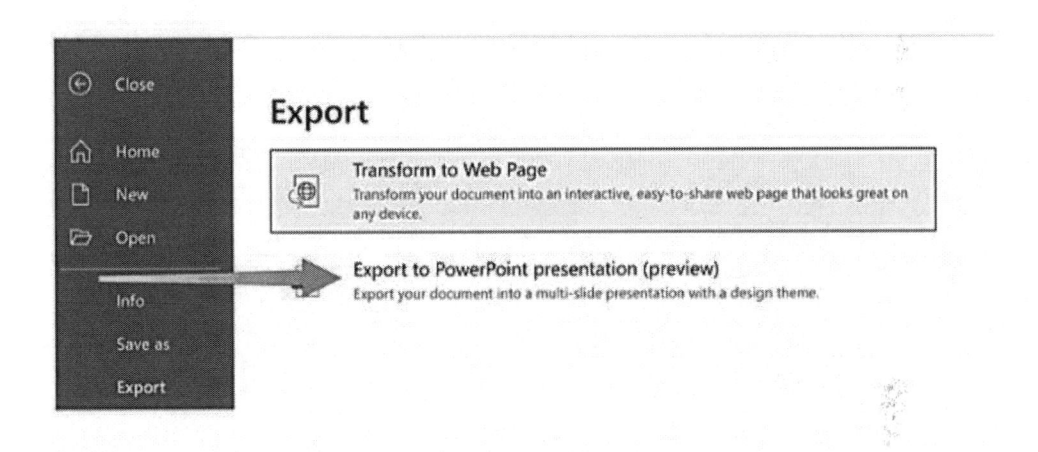

Text Prediction

This has been built-in words that you can turn on or off. Text prediction suggests the next word as you type on your word document. To put it on, go to the Review tab and click on Editor. On the drop-down arrow, click on text Prediction and turn it on. Then as you type, it predicts the word you want to type before you finish typing.

Autosave Option

Go to File and click on Options. Click on Save and you will see an option to 'save auto recover information every time' adjust the time and then mark the box.

Drop Cap

A drop cap is a large letter at the start of a paragraph as seen mostly in newspapers that covers two or more lines in your document as shown in figure 15 below. To create a drop cap, place your cursor on the paragraph that you want to format with the drop cap. Then select the Insert tab on the ribbon. Next, select the drop cap button in the text group and choose an option from the drop-down menu (None will remove an existing drop cap, the Dropped option will drop the first letter to about lines, and the In Margin option places the drop cap in the margin next to the paragraph and the drop cap options open the dialogue box with customization options) (figure 16). Choose any option of your choice. You can go further to choose additional options such as the font, lines to drop, distance from text, etc. Adjust it according to your choice. After making your choices, select the Ok button and the drop cap will appear in your text immediately.

Figure 15: Example of Drop Cap

The Drop cap is a large letter at the start of a paragraph as seen mostly in newspapers that covers two or more lines in your document. To create a drop cap, place your cursor on the paragraph that you want to format with the drop cap. Then select the **Insert cap** on the ribbon. Next, select the **drop cap** button in the text group. Then select an option from the drop-down menu (None will remove an existing drop cap, Dropped option will drop the first letter to about3 lines and the in margin option places the drop cap in the margin next to the paragraph and the drop cap options opens the dialogue box with customization options). Choose the drop cap options and on the ialogue box, choose dropped or in Margin and then choose additional options such as the font, lines to drop, distance from text etc. Adjust it according to your choice. After making your choices, select Ok button and the drop cap will appear in your text immediately.

Figure 16: The Drop Cap options

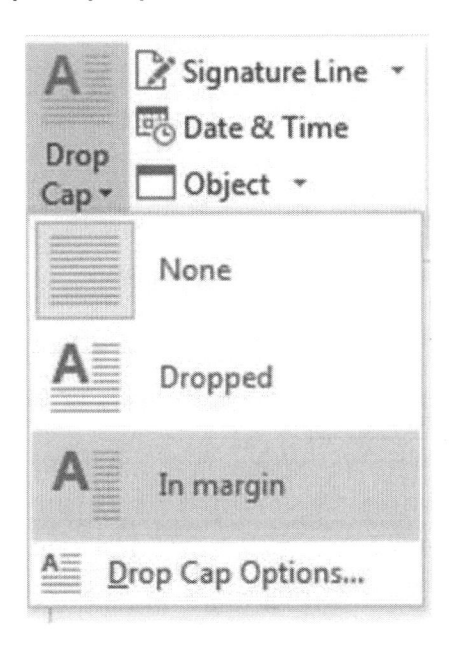

Lock Your Document on Microsoft Word

Open a blank document, input your writeup and go to the Save Option on the File Tab. Choose a location to save it and type in your document name. To lock that document, go to the Tool option beside the save option. Click on the drop-down arrow and click on the General option, it will require a password if you want to lock it, input a password and click Ok. It will ask you to reconfirm your password, type it in and click OK. That document has automatically been locked. To open it again, it requires your password.

Alternatively, click the File tab and select Info. Choose the Protect Document button.

There are different options (Mark as final, Encrypt depth a password, Restrict Editing). Choose an option and answer the question that appears on the dialogue box, then click Ok and your document is locked.

Bookmark in Words

Bookmarks are used for documents that contain several pages, you can add several bookmarks so that you can identify this bookmark easily for future reference. First, select the headings with the paragraph that you want to bookmark. Then go to the Insert tab and click on the Bookmark option under links and the bookmark window will appear on your screen. Give the bookmark a name in the popup window and click on Add.

Once you're done, click on the File Option. On the file option window, click on the Advanced tab and scroll down to the Show document content section. In that section, check the show bookmark option and click on the Ok button to save the changes. The brackets will mark the area you bookmarked.

Once you've added several bookmarks, click on the bookmark options again and the window will show you all the bookmarks you have. If you want to go to a particular bookmark, select that bookmark and click on the Go to Button. To delete a bookmark. Click on the bookmark and select Delete.

Figure 17: The Bookmark Option on Word

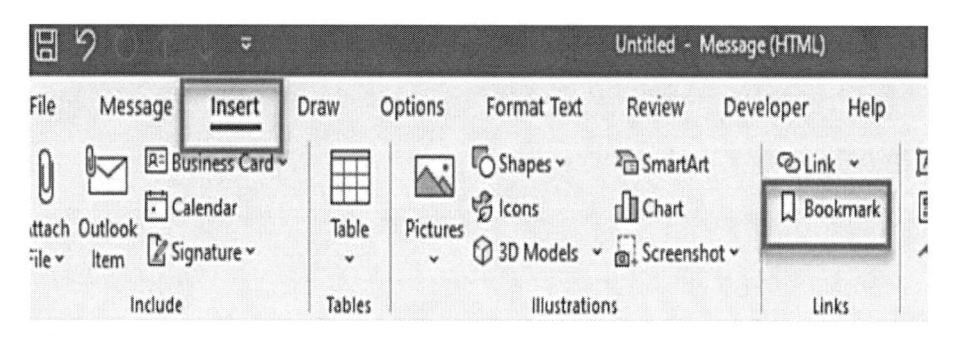

Side-to-Side Page Movement

You can arrange your document on Microsoft word to a side-by-side view. To do this; click on th**e View tab**. Select **side-to-Side** on the Page Movement group and it is automatically updated on the word document

Note that on this view tab, the zoom command becomes inactive and the horizontal scroll bar becomes more useful as you can use it to go through each page.

Accelerate the Ribbon

The keyboard accelerator can be used to access commands in the Ribbon. (Press **F10** key to access the Ribbon accelerator as a shortcut method) The best way to do this is to use the **Alt** Keys. When you click on Alt keys, letters in boxes appear on the Ribbon and each box contains one or two letters, which are the accelerator keys.

Note: You can click on a letter or the two letters in sequence to "click" a specific part of the Ribbon. To disable the accelerator mode, click on the Alt key again.

Click-and-Type

This is another feature of Word 365. The click-and-type is used to stab the mouse anywhere on the page and information can be typed in immediately.

Insert Video on Your Document

You can easily Insert videos on Microsoft word, 365. To do this; go to the **Insert tab** and click on Online Video. Before that, get the embed code or URL of the web page of the video. Then select where you want the video to be pasted on your document and click the **Insert tab,** select online video and paste the URL you copied then click Insert.

Figure 18: Online Video button

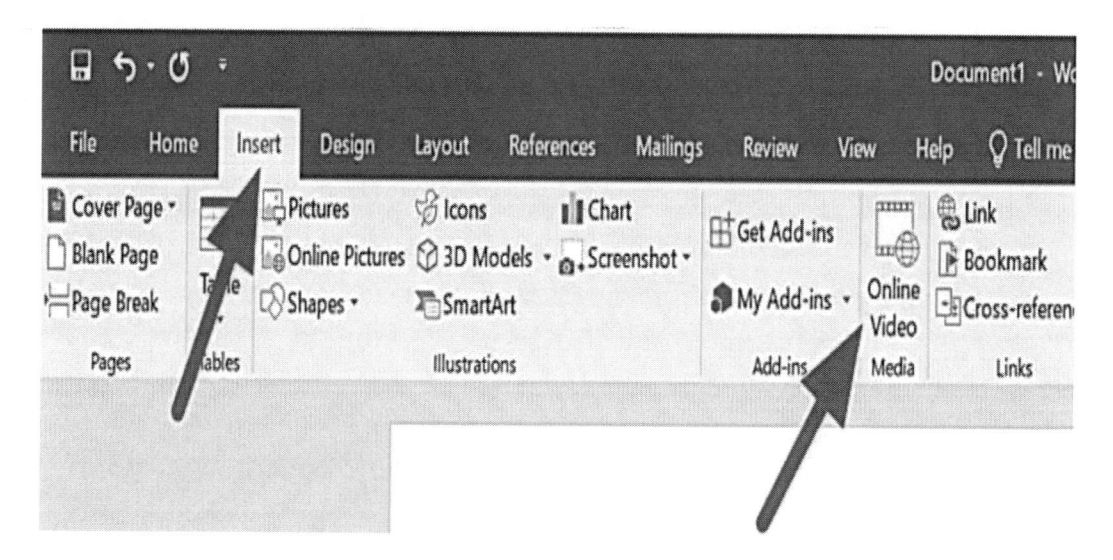

Hidden Text

Some texts are not visible on a document, they are hidden text. The only way to make this text visible is to click on the **Home Tab** ribbon and then on the **Paragraph group,** click on the **Show/Hide** command which looks like the paragraph symbol. When you enable it, the hidden text shows up in a document with a dotted line as shown below

Document Properties

To access a document property. Click the **File** tab and choose the **Info** option. The document Properties are displayed on the right-hand side which displays the document size, pages, word count, and other options. You can click on the **Properties button** and select **Advanced Properties** to see more options.

Document Version History

To View Previous Versions of Word Documents; click the "File" button on the Ribbon and select "Info." On this tab, click the "Version History" button and it will open up the Version History pane on the right. This Version History pane lists all major documents revised by date, time, and author.

To view any version of a document, click "Open version." This will open that version of the file and you can view the version of that document.

The Common Keyboard Shortcut for Shift Key

Shift + F1: Review text formatting

Shift + F2: Copy the selected text

Shift + F3: Change the case of the text (uppercase to lower case)

Shift + F4: Perform a Find or Go To action again

Shift + F5: Move to a previous revision

Shift + F6: Go to the previous pane

Shift + F7: Launch the Thesaurus

Shift + F8: Shrink the current selection

Shift + F9: Switch between field code and its results

Shift + F10: Display a shortcut menu

Shift + F11: Go to the previous field

Shift + F12: Save a document

Common Keyboard Shortcut for the Alt Key

Alt + F: To use backstage view open the file page

Alt + H: Move to the Home tab

Alt + M: Opens the Mailing tab to manage the Mail Merge task

Alt + N: Open the Insert tab

Alt + P: Open the page layout tab

Alt + R: Open the Review tab

Alt + S: Open the Reference tab

Alt + F4: Close Document

Alt + F5: Restore the document window size

Alt + F6: Switches to another document

Alt + F7: Find the misspelt word or grammatical error

Alt + F8: Open the Macro dialogue box

Alt + F10: Display the selection task pane.

Alt + F11: Display Microsoft Visual Basic code

Alt + Backspace: Undo the last action

Common Keyboard Shortcuts of the Control Key

Ctrl + A: To select all text	Ctrl + F1: Open a task pane
Ctrl + B: To apply a bold format to the selected text	Ctrl + F2: Display the print preview
Ctrl + C: Copy selected text	Ctrl + F4: Close the active window
Ctrl + D: Open font window to change font	Ctrl + F6: Switch to another open Ms word document
Ctrl + E: Align selected text to the centre	Ctrl + F9: Insert an empty field
Ctrl + F: Open the Find Dialogue box to search for words	Ctrl + F10: Maximize the document window
Ctrl + G: The Go-to dialogue box to search for a specific location in the current document	Ctrl + F12: Close the open command
Ctrl + H: Open the Replace dialogue box to replace text	Ctrl +]: Increase size of selected text
Ctrl + I: Italics	Ctrl + [: Decrease size of selected text
Ctrl + J: Align the selected to justify the screen	Ctrl + 0: Add/ remove 6pt of spacing above the paragraph
Ctrl + K: Insert a Hyperlink	
Ctrl + L: Align text left	

Ctrl + M: Indent a paragraph from the left/ Hanging indent	Ctrl + 1: Add a single space between two lines
Ctrl + N: New Document	Ctrl + 2: Add double space between two lines
Ctrl + O: Open other documents / open the dialogue box to select a file to open.	Ctrl + 5: Add 1.5 space between two line
Ctrl + P: Print	Ctrl +↓ Moves the cursor one paragraph to the down
Ctrl + Q: Add Space before paragraph / Remove paragraph formatting.	Ctrl + ← Moves the cursor to one word to the left
Ctrl + R: Align Text Right	Ctrl + → Moves the cursor to one word to the right
Ctrl + S: Save	
Ctrl + T: Left indent / to create the Hanging indent	Ctrl +↑ Moves the cursor one paragraph upward
Ctrl + U: Underline	Ctrl + Backspace: Delete one word to the left
Ctrl + V: Paste	Ctrl + Delete: Delete one word to the right
Ctrl + W: Close Document	
Ctrl + X: Cut selected text	Ctrl + End: Move the cursor to the end of the page
Ctrl + Y: Repeat / Redo	Ctrl + Home: Move the cursor to the beginning of the document
Ctrl + Z: Undo	
	Ctrl + Enter: insert a page

	Ctrl + Insert: Copy selected text
	Ctrl + Spacebar: Reset highlighted text to default the font
	Ctrl + Tab: Insert a tab character
	Ctrl + = Set selected text as subscript

As a way of conclusion, these are necessary things to note about Microsoft word 365;

- Always remember to save your work on Microsoft Word
- Be very vigilant when using the space bar
- Don't abuse the enter key
- To make your work easy and fast, use most of the keyboard shortcuts.
- Avoid manually numbering your pages and using the bullet in the wrong way
- Do not force a fresh/ new page and always remember the undo icon.
- Make sure your printer is in a good condition before you click on the print button to print any document

Printed in Great Britain
by Amazon